BECOMING A RELIABLE MAN

OF FAITH AND PRACTICE

D1376518

LARRY KENNEDY, PH.D.

To protect the privacy of individuals and families, I have changed the names of some persons and places, as well as other details not significant to the lesson. It is my desire to convey the important facts and principles necessary for spiritual and vocational growth without bringing harm to any person.

The historical facts and dates that appear in various portions of the text are widely accepted for their accuracy by scholars and historians, and/or, can be easily sourced through commonly available libraries and search engines on the Internet. For example, facts related to Constantine the Great can be found using the search format: constantine the great AND *the key word(s) from the text*. Some original sources are designated by their internet address. Please refer to the Appendix for further explanation.

Sometimes a very special person comes along who can make a great difference in your life. I am blessed to have married such a person. My precious wife, Dorothy, is not only my best friend and helpmate, she has been my faithful co-laborer in this work.

TABLE OF CONTENTS

Part Two
THE FOUR FOUNDATIONAL VALUES
OF SPIRITUAL GROWTH

Author's Preface

When I became a follower of Christ and began to study the Bible, I realized that the success I had always desired would not come from trying to obtain God's blessing on what I wanted, but in yielding to what He wanted me to do with my life. 2 Chronicles 16:9 (NAS) reminds us that "the eyes of the Lord move to and fro throughout the earth that He may strongly support those whose heart is completely His." As I began to learn what it meant to give Him all my heart, I also discovered that God's plan for each of us depends upon our *becoming a reliable man,* someone whom He, our family, and others can rely upon. I also learned that if I would let Him have His way in my life, He would bless and discipline my talents so that I could enjoy and be satisfied with my livelihood.

A man must divide his energies into two primary areas of responsibility: his personal life at home and his work. Although the things we do at home and at work are very different, the values that make us who we are at both places are the same, no matter how we earn our living. They directly influence our relationships and leadership style, how well we do our job, and every decision we make. These values, along with the strategies that support them, provide our family, friends, and co-workers with the sense of confidence they will need to respect and trust us. The Four Foundational Values of Personal Reliability are:

Personal Authenticity:
> a measure of our resolve to live a consistent life

Ethical Dependability:
> a measure of our trustworthiness in practical matters

Moral Purity:
> a measure of our cleansing and restoration from sin

Spiritual Authority:
> a measure of the power and favor of God in our life

Now, after more than twenty-five years of apprenticeship, I can testify both personally and professionally about the great benefit of living by these biblical values. But as I grew in personal reliability

11

and became a more disciplined follower of Christ, there was an ominous feeling growing in my heart that my church experiences were somehow in conflict with the purposes of God. I often found myself sitting in a typical "worship" service with a nagging feeling that something was not right. I wasn't thinking about my own personal preferences for music or what color the carpet should be, but about what scriptural purposes were being fulfilled by the church services my friends and I were attending. I wanted to know what things were essential for spiritual growth, what hindered it, and what a spiritually strong and emotionally mature man might do differently.

One of the primary purposes of the church is to fulfill the requirement found in Ephesians 4:13 to produce *teleios* men who are "mature or complete" in Christ. That means we should all be growing in our ability to think and behave like a disciple of Christ as a result of our participation in church life. But men often describe their experiences in church as dull or monotonous, with sometimes-manipulative sermons that have no relevance to their daily grind. Many are put off by the repeated emphasis on money, building programs, and membership which draw our attention away from the Lord to the institution's purposes. Some leave quietly, while others depart in anger because of inconsistencies that church leaders could not reasonably explain.

My research included an in-depth study of the mission of the church as found in the Scriptures; a review of church history and its effect on our current practices; a thorough evaluation of the administrative, educational and service processes of the church; and hundreds of counseling and consulting interviews. As my knowledge of these things increased, I began to understand why the church does not routinely produce mature, reliable men. Even a casual analysis of most people's church experience will reveal the inefficiencies, moral failures, idealistic delusions, and sincere miscalculations of its leaders. But it's not just that things don't always work the way they should, it's worse than that. The church often harms people instead of helping, producing spiritually emasculated and emotionally flawed men who only perpetuate its mistakes.

Even so, I found that most men are interested in a lifestyle with Christ that will pass the test of common sense. And when we read and interpret the Bible, free from institutional influences, we can see that God offers men a richly satisfying agenda for life. Isaiah 33:6 promises that "He will be the sure foundation for [our] times, a rich store of salvation and wisdom and knowledge." The Four Foundational Values of Spiritual Growth are:

Kingdom Identity:
a measure of our participation in genuine church life
Spiritual Accountability:
a measure of our practice of spiritual disciplines
Perceptual Clarity:
a measure of our training to discern good and evil
Sovereign Dependency:
a measure of our trust in God's provision

The most important part of a man's life and work is his commitment to becoming more reliable by allowing the Lord to make the essential changes that are needed in his heart. God has a specific plan for every man, and when our first priority is to seek His will, we are on our way to being restored or strengthened where we need it most. When Jesus said, "Come to me, all you who are weary and burdened, and I will give you rest." (Matthew 11:28), He was speaking to every man who is bearing the weight of his responsibilities at home and at work. And when He said, "Take my yoke upon you and learn from me" (verse 29), He was calling each of us to obey His Word.

This book was written for the man who has felt the Lord tugging at his heart to make some changes. It is my testimony to the grace of God and what I have learned about His purposes for men. With a background in engineering and business, I spent five years as an associate pastor at a large, ministry-oriented church, while I continued my graduate studies in management. Since 1985 I have spent about half my time making a living as a management consultant specializing in organizational design and process management. This has enabled me to fulfill my ministry calling in various missions to reach men for Christ, including extensive pastoral counseling and nine years traveling to St. Petersburg, Russia to develop charitable medical programs for the poor and elderly.

At the beginning of each chapter, I have written stories about some of the men I met in Russia and my encounters with them. Each account emphasizes the importance of the value in the chapter title. Then I have described five supporting strategies with stories and examples from my family, church, ministry, and business experiences over the span of my walk with Christ. To protect the privacy of individuals and families, I have changed the names of some persons and places, and other details not significant to the lesson. It is my desire to convey the important facts and principles of each story without bringing harm to any person. I hope that sharing these things will help you gain a clearer perspective of your own circumstances and connect more personally with the Lord.

Larry Kennedy

PART 1

THE FOUR FOUNDATIONAL VALUES
OF PERSONAL RELIABILITY

1

PERSONAL AUTHENTICITY:
A MEASURE OF OUR RESOLVE TO LIVE A CONSISTENT LIFE

I met Uncle Yuri at a luncheon that we held to inform local dignitaries about the gerontological hospital and other humanitarian medical services our foundation had helped establish. It was a happy public relations event with a simple meal and a few special introductions and speeches like most luncheons with a purpose. We wanted to inform as many influential people as possible about the kinds of clinics we were sponsoring for the elderly. Besides getting acquainted and allowing them to tour our facilities, we also provided everyone with free medical exams and a small pack of over-the-counter medicines to take home with them. We wanted them to experience first-hand the kind of loving care our patients could expect to receive.

When I sat down next to Yuri, I had no idea what he did for a living. He was a big imposing man about my father's age with a deep authoritative voice and a strong handshake. We quickly entered into a conversation about how a Floridian like me was coping with the cold and sunless days of Russian winter. It was a brisk exchange that was, at times, very funny, with good-natured bantering back and forth. Yuri had a surprisingly quick wit and he loved to tell Russian proverbs and riddles. It was as though we had been friends from the beginning and I felt free to kibitz and joke around with him just like anyone would with their uncle. I don't remember when

I started calling him Uncle Yuri, but it felt completely natural to both of us.

When I asked him about his wife, his eyes misted. She was frail and weak from a long-time illness and was not expected to get better. I wanted to help if I could, so we arranged to meet her for tea and to pick up her medical file. An American missionary doctor volunteered to help me obtain the specialized medicine she required and coordinate her treatment in Russia. Yuri could not have been more appreciative and those simple efforts deeply cemented our relationship. He soon invited me to his office, a common ritual among Russians, to visit and get to know his colleagues. It was like any family-man's office, with pictures of his grandchildren on his desk and mementos scattered about. And like any proud grandpa, he had stories to tell about each of his "babies." Yuri was a perfect example of how you can be misled about a person's personality or character if you are exposed to only one dimension of his life. This articulate and playful older man with a "Papa's" demeanor was a KGB General.

Russians often referred to KGB headquarters as the "Big House." It was a place they feared because of its history of terrifying interrogations, torture, and murder during the Soviet years. None of my Russian friends would go with me to visit Uncle Yuri; even finding an interpreter was a problem. When we pulled up in front of the building, they would become visibly shaken and refuse to go in with me. It was a demonic stronghold that represented the most evil part of communism, but the Lord wanted me to go there whether it gave me the creeps or not. His grace allowed me to remain natural and friendly, even though I was always closely scrutinized by everyone from the guards downstairs to the people I passed in the hallways. Apparently, I didn't look like I belonged there, which was strange, because some of them didn't either.

Yuri and his colleagues had been taught to rationalize the things they did at work as necessary for the state. This allowed them to close off their consciences so that they could live what was an otherwise normal life. I wasn't too surprised by this because I understood from my consulting experiences how businessmen can rationalize the dishonest things they might be doing either personally or professionally in order to keep functioning. Just like some of the men I knew who were trapped behind a religious facade, I was sure that Yuri would like to find a way out. When we talked about the Kingdom of God, I could see the desire in his eyes, but there was always something holding him back. One night after we had shared dinner at his apartment, the Lord opened my heart to understand. His reluctance wasn't related to the personal and financial risks involved. He had done such terrible things, he didn't think that he could be forgiven.

I suddenly realized that the Lord wanted to give Yuri a miracle, and in a moment of calm boldness I began to speak to him on behalf of the Lord. "Uncle Yuri, you believe God speaks to men don't you?" "I suppose," he said, "but He has never spoken to me." It was a startling response because there was absolutely no reluctance on his part to speak about God as a person. I could see that His heart was wide open and ready to believe, so I continued. "Well, He just spoke to me about you," I said, "and He wants me to convey a message. Would you like to hear it?" His eyes widened, and in the quiet voice of a frightened little boy he said, "Yes, please." "I think He said that at this very moment He is bringing things to your memory, bad things that you have done that you have not believed that even He could forgive. Is that true?" He nodded yes, as though he was unable to speak. "Well, the Lord wants to forgive you for these and all your sins. All you have to do is accept His forgiveness and you can be free."

Tears started streaming down his face and mine. For a long time he sat silently in the presence of the Lord, crying and being cleansed from the sin-guilt of the horrors in which he had participated. His prayer was a simple and repeated, "Thank you," as he expressed his deep appreciation to the Lord. I don't know what else the Lord said to him that night, but it was obviously a lengthy conversation. Not long afterwards, without any prompting from me, he was baptized. He eventually left the KGB for a job in industrial security, leaving behind the glaring inconsistencies of his double life.

Personal authenticity is a measure of our resolve to live a consistent life. It is an indicator of the sensitivity of our conscience and how obediently we respond to the conviction of the Holy Spirit. True accountability begins in the recesses of the heart, where our hidden will and desires are tested by our knowledge of the will of God. The choices we make to discipline our souls, bring consistency to our words and deeds, and obey the Lord, are the ultimate proof of our credibility. As followers of Christ, "the goal of our instruction is love from a pure heart and a good conscience and a sincere faith" (1 Timothy 1:5 NAS). These inner attributes are essential for becoming a reliable man.

Like Uncle Yuri, too many men have believed that they are in a special category of sinners that will prevent them from fully obeying Christ. They either believe they are too entangled in their sinful desires and indulgences to be able to follow the Lord, or that they can't fit into the unlivable models that religion has offered. A man who has tried to turn away from his sin and naively reached out to the church for help can find himself trapped between his desires for something real and lasting in Christ, and his refusal to continue in a religious system that has failed him. But ultimately, each of us owns our sins and can blame them on no one. Our choices are simple: We can ignore the important issues of life, or we can turn our hearts to obeying Christ first and above all else "forgetting what lies behind and reaching forward to what lies ahead . . . press[ing] on toward the goal for the prize of the upward call of God in Christ Jesus" (Philippians 3:13-14 NAS).

And what a goal, prize, and upward calling it is! When God spoke through the prophet Isaiah about the coming of Jesus, He described His fantastic plans and purposes for men. About Christ's ministry to those who would believe in Him, He said:

> The Spirit of the Sovereign Lord is on me, because the Lord has anointed me to preach good news *to the poor*. He has sent me to bind up *the brokenhearted*, to proclaim freedom *for the captives* and release from darkness *for the prisoners*, to proclaim the year of the Lord's favor and the day of vengeance of our God, to comfort *all who mourn*, and provide for *those who grieve* in Zion to bestow on them a crown of beauty instead of ashes, the oil of gladness instead

of mourning, and a garment of praise instead of a spirit of despair.

Isaiah 61:1-3

And about His vision for men and the effect His restoring power would have on those who obey Him, He continued:

They (those who *were* poor, brokenhearted, captives, prisoners, or who mourned or grieved) will be called oaks (#352, or strong men) of righteousness (#6664, justice, and the right thing to do ethically, morally, and legally), a planting of the Lord for the display of His splendor.

Isaiah 61:3

This is what Christ died for and the kind of vision that makes life vital and satisfying for those who follow Him. What could be more relevant than to be God's men of "righteousness and justice" at home and at work.

Embrace the Obligations of Manhood

The subject of manhood has been written and argued about for centuries with various theories on how to identify and measure masculinity and know when manhood actually occurs. But I remember very well when I first stepped across the line of demarcation between adolescence and adulthood. I was standing in a hot, muggy telephone booth next to the post office in Cocoa Beach, Florida. It wasn't exactly what I had in mind; not a grand entrance, but it was more than conspicuous. The street noise was so loud that I could barely hear the voice on the other end of the line say, "I'm pregnant." The crush of that moment was indescribable. As the weight of responsibility settled across my shoulders, I understood for the first time that life had the potential of being more than I could handle. I was gripped with the fear of failure, thinking I might not be capable of caring for myself and a new family. But down deep inside I heard a voice speak to me, "be a man." I don't know if it was a memory of the things I had heard my Dad say, or the voice of God pushing me to embrace my obligations, but it strengthened my resolve and in just two weeks I was married and on my way to figuring out life.

Just a few days before I heard I was going to be a Dad, I had made a deposit on a bright red Corvette Stingray. So when I stopped by to tell my parents that I was getting married, my Mother craftily tested my will by saying, "You can't afford to buy a new car *and* get married." I sat at the kitchen table and thought for a moment. I wasn't wise or godly, but I could add and subtract in my head. And there were going to be more important expenses to consider. So I picked up the phone, called the dealer and canceled the order. Looking back, that was a clear indicator that our marriage would survive life's pressures. Actually, Dorothy and I had both done much better selecting a mate than we could have imagined at the time. Each of us was part of God's plan for the other. But although we worked very hard and shouldered our responsibilities well, the love that had brought us together in the beginning was clearly not going to sustain us without some adjustments. Within a short time I seriously damaged our marriage with my misguided and selfish attempts to "be a man" without God.

Whether we are aware of it or not, almost every man has argued against the Lordship of Christ at one time or another. It's not something we do consciously. In fact, our arguments sometimes sound very noble, especially when we say (as I once did), "I'm not going to try following Christ until I am really ready, because I don't want to be a hypocrite." But there is nothing wise or noble about saying "No" to the Lord. In my own case it would have been more honest to say, "I have good feelings about the Lord when I think of Him, but I like doing things my own way and I'm enjoying my sins far too much to consider obeying Him right now." Like most men, I was too proud to say anything quite so honest. And it would be many years before I realized how ridiculous my reasons for not following Christ had become. Eventually though, every one of us must settle his differences with his Maker and obey Him if we want to reach our full potential as a man.

When God made man, He gave him the freedom to reject having a relationship with Him. He also gave him the freedom to not trust in or rely upon Him. But there is an undeniable capacity within man to know that God exists and it is out of that conflict–the truth of God's sovereign existence against the hardness of man's will–from which all arguments against His Lordship arise. The extreme is atheism, although I've discussed the impossibility of it with many avowed atheists (especially in Russia) and each of them quickly retreated to agnosticism. The agnostic, unlike the so-called atheist, does not deny the existence of God. He backs slightly away from that hard line and says it is impossible to prove the existence of God. Each step away from atheism modifies slightly what a man is willing to admit without submitting to Jesus as Lord. "Oh yes, there is a God, but his name is _____, not Jehovah." "Oh yes, I believe in God, but Jesus was not the Son of God." "Oh yes, I believe that Jehovah is God, and that Jesus is His Son, but I don't believe the entire Bible," and so on.

One night I was sharing my faith with an industrialist who had built textile plants around the world. He was very firm in his position of "unbelief" and when I had finished sharing about Christ's work in my life he said very succinctly, "That's a very nice fairy tale, but I'm sorry, I don't believe it." He was not offended or offensive, just unbelieving, so I thought we should change the subject. I asked him to tell me more about his work. For the next couple of hours he told me about the various factories he had built, the difficulties of international finance, and even details about the textile machines he manufactured. It was a fascinating discussion that would hold the interest of almost anyone. I learned a lot and was sincerely interested in knowing more about him. At the end of our discussion I turned to him and said, "That's a very nice fairy tale, but I'm sorry, I don't believe it." He was dumfounded and sat quietly for a moment. Then he said, "I get your point." We went back to our discussion of faith and he became a follower of Christ.

Every obstacle to the Lordship of Christ rests upon a foundation of unbelief. Whether it represents a logical, illogical, rational, or irrational perspective, unbelief is very often rooted in the pain or disappointment of real-life events that didn't turn out the way we wanted. Some unbelieving arguments are based upon misstated or confused facts or even false doctrine. But if they are repeated often enough, they can begin to sound reasonable and provide a man with the excuse he needs for hardening his will against God. No matter how carefully a man may have been nurtured and trained by his parents, how much life experience he has, or how well-intentioned he may be, if he does not know the Lord, understand what He requires of him, and learn how to obey Him, he can expect only limited success in dealing with life's problems.

Ironically, one of the most common sources of unbelief is the church's many denominations. When you analyze the theologies of most "Christian" religions, you discover that most have congregated around their common unbelief of one or more parts of the Bible. As a result, their ministries are able to produce no better than partially committed men–partially committed to God through Christ, and partially committed to the limiting doctrines of a religious institution calling itself "the church." The man whose faith has been divided by his commitment to both God and an institutional agenda is like the man described in James 1:8 whose faith is divided by doubts. He is "double-minded" and plagued by recurring episodes of his failed personal reliability. The Apostle Paul clearly warned us about dividing our hearts between the Lord and even our most respected brothers in Christ. In 1 Corinthians 1:11-13 he said:

> My brothers, some from Chloe's household have informed me that there are quarrels among you. What I mean is this: One of you says, "I follow Paul"; another, "I follow Apollos"; another, "I follow Cephas"; still another, "I follow Christ." Is Christ divided? Was Paul crucified for you? Were you baptized into the name of Paul?

Having been a Pharisee and the son of a Pharisee (Acts 23:6), Paul understood the kind of institutional pride and idolatry that can grow from sincere and misguided acts of loyalty. It can become divisive to the body of Christ in general, and to a man's personal devotion to the Lord. Instead of finding his identity in the Lordship of Christ, a man's need to belong, to participate in something bigger than himself, or to be associated with power, can draw him into the captivating agendas of organized religion. Whether you're just becoming a follower of Christ or you're a weary veteran looking for a fresh start, the Lord's message has always been the same. He consistently calls us to turn away from the temptations of the world or the disappointments of institutional religion and to turn to Him. So when He speaks to men, there is no confusion about His purpose.

To Thomas, who needed help in overcoming his doubts, He said, "Be not unbelieving, but believing" (John 20:27 NAS).

To Peter, who had denied Him and failed miserably in his time of testing, He asked, "Do you love Me more than these?" (John 21:15 NAS).

To the proud and rebellious Pharisees He said, "Either make the tree good and its fruit good, or make the tree bad, and its fruit bad. . ." (Matthew 12:33 NAS).

In Isaiah 46 the Lord exhorts the men of Israel to turn away from their numerous sins and return to Him alone as their protector and provider. He makes this simple, clear, and direct appeal:

> Remember this, and show yourselves men (#377, be a man, act in a masculine, manly way); Recall to mind, O you transgressors. Remember the former things of old, for I am God, and there is no other; I am God, and there is none like Me.
>
> Isaiah 46:8-9 NKJ

Be Diligent in the Use of Your Faith

The first twenty-four hours after I became a follower of Christ is a blur in my memory. All I can remember is the sweet, mellow, peace of the Lord's presence. It was clear to me what I had done: I had committed to a complete surrender of my will to His. In return, He had mercifully forgiven me of my sins and was going to teach me how to follow Him. And, because He loved me, He would stick closer to me than any mentor I'd had, convicting me of my sins and giving me wisdom so that I could become a better man. To remain in the peaceful presence of the Lord, all I had to do was apologize to Him and ask for His forgiveness (or repent) when I made a mistake.

On the evening of the second day, I faced the first major challenge to my faith. As I stood in the bathroom brushing my teeth, I suddenly remembered the magazines that were tucked away in the cabinet just below the counter where I was standing. And I immediately felt ashamed that they were still there. The Holy Spirit was doing His job of convicting, now it was my turn to obey. But instead, I closed the door and reached under the counter fully intending to indulge in one more act of lust. Evil was still trying to control my life and something within me wanted to take just one more look. It was an impulse that went completely against the desire to obey that I had felt only a few seconds before. Then, just as though a friendly counselor was speaking to my soul, the Lord simply said, "Don't do it." His voice reminded me that what I now had was far too valuable to risk taking even one more look. I asked God to forgive me for having considered it. Then I yelled at the top of my voice to my invisible, unknown foe, "No, never again. In the name of Jesus, leave me alone!" As suddenly as the episode had begun, I was free.

A strategic fragment of Satan's grip on my soul was broken that night. And the Lord wasted no time in consolidating His gains. Almost immediately, other sins associated with lust began to come to my memory as the Lord led me in a thorough renunciation of each facet of this evil scheme in my life. I had sneaked around, lied, and done many other things that were in violation of my marriage covenant in order to support my habit. Not only that, I had feelings of insecurity and rejection that gave lust validating powers it should never have had. That night the Lord began a dialogue about a number of things that needed correcting before they produced further sin and torment in my life. I had already been forgiven of my past sins, but God wanted to eliminate the *sources* of sin in my life. Instead of spending my entire life repenting of the same old sins, He wanted me to work at identifying and removing the root causes.

In John 6:29 Jesus said, "The work of God is this: to believe in the one He has sent." The easiest and most obvious step we can take to help ourselves believe is reading God's Word. But the toughest work in believing is obeying the conviction of the Holy

Spirit to rid ourselves of "unbelief" that causes us to resist God's Word or to argue against His way of doing things. The simplest definition of "faith" (#4102) is "being morally persuaded of the truth." And the simplest way to express faith is through repentance and obedience. So when we become morally persuaded that we are routinely thinking or acting in a way that is contrary to the will of God, we can ask Him to help us see the reason why. We can then express our faith by repenting and taking actions consistent with obedience.

This kind of introspection might require layers of repentance. For instance, cursing could be rooted in anger, and anger could be rooted in an injustice that needs to be forgiven. By forgiving the injustice and then repenting of the anger associated with it, we might lose the powerful urge to curse. If we don't we might become so frustrated at our inability to stop cursing that we become even more unbelieving. Ridding ourselves of unbelief is the most important work that God requires of us as followers of Christ. And it is the most effective way to seek personal improvement because it relies upon an active relationship with the Lord. The success we experience will depend upon how persuaded we are that:

> The law of the Lord is perfect, reviving the soul. The statutes of the Lord are trustworthy, making wise the simple. The precepts of the Lord are right, giving joy to the heart. The commands of the Lord are radiant, giving light to the eyes. The fear of the Lord is pure, enduring forever. The ordinances of the Lord are sure and altogether righteous. They are more precious than gold, than much pure gold; they are sweeter than honey, than honey from the comb. By them is your servant warned; in keeping them there is great reward.
>
> Psalms19: 7-11

All of the men I've known who said they were followers of Christ, yet argued against this practical approach to faith, had focused their believing on external goals. Instead of working to bring their soul into submission to God's will, they were striving to gain God's blessing on what they wanted to do; and that didn't include a lot of time digging into their past. In virtually every case the results were tragic, as root causes that had been ignored or rationalized eventually overtook their lives. Whether it was a businessman using his faith in God to believe for greater success, a family man leaving his job to minister and do great exploits for God, a man-child allowing his wife to carry the emotional and spiritual burdens of their family, or a religious loyalist who believed he had fulfilled his obligations to God by supporting the local church, they were each blinded by unbelief. Eventually though, a man will reap the consequences of failing to do the "work of God."

Karl was a residential real estate broker who had started out as a salesman for a tiny firm. He was a handsome, bright, articulate man who had worked hard at his profession and had already become reasonably successful. Not long after he became a follower of Christ he attended a men's meeting where he was encouraged to demonstrate his faith in God by "calling those things which be not as though they were" (Romans 4:17 KJV). This was a reference to Abraham's faith to believe that he would become the father of nations. Each man was encouraged to think of the thing he wanted most in his business (and that would bring glory to God) and to begin speaking about it in such a way as to believe it had already happened. Karl quickly saw himself as "the largest broker in his city" and began to say it to nearly every person he encountered.

Since his "confession" was consistent with almost every motivational speaker's idea of a visionary, and the goal-oriented methodology of most leadership seminars, it was easy to see how Karl had overlooked one very strategically flawed nuance of the principle his seminar leader had failed to convey: Abraham was being encouraged to believe *what God had told him*, not what he imagined himself to be. Nonetheless, for several years Karl repeated his goal as though it had already come to pass. As his business steadily expanded he became increasingly convinced of his ability to "believe God for great things" and he could not be persuaded that he was the willing captive of unbelief, and that what he did believe was inconsistent with the truth of Scripture. In fact, the success of his business had become the defining virtue of his walk with Christ. He gave his testimony at churches, traveled on volunteer mission trips to speak about faith, and demonstrated his prosperity as a generous contributor to many programs as the evidence of God's approval of his use of his faith.

But Karl had brought unfinished business into his walk with Christ. He had a serious problem with "the ladies," as he called it. He was constantly flirting with women and was involved in more than one adulterous relationship prior to coming to Christ. He had made a new commitment to his wife, resolving to never again be unfaithful. However, on my occasional visits to his office, I noticed that Karl continued to be flirtatious (or at least overly familiar) with women. When I asked him about it, he would deny any wrongdoing and defend it as part of his "sales" personality. But I knew it went deeper than that and kept encouraging him to pray about it. Each time we talked he would lament that he hadn't taken time to be with the Lord and talk to Him about his problem. Eventually, I heard rumors that Karl's marriage was breaking up. It wasn't long before he called me for an appointment to seek counsel.

He had gotten involved with a young girl about half his age who was, of all things, a stripper in a nightclub. I had only one question for him, "How does a follower of Christ find himself in a night club, watching strippers in the first place?" He hung his head and said, "I know, but she really is a great gal, and I love her. She wants to be a Christian and get married, and I believe it's God's will." There were so many things wrong with his thinking that I barely knew where to start. He wasn't even considering repentance. He had long since rejected what I had told him about root causes and their consequences. In fact, he had mildly mocked my faith as being "hung up on the past." Although he knew he had a sin from which he could not shake loose, he had depended upon "calling those things which be not as though they were" instead of working to find the cause of his unbelief. Now, all he wanted was someone to approve his mistaken plan. The ridiculous part of this story is that he probably would have been a very successful realtor anyway. But his choice to follow an easy path of unbelief cost him his family, his business, and the relationship he could have had with the Lord.

Not long after our last meeting, he filed for bankruptcy and was nearly destitute from the drinking, drugs, and immoral lifestyle he and his new "Christian" wife had built for themselves.

> Now for this very reason also, applying all diligence, in your faith supply moral excellence, and in your moral excellence, knowledge, and in your knowledge, self-control, and in your self-control, perseverance, and in your perseverance, godliness, and in your godliness, brotherly kindness, and in your brotherly kindness, love. For if these qualities are yours and are increasing, they render you neither useless nor unfruitful in the true knowledge of our Lord Jesus Christ.
>
> 2 Peter 1:5-8 NAS

Work to Keep a Clear Conscience

The kind of cold, heartless arguments against truth that at one time were the private venue of hardened criminals are now routinely heard in our homes, schools, businesses, and yes, churches. While young and old alike argue for their right to exhibit selfish, vulgar, unethical, and insensitive behaviors, "don't judge me," has become the standard defense for a worldwide culture that rejects defining right and wrong. We are living in an era where people have little concern for their neighbor's rights or about matters of personal conscience. It is a time when large numbers of our citizens, from every walk of life, have learned to ignore the facts and switch the rules when it suits them and to rehearse their lies until they show no conscience.

One of the most pathetic and terrifying things to see is a man who has lost or is losing his conscience. In both my business and pastoral counseling, I have encountered several men who were so stunningly without conscience that they defied understanding. A businessman once came to my office to discuss what he called "personal problems." I occasionally had interviews with men whose friends had referred them to me for spiritual counsel, so I expected it to be a routine first visit. But not long into our discussion, he very casually mentioned that he was facing legal charges for "touching" a little girl in his neighborhood. He said it in such a matter-of-fact manner that he might as well have been talking about a business loan. There was no sense of urgency or remorse about the man whatsoever and when I made a comment about the seriousness of the charges he looked me straight in the eye and said with a light chuckle, "I don't get it. I mean, what's all of the fuss about. She's only six years old. She doesn't even know what I did. There's really been no harm."

The pedophile who sat across from me in my office that day was dressed in a conservative business suit and looked like any middle-aged family man. He had a wife and children of his own and lived in a nice neighborhood where families thought they could trust one another. He went to work every day and even attended church, so there was no reason for his neighbors to have suspected what he was capable of doing, unless they had known about the video tapes he had stashed around his home, or his choice of websites. If they had followed him to work and witnessed the cool manipulation of his customers, they might have been alarmed. Or if they had called one of the business contacts he bragged about, they might have discovered, as his mortgage banker had done, that his work history was not as impressive as he had often stated. But whenever he was caught in a misdeed, he would calmly lie and discredit his accuser. He was a special kind of predator called the "white-collar psychopath," (Hare 1993) whose smooth, articulate demeanor allowed him to blend into almost any community undetected.

My first encounter with someone who demonstrated such an extreme lack of conscience had come years before when a friend asked me to help counsel a man from a prominent Christian family who had left the church and actually become a Satanist. He had become violently angry when his parents confronted him with his sins, but had agreed to attend a counseling session to appease his mother. For our entire session he boldly and defiantly described his participation in unspeakable rites and sacrifices, including murder. I was so shocked that I had trouble breathing. As I sat there praying about this hollow shell of a man, I asked the Lord, "How could he possibly have declined from reciting Scripture in Bible class to where he is now?" His answer came with clear and unequivocal precision, "One step at a time." Just like a young man learning to smoke or to drink scotch, he had to have ignored and overcome the nauseating natural repulsions of his body and soul, and willed himself to continue. Although his story was heartbreaking and gruesome, it was a good lesson how each of us is capable of sinking deep into sin and depravation.

Speaking to someone who has slipped over the edge of humane behavior into what might be an irreversible spiritual condition has always had a very sobering effect on my own attitudes. It makes me more thankful for God's grace in my life, and a lot more sensitive to what I might be doing to grieve the Holy Spirit. I've also realized how easy it is to continue doing little things that dull our spiritual senses and eventually lose our sense of shame about sin. When that happens, a little piece of our conscience is gasping for breath and has already weakened a part of our will to be further tempted. What we're doing wrong might appear almost indiscernible or harmless by itself. But when it becomes part of a pattern of disobedience, it can accumulate into the spiritual leverage the devil needs to draw us into more serious sins, ones that we might not have considered had we obeyed our first convictions about the little things.

One afternoon I received an urgent call from a family asking me to visit their son who had just been arrested. I didn't ask why but assumed it was on another drug charge. When I arrived at the jail, the chaplain, who escorted me to the young man's cell, spoke to me in a fatherly tone and said, "Remember where you are and what you're doing. Keep alert. If you need help, just wave to the guard." It was a rather ominous instruction for a visit with a young drug addict. But as soon as I sat down, I realized why. The young man began sobbing and cried out, "I did it! I did it! I'm so sorry; I don't know what came over me." He then described in excruciating detail how, only hours before, he had murdered an innocent storekeeper who had refused to give him money so that he could buy drugs. It was a despicable and bloody crime and an act of senseless rage. But as unbelievable as it sounded, almost any addict could relate to the reservoir of anger that had accumulated within him, if not the crime. The habit that had started out years before with marijuana had become a consuming heroin addiction, creating the potential for any act that would satisfy his craving.

My next visit was even more startling. I found quite a different young man this time. If I had not already heard his horrific confession, he would have sounded completely believable when he said, "I'm innocent you know. My parents have hired a good lawyer and he says we can beat the charge." After spending time with his lawyer, he was intent on speaking the legal language of the courtroom. Apparently, he had rejected the Lord's conviction and decided to rely upon his proven ability to manipulate his parents with lies. Before he was finished with them, they had spent all of their savings, re-mortgaged their home, and even asked me to be a character witness at his trial. I was so saddened by their plight that I only said this, "Tell your son I will be very happy to tell the truth and the whole truth, but he might prefer that I invoke my right to pastoral confidentiality and remain silent. Let it be his choice." Instead of clearing his conscience, pleading guilty, and probably getting a lighter sentence, he ended up on death row.

Ecclesiastes 1:9 says, "What has been will be again, what has been done will be done again; there is nothing new under the sun." There are no especially "modern" sins, only new ways to commit old ones. But one thing is abundantly clear; the frequency, intensity, and widespread acceptance of the no-conscience attitude has had an alarming influence on the world, and even on believers. Some men I've known have even started comparing their behaviors to the rest of the world instead of the Scriptures, as a way of arguing against their need for change. No one but God really knows what combination of pain, rejection, unbelief, and rebellion it takes to gradually turn a person's heart to defiant disobedience, or just how far we can go before the Lord calls us to accountability. But why take the risks of ignoring the conviction of the Holy Spirit upon our heart? It's too easy to slide, one step at a time, toward a personal disaster. Instead, we should work to keep a clear conscience and pray as King David did in Psalms 51:10-12:

Create in me a pure heart, O God, and renew a steadfast spirit within me. Do not cast me from your presence or take your Holy Spirit from me. Restore to me the joy of your salvation and grant me a willing spirit, to sustain me.

Subject Yourself to Reality Checks

When our focus is first of all on the Lord and His will, He helps us overcome the challenges of each day, sometimes by causing us to avoid troubles and sometimes by strengthening us to go through them. In 2 Corinthians 12:9, the Lord said to the Apostle Paul, "My grace is sufficient for you." There is no truer test of our faith than when we trust the Lord to establish our agenda, including who and what comes into it each day. King David said to the Lord, "Blessed are those whose strength is in you, who have set their hearts on pilgrimage" (Psalms 84:2-5).

The Hebrew word here translated as pilgrimage (#4546) also means "a highway, course, path, staircase, or terrace," indicating a way or means to a destination. One of the greatest mistakes made by new followers of Christ is to think of our salvation experience and forgiveness for all our past sins as the culmination of our journey instead of the beginning. The restoration of our soul can be a life-long process. And it is founded upon a very involved personal relationship with the Lord. There is much more to a walk with Christ than stumbling along in life and occasionally repenting and getting back on track in our pilgrimage. He wants us to dig deep into our souls to seek improvement and grow into strong, reliable men who can be trusted. Becoming a follower of Christ is not like joining a political party or a service club. It is a learning experience that allows us to enjoy wonderful fellowship with our Maker.

I had two failed attempts to find a sustaining faith (at ages twelve and twenty) probably because I had only decided to "be a Christian," instead of beginning a pilgrimage. Each time, I sincerely repented of my sins and felt God's forgiveness. But without setting my heart to learn His ways and do what I read in the Bible, I was destined to have sins pile up day after day until I gave up. Then, after a few years under the pressures of family life, I realized how poorly I had managed things. The third time I came to Christ as a learner and I was able to share the same testimony as the Prophet Jeremiah, who said, "Your words were found and I ate them, and Your words became for me a joy and the delight of my heart" (Jeremiah 15:16 NAS). From that day forward, I was committed to practicing the ways of the Lord. And nothing or no one would ever again be allowed to take the place of His presence in my life. It is that intensity of love and appreciation for who He is and what He has done for us that releases His grace to help us each day.

You may have heard the story of the chicken and the pig that were wandering around the barnyard, watching the farmer complete his chores. The chicken said to the pig, "You know, he's a really nice guy and he's been good to us. Why don't we give him a ham and eggs breakfast to show our appreciation?" The pig looked at the chicken with a frown and said, "That's easy for you to say. For you it's just a contribution, but for me it would mean total commitment." Over the years, I've heard countless discussions like that between men who were trying to decide whether or not they wanted to take an easy doable path that required little or no sacrifice, or to lay down their lives as they knew them to obey Christ. Jesus said, "Whoever wants to save his life will lose it, but whoever loses his life for me and for the gospel will save it. What good is it for a man to gain the whole world, yet forfeit his soul?" (Mark 8:35-36). The Scriptures provide many penetrating reality checks like this one to which a man must subject himself if he is going to continue to follow Christ. No one can press these things upon us. Our embrace of them must be an authentic expression of our love for Him.

Spiritual confrontation can be one of the purest expressions of real love. This is especially the case when it takes place between a husband and wife who are both dedicated followers of Christ. Second only to the Lord Himself, no one knows or loves a man like his wife. Although it took me too long to appreciate her perspective on my life, I have come to trust Dorothy first among all others, not just to love me, but to know something about me that no one else could tell me, and to tell me for my own good, not just to even the score from a previous hurt. And she feels the same way about me.

But with all that said, we both realize that nothing or no one can take the place of our personal pursuit of the Lord's perspective on our life. Everyone else—friends, family, and members of small groups—are just helpers for those times when we're having trouble receiving the truth about ourselves.

Recognizing their limitations, small groups can be very helpful in sorting through issues and providing a needed perspective. But unless the people from whom we seek advice have reliable knowledge and experience, they might hinder rather than help. I've counseled with several men who say they have attended small groups seeking help to overcome lust or another equally tormenting sin, only to have their hearts turned away from the power of God to the unbelieving view that "we can never really be free." It's like telling someone that they can never be free from the compulsion to open the hood of their car, pop open the battery, and drink the acid from it. No matter how many enticing ways someone might try to tempt a man to take those fatal steps, he could never be convinced to do it if he knew what the results would be. When a man thoroughly understands the realities of his sin, and the full effect it has had on him, his relationship with the Lord, his family, job, etc., it will become relatively easy for him to hate his sin and repent deeply enough to get free. Then, with a little common sense and discipline, he can resist the temptation of sin just like it was acid, in a sealed battery, in a locked car, in a distant parking lot.

A man can also attend a small group but not have the humility to honestly participate and take it to heart when he receives godly counsel. I attended a men's prayer group that occasionally spent a whole day together just to talk about our walk with the Lord and pray for one another. Our "prayer day" was a priority that each person considered an almost sacred appointment. We were a group of only six men with very diverse backgrounds and careers. And even though we felt like brothers from the beginning, one of the men never got connected to what we were doing. He was just too proud to be real, and when he came to our meetings he was always in the middle of a business crisis that sounded very similar to the ones we had heard before. It soon became clear to us that he was using our prayer time to show off a little and brag about his business exploits. Like a lot of men, he was more interested in money and toys than in taking serious steps to pursue the Lord. Unfortunately, his religious experiences had only taught him how to "act spiritual" instead of being led by the Spirit. He had not yet learned the importance of Jeremiah 9:23-24, which says:

> "Let not the wise man boast of his wisdom or the strong man boast of his strength or the rich man boast of his riches, but let him who boasts boast about this: that he understands and knows me, that I am the Lord, who exercises kindness, justice and righteousness on earth, for in these I delight," declares the Lord.

I've been a part of several small groups for fellowship, prayer, and Bible study—some with just men, others with just couples, and still others with a mix of single and married male and female participants. Although each of these groups had its own sweet moments and fulfilled a portion of God's plan for my life and marriage, the "men-only" format had a far more powerful effect on its participants because it created situations where we had to humble ourselves and tell the truth or be exposed as phony. The corporate wisdom that God releases when men get real and join together to help one another do the right thing can be astonishing. In a mixed group, people are often reluctant to do the kind of confronting that can be done in a men-only setting, probably because men have a tendency to be more easily embarrassed and become defensive when they are in a mixed setting. They may also harbor hurt feelings or frustration in a mixed group that in a men-only meeting might be taken head-on, just like flesh and blood brothers would do. Done with love and care, it's usually better to get our issues out in the open and talk about them. Each man must decide between the Lord and himself what kind of group, if any, suits the Lord's purposes for his life and which relationships can be depended upon to provide wise counsel. As King David said:

O Lord, you have searched me and you know me.
You know when I sit and when I rise; you perceive
my thoughts from afar. You discern my going out
and my lying down; you are familiar with all my
ways. Before a word is on my tongue you know it
completely, O Lord. You hem me in–behind and
before; you have laid your hand upon me. Such
knowledge is too wonderful for me, too lofty for
me to attain.

Psalms 139:1-6

Let Your Life Be Your Message

In over twenty-five years of ministry I've found that one of the most imposing obstacles to men becoming more reliable is the inconsistent behavior of those who teach and lead in the church. The religious denominations within the church have done such a good job of convincing people that they are God's representatives on the earth that men who turn away from their unbelieving inconsistencies often give up on the pilgrimage they have begun with Christ. They don't stop believing in Christ, but their faith and motivation are often so dramatically shaken that they cynically withdraw from their daily pursuit of His will. Since men often believe that there are no other options but the secular world or institutional religion, they are likely to wander through life frustrated and confused about God's purposes.

Barry was a guy I had met at a men's prayer breakfast. He was a country boy who had grown up in rural Arkansas and become entangled in guns and violence as a teenager. After spending several years in prison he had worked cutting lawns and doing hard labor until he eventually established a very profitable landscape business. Since he had come to Christ, he had settled down and become a gentle and devoted family man. He was also a practical person who was very sensitive to people's needs and often bought groceries or paid the rent for folks who were struggling. His entire church life centered on his personal ministry to the poor and the relationships he had built with a small group of fellow-believers. He had also influenced other men to follow the Lord. Barry was an uncomplicated believer who had continued to grow spiritually until someone urged him to become more involved in his local church.

Like so many men, he soon found that the church was absorbing his time and energy, limiting his fellowship with friends and family. As he became immersed in the church's programs and organizational issues, he realized that he could not conform to its man-made rules nor defend its leaders whose messages were often grossly inconsistent with the way they conducted their lives. Not only that, he had begun to invite people to listen to an "inspiring message" rather than serving and loving them until they asked him about his faith. He knew that his own life wasn't working as well as before and the people whom he had invited to church were regularly falling out of sync with the church's agenda and leaving. Finally, he erupted in anger, "backslid," and left for Las Vegas where "everyone was doing exactly what they looked like they were doing." However, he soon realized that the people in Las Vegas were no more real than some of the "hypocrites" who had caused him to leave the church. They were both just acting in ways they thought were expected of them. Barry had discovered how dysfunctional a life dominated by either worldliness or religion could become and thought that he was trapped between two losing choices. But when he remembered his roots were in Christ and the relationships God had given him, he found real joy again.

Barry's testimony is typical of a lot of men I have known who start out serving the Lord with all their heart only to become side-tracked into institutional life. Far too often, men either give up their faith and return to their worldly ways, or yield control of their lives to organized religion, missing the very best that God has to offer—a life of freedom in Christ. There is no more powerful force against the Lordship of Christ than religion, which slowly enslaves and emasculates men by pressing institutional authority between them and God. As men relinquish their leadership responsibilities to an institution, they begin to believe that a professional minister can exert more influence for Christ than men who are just being themselves at home, at work, or meeting with a few close friends. In Matthew 5:13-16, Jesus said:

You are the salt of the earth. But if the salt loses its saltiness, how can it be made salty again? It is no longer good for anything, except to be thrown out and trampled by men. You are the light of the world. A city on a hill cannot be hidden. Neither do people light a lamp and put it under a bowl. Instead they put it on its stand, and it gives light to everyone in the house. In the same way, let your light shine before men, that they may see your good deeds and praise your Father in heaven.

When we choose to let our light shine through the filter of a religious institution and its programs instead of allowing the Lord to direct our energy where it's needed, the light of Christ does not shine as clearly as it should. One of the most compelling examples I have known was that of George and Frances Lanier. I met for several days with Pastor Lanier, his wife, and their Board of Directors, discussing what had become an embarrassing list of personal inconsistencies in their life and ministry. Having begun as an evangelist, Pastor Lanier had become a Christian celebrity, with invitations to speak coming from literally around the world. The church had applauded almost everything that George and Frances had done and they were perceived by most people to be two servants perfectly harnessed into God's work. But the marital and ministry harmony they projected in public was not at all the real story. They had almost constant battles about the differences between Pastor Lanier's sermon's and his private practices at home and in the office.

While Pastor Lanier appeared transparent and vulnerable in his public life, he could turn cold and demanding in private, and he had regularly ended relationships with people who had pointed out his frailties. Frances had often come to tears during board meetings, alternately lashing out in rage at her husband's lifestyle or neurotically defending him from inquiries that might threaten either his mission or their financial stability. Somewhat intimidated by the Laniers' public stature and the practical eloquence of Pastor Laniers' work, several groups of board members, over many years, had struggled to help them find healing. There had been angry separations and reconciliations, lots of board turnover, and a fragmented family that followed dutifully along, thinking that the chaos they endured was part of their burden in Christian ministry. Every family and board member I spoke with said they felt obligated to protect what they called "the message" Pastor Lanier "carried" by keeping the knowledge of his personal life as secretive as possible. They knew that if his constituents became aware of how often they had caught him lying, manipulating, and breaking his word that the validity of what he had to say would suffer.

But after extended prayer and discussions, the Board agreed on the necessity of confronting the Laniers once again. One entire morning had been spent laying out specifics as lovingly as possible, so that the Board's position on each fact was clear and unmistakable. After giving the Laniers some time alone, we had reconvened to discuss any questions they may have had. As we got started, Frances said, "I have an important question. Is the Board saying that we have to be, or that they are requiring us to be, authentic Christians? In other words are you saying that we are not authentic?" Realizing the pain of that moment, I answered in as subdued manner as possible, "Yes, that's what the Board is saying." She motioned to her husband and spoke with disgust in her voice saying, "Then why have I had to endure 'this' all these years?" She raised her hands and arms, as if to worship the Lord, leaned back in her chair, gazed upward and prayed hopeless words of unbelief that almost stopped our hearts, "Lord help me. I'm drowning in 'Lanier.' Just give me cancer and let me die. I can't stand it anymore."

It was one of the most chilling moments in my spiritual life and an exclamation point to the list of failures Frances had complained about for many years. But each time their friends had attempted to reconcile Frances' accusations about George's lies, financial mismanagement, and general unreliability with his complaints about an unloving, vindictive wife with signs of mental instability, they had failed. The problem with their counter-accusations was simple. Each of them was telling the truth about the other. But neither of them was willing to take responsibility for his or her own sins. When each of a series of counselors discovered the unyielding nature of their conflicts and the fraudulence of their public image, the Laniers quickly joined forces to escape exposure and keep the cloak of authenticity draped over their ministry. One disappointed constituent who had first-hand knowledge of their deceptions had frustratingly labeled their life together as "the Lanier conspiracy."

The Laniers are a good example of how people can become caught up in the "profession" of ministry and/or the development of their "message" instead of doing what's necessary to let the Lord's light shine through their lives. Even though counselors and board members with whom they had supposedly maintained close relationships for many years surrounded them, they chose to live a double life that was completely inconsistent with the mandates of Christ. Rather than develop an authentic inner life with Christ and an honest relationship with one another (as they had often preached) they had been acting happy and unified in the presence of their Board and constituents and quite another way at home. Theirs is one of many sad stories in the long history of the church, and the negative effect its leaders' inconsistent behaviors have had on the lives of people like Barry.

All that most of us can do to help people like the Laniers, or someone they may have harmed or discouraged, is to pray for them and occasionally provide opportunities for correction or healing they may have missed in the quietness of a prayer closet. Even so, the final responsibility for authenticity rests squarely on the shoulders of each believer who must bear the consequences of his or her failure to obey the Lord. In Psalm 86:11, King David prayed, "Teach me your way, O Lord, and I will walk in your truth; give me an undivided heart, that I may fear your name."

2

ETHICAL DEPENDABILITY:
A MEASURE OF OUR TRUSTWORTHINESS IN PRACTICAL MATTERS

We were considering several remodeling projects that were critical to the success of our Russian medical programs. Although we had solved the design and financing problems, the toughest challenges were still ahead. Russian construction standards were arcane at best and we knew that there would be dishonest building inspectors at every turn, trying to squeeze bribes out of us with trumped up issues. We had interviewed a number of construction companies, even some from Finland and Germany, but they were all far too expensive or lacked the experience we needed. We decided to investigate the possibility of doing the work ourselves, but to do so we had to have someone who really knew his way around a construction site and could handle the pressures of managing a crew of Russian laborers. However, there was one thing sadly lacking–ethically dependable men from which to choose a construction manager.

Russia's tradesmen had been trained to operate within the confines of a godless bureaucracy. Their daily activities were shaped by time-consuming and wasteful rules that were strictly imposed and anyone who got out of step could easily suffer the loss of his job, social standing, or much worse. A man's work was not judged on its merits, but on how it supported the narrow doctrines of the

Soviet "vision." Over time, the cynical effects of loyalty to inept and corrupt managers and a doctrinally controlled culture that could not fulfill its own mandates, had caused most workers to abandon any thought of doing things efficiently or with excellence. In order to advance in pay grade they had to lie, manipulate the facts, and report progress, even where there was none. It was the same kind of mentality that's found in mafia-run labor unions. I knew it was asking a lot, but I was sure that the Lord could lead us to the right person.

I was scheduled to attend a chapel service at one of the prisons and was looking forward to the diversion it would bring from my construction planning. Visiting inmates has been a vital part of my ministry and in Russia it was an especially rewarding experience. Russian prisons are brutal and when you meet a fellow-believer in one of them, he is likely to be a serious man of God. To fellowship with such men is an honor that I greatly appreciated. A local priest (with help from an accommodating prison official) had been sneaking communion in to a small group of believers in this particular prison for several years. Now that they were free to assemble and have Bible studies, they had a thriving fellowship of about fifty men and they were beginning to have a very stabilizing affect on the compound. Violence among inmates was down and the warden had given them permission to have regular meetings. In fact, on the day of my visit, they were planning to dedicate a new chapel, which was usually little more than a small one-man prayer closet, but precious to them.

The leader of the prayer group met us just inside the gates and escorted us across the compound. His name was Gregori. He was a middle-aged man with clear blue eyes, gray hair, and the humility of an elder. He bear-hugged the priest and then me and I felt as comfortable and welcome as if I were attending someone's home church. As we walked across the compound, Gregori introduced us to various inmates and officers who were also on their way to the chapel. There was an excitement or "buzz" among the men that was quite unusual for a prison. And as we cut through a run-down dormitory and out into an enthusiastic crowd, I understood why. Gregori's face beamed with pride as he pointed toward a beautifully constructed miniature of a Russian Orthodox cathedral, spires and all. About sixty people could jam into it and there were several hundred men gathered in and around it for the dedication.

The families of the inmates, and even some prison guards, had donated every brick, board, and nail. Gregori had designed, organized, and managed the entire project using volunteer inmate labor. It was an astonishing accomplishment and the quality of the work was outstanding. "It is for the Lord," Gregori said, "we did our best work for Him." It was a special triumph for Gregori because he had just completed two years of a five year sentence for "mismanaging" a construction project. Actually, he was more of a political prisoner than anything else. He had become a believer during the period of "Glasnost" (or openness) that had preceded the fall of communism and had refused to cooperate with corrupt administrators who were routinely stealing materials from the jobs they supervised to either sell on the black market or use them to build their summer homes. He had also finished his project under budget and ahead of schedule making the "skim" that his colleagues were trying to run more difficult to disguise and exposing their mindless work ethic. So he was charged and convicted–a common event in Soviet Russia, but he was the hero of the men who had defiantly stood with him.

Gregori was a "stand up" guy who had the courage to take the heat for doing what was right. Because of his consistent testimony for Christ, he was respected by believers and non-believers alike within the prison, and had even won the admiration of the staff. He was the real thing, and I knew he was God's man for our project. Sometimes our most impressive credentials are related to the reputation of our enemies or the groups or organizations that have rejected us. It helped that Gregori had a legitimate argument for release and with political support from some friends and local dignitaries, the corrections officials were soon convinced to release him back to society where he could return to a productive life. As soon as he was released from prison he came to work for us. He did a phenomenal job and everyone who visited our facilities was impressed by the work that had been done, under budget and ahead of schedule.

Ethical dependability is a measure of our trustworthiness in practical matters. It's an indicator of the confidence that others have in us that we will be honest, fair, and faithful. These qualities are critical in a man if people are going to rely on him to make good decisions. They are essential not only in his personal life and family, but also to the success of any career he will have. If a man wants to be trusted, he should strive to develop reliable ethics and good judgment because "even a child is known by his actions, by whether his conduct is pure and right" (Proverbs 20:11).

I know from personal experience what the Lord can do with a man's life. When I first became a follower of Christ and began to rethink my values, I was shocked to discover the mess I had made both at home and at work. I had become unethical, immoral, and generally a tyrant. I had not been a reliable man, especially at home, and the Lord was challenging me to make things right with my wife, son, and many others. Because of all the instability and chaos I had caused, my family had been afraid to follow me. I knew that I had to earn back their trust, and rebuild their confidence in my ideas and judgments. My primary goal was to improve enough to be able to credibly say to my family, "Follow my example, as I follow the example of Christ" (1 Corinthians 11:1).

For instance, I knew that I had to stop lying to others and myself. I had become very adept at disguising my failures and avoiding accountability, but the more I lied, the more tangled my life became. So one of the first things I did was establish a new value of *truthfulness*. When we decide to change our values we must carefully consider the strategies that support them. Old ways of thinking can undermine new values, and they must be eliminated and replaced so that we can be more certain of reaching our goals. The strategy required to support my new value was very simple. When I was asked a question, all I had to do was tell the truth about the facts, as I knew them. But it was not long until I realized from reading the Scriptures that I needed to raise my standard again to "speaking the truth in love" (Ephesians 4:15). This more demanding value required a more refined communications strategy. When asked a question, I would still speak the truth, but hopefully with sensitivity to the circumstances of the listener and how what I say might cause them pain or suffering.

This would be one of many corrections that the Lord would require of me. Each improvement not only set me free from the causes of sin, but also increased my credibility and made me a more reliable man. As followers of Christ, one of our primary activities should be evaluating what we believe and how we do things, comparing them to what the Scriptures describe, and, with His help, making the appropriate changes. Learning from the Lord can become life's greatest adventure. It can also bring tremendous relief from its uncertainties. Jesus said, "He who sent me is reliable, and what I have heard from Him, I tell the world" (John 8:26).

Acquire a Disciplined and Prudent Life

Who among us has not said, "I would like to do that all over again with what I now know"? When we look back at how things "could have been," we can see how some of the most important decisions we have made were affected by our character. Greed, passion, or the personal need for power may have caused us to say "yes" to a risky idea when a more secure, disciplined person would have declined. Or careful and prudent analysis could have helped us properly evaluate the ethics of a business relationship that would later prove to be unsavory. There might also have been times when the fear of failure or our questionable judgment neutralized us, and left us unable to take advantage of reasonable opportunities when they occurred. As we gain experience in life, we can begin to figure out what did or did not work for us in different situations, and decide how things can be done better in the future. When these reflective times reveal problems with our values and strategies, they become opportunities "for acquiring a disciplined and prudent life" and "doing what is right and just and fair" (Proverbs 1:3).

In Romans 12:2 the Apostle Paul exhorts us not to "conform any longer to the pattern of this world, but be transformed by the renewing of your mind." This is a difficult concept for most men because we don't easily change how we think. We often have "war stories" about how we have learned our lessons, and why and how we do things. While these stories may be colorful and interesting, they tend to disguise the weaknesses of our logic. There may also be an underlying trauma or emotional reaction that has shaped our thinking. Along with the unique facets of each person's personality, these things can blur our ability to see and accept our flaws. Our pride can also get in the way and cause us to resist the insights and opinions that could help us improve. For most of us it will take a deliberate act of our will to humbly reconsider our viewpoint. But as Jesus said in Matthew 23:12 (NAS), "whoever humbles himself shall be exalted."

A person's value system operates like a program in a computer. It is a complex set of interrelated ideas, learned experiences, and personal theories through which information is processed, analyzed, and converted to action. It includes all the values and strategies a man has collected over his lifetime along with the various priorities he has assigned them. When he has to make a decision, this program with all of its preset ideas and concepts (good and bad, accurate and inaccurate) begin to converge on the problem in an effort to come to a conclusion about the correct action to take and the strength with which it should be executed. Changing the viewpoint of just one item in our program from a worldly to a biblical pattern can have enormously positive effects.

So when the Apostle Paul exhorts us to "be transformed by the renewing of our mind," his purpose is for us to change some of our ideas and concepts so that we may "prove what the will of God is, that which is good and acceptable and perfect" (Romans 12:2 NAS). Actually, the man who wants to be a follower of Christ should settle for nothing less. But Paul knew how hard it would be for men to so easily give up the things they have learned in the world. So he further challenges us in verse 3, "for through the grace given to me I say to everyone among you not to think more highly of himself than he ought to think; but to think so as to have sound judgment, as God has allotted to each a measure of faith."

Too often, I have heard someone describe a very questionable attribute about a man's behaviors or methods only to hear another person come to his defense and say "maybe so, but he gets results." The possibility that the behavior could be an indicator of a deeper, more serious problem with his values or strategies is naively overlooked because of what appears to be the achievement of the "desired results." This unrealistically tolerant attitude has a tendency to change when you are the person who has to endure the consequences of someone's faulty methods or personality quirks, or if the results of his inappropriate actions end up on the front page of the newspaper. Achieving desired results is no license for misbehavior. Nothing is more essential to a family or an organization than having a man's practiced values be consistent with his stated values.

Proverbs 29:19 (NAS) says, "A slave will not be instructed by words alone; for though he understands, there will be no response." In other words, people need a consistent role model of what is being said before they will trust someone and respond to them properly. Without it people will either refuse to follow the one who is trying to lead them or will cooperate for the wrong reasons, such as fear, idolatry, or intimidation. The influence character has on good judgment and behavior cannot be minimized. It is the real issue behind many of the failures that occur at home and at work. In fact, reliable character is a man's most important asset.

We begin to shape our character early in life as we learn the principles that will become the foundation for our values and strategies. They include the significance of truth, what is just and fair, the difference between responsible and irresponsible actions, respect for the rights and property of others, the need for compassion and faithfulness in relationships, and how to exercise moral restraint. Everything else we learn or do is affected by these fundamentals. Since many of us didn't become followers of Christ until adulthood, it's always a good idea to renew our ethics according to the Scriptures.

Communicate with Intellectual Integrity

A person with intellectual integrity thinks and communicates with honesty and fairness. He presents his opinions and evaluations honorably and with propriety, always trying to give an accurate representation of what he believes are the facts in any situation. He is guided by a sense of principle that is above self-interest and which is comfortable with even the most intense scrutiny. These are essential attributes in any man because the credibility of political, social, or economic debate, the soundness of democratic processes, and the reliability of relationships are in question when the intellectual integrity of a person is in doubt. Solomon said that "Truth stands the test of time; lies are soon exposed" (Proverbs 12:19 TLB).

Breaches of intellectual integrity are emerging in all parts of our society. The honest representation of facts and figures is routinely being displaced by lying, deception, and various forms of manipulation. A war of perception–waged through what is tactically viable for the moment, not on what is fair, right, or true–dominates the media and the marketplace. In advertising, social actions, and political debates, the presenters are often depending on the listeners' ignorance of the manipulative methods they have used in their opinion polls. Or they may be relying on their ability to sway the listener with deliberately inaccurate rhetoric. The self-serving manipulation of words–or spin–has become an accepted professional skill. Although spin can produce the desired results in sales, memberships, contributions, and votes, its benefits are short-lived. Solomon said that we should "have two goals: wisdom–that is, knowing and doing right–and common sense" (Proverbs 3:21 TLB). But more often we see men making decisions based upon what is good for them alone, notwithstanding what is fair or just.

I worked with a client a few years ago who asked me to help him review the organizational design of his already quite profitable business. As we went through the preliminary training with his senior staff, we quickly discovered that there were serious differences of opinion about how the company's goals would be changed. This kind of conflict is not unusual, since there is always some resistance associated with organizational change. We knew that we would have to discuss the ideas and viewpoints of everyone that would be affected until we reached agreement. It was important to patiently move toward the new vision. But as our training progressed, this particular situation became unusually combative.

One day during a coffee break, we were all sharing stories about week-end interests, when I realized what was wrong. Everyone in the room was much younger than the CEO and myself and had participated in what is commonly referred to as public education's Values Clarification Programs. These programs were intended to make them free thinkers by teaching them not to allow anyone to impose values on them. While the CEO and I had been educated in a public school environment which taught the importance of intellectual integrity, the others had been taught that integrity was a relative concept with no absolute borders. They had been trained to resist values-based accountability and thus had been intellectually and morally crippled, unable to unselfishly negotiate for the common good. This is one reason that so many people we encounter each day really do not believe that "a good man is guided by his honesty" (Proverbs 11:3 TLB).

In Matthew 23:21 (NAS) Jesus said, "He who swears by the temple, swears both by the temple and by Him who dwells within it." This implies that when a follower of Christ speaks, what he says is spoken in the presence of God because the Holy Spirit dwells within him. So we have a great responsibility to speak with intellectual integrity. Only a few months after I became a believer, I went on a sales call with an important prospect for whom I had been designing a pension plan. Earl was a coarse old man who had made his fortune selling sand for construction projects. I followed him around that day from one sand mine to the next, answering his questions and hoping that the relationship we were building would help lead to a sale. Earl was a careful buyer and he kept asking me the same questions in different ways during the day. It wasn't long until I noticed that I was repeating myself. Finally, growing frustrated, I asked him if he had read the proposal I had given him. He responded sharply, "Of course I've read it. And I know all of these figures by heart. I'm just checking out your honesty." At first I was stunned and a little bit disoriented. Then I blurted back, "Did you think I might be lying to you?" For just a moment the gentle fatherly side of him came through and I felt the kindness in his voice. "Son," he said, "you can never be too careful." "But Earl," I said, "I could never lie to you about these things, I am a Christian."

He laughed, shrugged his shoulders and said, "Come with me." He led me across the parking lot to his shiny Cadillac. Then he said, "What do you see on the front seat of this car?" I looked in and, of course, saw the big black Bible which I had noticed the first time I got in the car. It had made me feel comfortable because I thought it meant I was dealing with a brother, although some of the things Earl had said throughout the day had made me wonder. I answered, "Do you mean the Bible?" "Yes," he said, "And do you know why I carry that Bible with me in the car everywhere I go? It is to remind me that the biggest mistake I ever made in a business deal was trusting the word of a man who was carrying one just like it. I know you are a Christian, but as to my dealings with you in business, it means absolutely nothing, until you prove yourself."

Earl said he was not a believer because he had seen enough of what Christians could do to him and to one another. I spent several hours listening to him unload his frustrations about the church. Earl is a reminder that the church has had a great audience who has seen and heard our behaviors over the years and been disappointed. It has been difficult at times to understand the behaviors of some of our leaders. Too often what we have seen and heard has been inconsistent with intellectual integrity. But when a man chooses to risk the consequences of dishonesty for some immediate gain, he is sacrificing a far more important goal in life. As David said in Psalm 15:1-2 (NAS), "O Lord, who may abide in Thy tent? Who may dwell on Thy holy hill? He who walks with integrity, and works righteousness, and speaks truth in his heart."

Be Governed by Moral Conscience

Moral conscience is the power source for our moral behavior. It refers to much more than the chasteness or modesty of our sexual life and other private behaviors. It includes the concepts of self-restraint, the decent and humane treatment of others, respect for life and authority, principled and responsible policies, and all of the values which consider the common good as an outcome. It is broader than intellectual integrity. Moral conscience is the traffic director of our thought processes and moral behaviors. It gives us the strength to make difficult choices and stay the course in hard times.

The loss of our moral conscience as a nation has become very problematic. People have dramatically lowered their moral standards. Rape, sexual harassment, pedophilia, drug abuse, and fraud, along with other dangerous expressions of personal moral failures, have hit our country like an epidemic. The lack of moral conscience that has been demonstrated by some of our leaders has resulted in defiant attitudes which are astonishing when compared with the heritage we have as a nation. We in the church are supposed to be different. We should be prepared to offer hope and demonstrate moral authority to the world around us. There must be trustworthy, reliable people in our society where others can turn for solace, support, and direction. Proverbs 28:2 (TLB) tells us that "When there is moral rot within a nation, its government topples easily; but with honest, sensible leaders there is stability."

In Matthew 23:27-28 (NAS) Jesus rebuked the Jewish leaders by saying,

> For you are like whitewashed tombs which on the outside appear beautiful, but inside they are full of dead men's bones and all uncleanness. Even so you too outwardly appear righteous to men, but inwardly you are full of hypocrisy and lawlessness.

This Scripture reminds me of how many men I have known who were faking their morality. They attended church regularly and had learned how to act moral, but inwardly they were tormented and like volcanoes ready to erupt. They were "on the verge of total ruin, in the midst of the assembly and the congregation" (Proverbs 5:14 NKJ). This is particularly the case regarding sexual lust. We expect that God can deliver us from drugs or a life of crime, but to live life free from the torment of fantasies or unclean thoughts and desires is considered by too many men as impossible. I have often heard preachers describe the battle with lust as though it were an unsolvable problem. One pastor exhorted the men in his congregation to avoid the temptation of lust by volunteering at the church to change light bulbs. The idea was to occupy the mind and body doing some godly activity.

I have both bad news and good news for the man who has heard and believed such unbiblical views about sexual immorality. The bad news is that unhealed sexual lust will undermine your manliness. It softens your character and confuses your ability to make sharp, clear decisions. It can destroy your finances, weaken your self-confidence, torment you with guilt, and leave you unable to lead effectively at home and at work. If you have any doubt about these consequences, read chapters five through seven of Proverbs in any version of the Bible. Scattered among these chapters is an astounding compendium of the results of lust, and the margin references will take you to other Scriptures throughout the Bible.

The good news is that you can be healed and set free. The reason most men think it is impossible is because it is not easy. Getting free from lust requires gritty determination and the right spiritual strategy. There must be a severe split in your friendship with lust and all of its sources. As someone once said, "It is hard enough to be delivered from your enemies, but you can't be delivered from your friends." If lust is secretly your friend–forget it! You will not get free.

Being set free from sexual immorality and lust is a big part of my own testimony, so when I approach this subject with men I have both sympathy and no misgivings about what is required. Over the years, I have counseled with dozens of men about how to solve problems in their business, finances, or family only to discover that the root problem in their lives was lust. After going through the routine reviews of their business disciplines, financial management, family lives, etc., without uncovering a clear root cause for the apparent problem, I would ask them this question; "Is there some kind of secret and/or sexual sin in your life?" The following paragraphs recap their most common responses, my comments, and a strategy for eliminating lust:

"Well, I do have a little problem with pornography, but it is not real bad." Men sometimes think they are not doing anything really bad if they are not physically committing adultery with another woman (or man). Looking at pornography is sinful in and of itself because it is mental fornication (or adultery, if you are married); it also sows seeds of rebellion throughout your soul. Remember, under the new covenant, if you even fantasize about it, you have done it. Saying you have a little problem with pornography is like saying you have a little problem with cancer. Left unopposed it can destroy you.

"No, my wife and I have a good sex life, although it's not completely satisfying to me." Are you asking her to do things that she does not feel comfortable with? There are some things, even between married consenting adults, that are "unnatural." Just use a little common sense and think about what you are asking her to do.

"I sometimes flirt with women, but it's not a serious thing with me." All women should take flirting seriously, because it is serious. It is an enticement for further contact, and you have probably already committed sin in your heart when you flirt.

"I committed adultery. But even though I repented I still have the desire." When we commit adultery, any kind, we have broken our covenant with our spouse. If we broke our covenant with our wife in any other area, we would know that we had to confess it to her to be completely free. Confessing sexual sin is no different, but it does require some wisdom and God's timing so that it will be a healing event and not destructive.

Here are some ideas that can be helpful:

1) You must hate the sin of lust, deeply repent, and call on the Lord for deliverance. If you read carefully what the Bible has to say about lust and look closely at what it has done in your life (remember Proverbs chapters 5 through 7), it should be easy to hate this sin. "The fear of the Lord is to hate evil" (Proverbs 8:13 NKJ). Repentance will come naturally when you have a clear revelation of what you have done. Ask the Lord to help you become free of your sinful ways.

2) You must set your will against all sources of lust in your life with a vengeance. Your soul has probably been working in concert with lust for a long time. Being forgiven is wonderful, but learning a new way of life is a little more challenging. The Holy Spirit will convict you of things that are allowing lust into your life. All you have to do is resist by changing the channel, putting down the magazine, etc. If you have any question about what is allowable, I recommend that you err to the side of purity, lest "as the serpent deceived Eve by his craftiness, your minds should be led astray from the simplicity and purity of devotion to Christ" (2 Corinthians 11:3 NAS).

3) You must confess to everyone who has a right and need to know. The power of lust is very often tied to the secrecy of it, and the appropriate confession can bring deep and permanent healing.

Once you have had to work through the fear and humiliation of confessing your sins and rebuilding trust in your relationships, you will be much more motivated to resist lust. If you are worried about how your wife will react, you have good reason to be concerned; but you have already done much more damage to her than a confession ever could. She needs healing too. Stand up like a man, take the heat, don't make any excuses, and pray for God's mercy. "He who conceals his transgressions will not prosper, but he who confesses and forsakes them will find compassion" (Proverbs 28:13 NAS).

Demonstrate Task Faithfulness

Personal responsibility is the hallmark of task faithfulness. A person who is task faithful can be depended upon. He is dutiful, constant, dedicated to his responsibilities, and unwavering in the fulfillment of his word. His stewardship is proven and he has the confidence of his superiors, peers, and subordinates. He is the one people turn to when they want things to work right, run on time, and be there when they are needed. He is devoted to his relationships and his family is carefully nurtured. His presence adds a level of certainty to any endeavor, and he carefully manages his time, energy, and resources. A faithful man generates faith and hope in those around him and brings a sense of security to his family and work.

Proverbs 20:6 (NAS) tells us that "Many a man proclaims his own loyalty, but who can find a trustworthy [or faithful, NKJ] man?" This is a question in the mind of most people, especially women. And just like the admonition of Paul to Timothy in 2 Timothy 2:2 (NKJ), educators and businessmen are once again seeking "faithful men who will be able to teach others," and steward the processes of service and industry. Over the years, I have had a number of discussions with my son about the management of his business and career. I have assured him that in today's marketplace, his faithfulness, alone, will cause him to stand out among his competitors. By adding to his faithfulness the disciplined mastery of his field, a young man can offer his customers a unique experience of satisfaction. It is ironic that in a time when unfaithfulness is growing, society is more and more demanding of certainty. A faithful and competent man can find himself with a great advantage, and have all of the customers or clients he will ever want.

Being faithful is so fundamental to a man's stewardship of authority and processes that when it is not proven, it is certain to create unwanted surprises. Faithful people can be taught the information, skills, and methods they will need to perform well, but building an organization with even the most highly-educated and talented people whose faithfulness is in question, is a recipe for crisis. Every man will face crunch-times when the commitments he has made are tested by the shortage of time, money, and energy. It is when we tackle these challenges that we discover the importance of faithfulness. When I think back through all the instances where I struggled to make a deadline and succeeded; it was faithful people who made the difference, not money or resources. It is during those pressurized events that human bonds are built and trustworthiness is proven. If we have noticed the signs of unfaithfulness in a person and have ignored or rationalized them away, we can be assured that we will pay the penalty when crunch-times come. "Like a bad tooth and an unsteady foot [or slippery footing] is confidence in a faithless man in time of trouble" (Proverbs 25:19 NAS).

The importance of faithfulness was wisely explained to me by my grandmother when I was only a child. She would tell me stories with scriptural morals and lessons about stewardship. They sounded like proverbs and they always emphasized a simple value like: "Don't take anything that is not yours. If you steal little things when you are little, you will steal bigger things when you are big." She knew that a person who is "faithful in a very little thing is faithful also in much; and he who is unrighteous in a very little thing is unrighteous also in much" (Luke 16:10 NAS). She also knew the temptations I would face in life and was teaching me to be faithful as early as possible.

We should always test people's faithfulness in little things before giving them authority over people or processes. Of course, we can't take them back to their childhood and teach them grandmothers' proverbs. But we can give them little responsibilities and carefully hold them accountable for those little things. If they are found to be faithful, we can give them more little responsibilities. Then, if they continue to be found faithful, we can begin to give them a few bigger responsibilities mixed in with the little ones. Eventually we can prove the stewardship of a person who is trustworthy in much. But what are the little things? Believe it or not, the Scriptures teach us that money is one of the little things. "If you have not been faithful in the use of unrighteous mammon (or worldly riches, NIV), who will entrust the true riches to you" (Luke 16:11 NAS)? So test a man early with little amounts of money and continue testing him until you are confident that he will handle authority over people and decision-making properly.

There is a Russian proverb which President Ronald Reagan made famous during the negotiation of the nuclear treaties with Russia. It is simply "trust, but verify." It means that two people can make an agreement that each trusts the other will fulfill. But to be sure, they should verify each other's actions. Sometimes people act offended when you verify their faithfulness. When you come back to check their work, count the money, or talk to a client or customer, they feel like it is an expression of your lack of trust in them. I have learned to explain to people that I can confidently verify their work because I do trust them, and I am sure that I will find faithfulness in the accounting or analysis. It is helpful to our working relationship for them to know that I trust them because I have verified so many times and found them to be faithful. And it is particularly important for both of us when I must give an account to others about the faithfulness of those under my authority. To a faithful person, accountability is not a threat, it is a friend. It is another opportunity to allow his faithfulness to shine through.

In Matthew 23:23 (NAS) Jesus said, "Woe to you, scribes and Pharisees, hypocrites! For you tithe mint and dill and cumin, and have neglected the weightier provisions of the law: justice and mercy and faithfulness." These people had busied themselves with details, giving a tenth of even their spices to the Lord, but had failed to become men who were faithful to dispense justice and mercy through reasonable judgments. By saying, "these are the things you should have done, without neglecting the others," Jesus is clearly telling them that they are responsible not to neglect any area of their responsibilities. I have counseled many men who were facing business failure because they had focused their energies only on those parts of their businesses they most enjoyed. They had either ignored other essential areas or delegated them to people they later discovered to be unfaithful.

Others had failed to show the proper attention to their wives or children while they poured their lives into their businesses. When a crisis developed, they might confess having had a nagging concern that they were not paying enough attention to the areas from which the problems originated. But then they would say something like, "I can't do everything and be everywhere," "nobody's perfect," "I kept trying to find the time," or "I'm just not very good at that." These comments may sound reasonable, but most of the time they are just cop-outs. They are unanswerable defenses which are intended to produce sympathy or deflect guilt. The truth is that men always find a way to do the things that are important to them. When they don't give a responsibility the time and energy it deserves, there is usually a specific reason. Here are a few to consider:

1) Sometimes it's inexperience. One of the best ways to gain experience is to be faithful in another man's business or ministry. Apprenticing can provide insight and wisdom that education alone can't provide. It can be very enlightening to observe the processes and pressures of leading an organization without having to suffer the full consequences. It is a luxury which is often overlooked by young people who have ambitions and visions of their own. Those of us who didn't serve an apprenticeship, or who failed to pay attention when we did, have missed important opportunities to learn how to set priorities, test our motivations, and understand the consequences of neglected responsibilities. The things we experience as an apprentice can mature our attitudes and help us gain the advantage of being able to more correctly judge our own or another person's faithfulness. "If you have not been faithful in the use of that which is another's, who will give you that which is your own?" (Luke 16:12 NAS).

2) Sometimes we're serving the wrong master. The way a man conducts his responsibilities exposes his motives. For instance, if your primary goal in life is earning money or having things, then everything you do points to that fact. The decisions you make and

the way you treat people reflects what you think their value is to you in dollars. However, when your primary goal in life is to serve the Lord faithfully, your actions will have more to do with the proper stewarding of your responsibilities, knowing that everything you do is done in His presence. A man really cannot serve two masters, "for either he will hate the one, and love the other, or else he will hold to one, and despise the other" (Luke 16:13 NAS). If money is your master, you will consistently treat people in a way that reflects your own desires. If the Lord is your Master, the things you say and do will more commonly reflect God's purposes and attitudes, and you will prosper. This means more than just being a good guy. It is a commitment to be faithful to the things that are important to Christ. "A faithful man will abound with blessings, but he who makes haste to be rich will not go unpunished" (Proverbs 28:20 NAS).

3) Sometimes we are naive or undisciplined. While I was going to college, I worked at a car dealership. Working there was chaotic and there were all kinds of things that could go wrong to make a customer unhappy and spoil a deal. I learned quickly that unless I followed up on every phase of the sale, financing, preparation, and delivery of a customer's car, the result could be an unsatisfied customer and the loss of a commission. It made me angry that other people's mistakes kept costing me money and that I had to do so much follow-up. It probably was unfair, but grumbling didn't change the circumstances. I finally stopped complaining about everyone else's failures and disciplined myself to regularly visit the finance office and service department to make sure that the things the customer had specifically asked for, as well as those that I knew he would expect, were completed properly and on time. Sometimes I found that I had made errors in submitting paperwork. But even when I had done everything right, I learned how easily unintentional mistakes could be made by others. This required me to develop relationships in every part of the organization. Doing so helped me to gain a greater appreciation for what each person did in making my sale complete. I learned to "trust in the Lord and do good; dwell in the land and cultivate faithfulness" (Psalms 37:3 NAS). And I made great money doing it.

4) Sometimes our priorities are not properly balanced. Even when we have made Christ the master of our life, keeping our priorities balanced can be difficult. A man's work is usually so much a part of his life that he tends to spend the majority of his time and energy there. And rightly so, because being faithful to our work is an important measure of our faithfulness with our gifts and talents. In Ecclesiastes 3:12-13 (NAS), Solomon says, "I know that there is nothing better for them than to rejoice and to do good in one's lifetime; moreover, that every man who eats and drinks sees good in all his labor–it is the gift of God." Solomon understood that part of God's design for man is that he would find satisfaction through his work. But men often become so absorbed in their work they forget its purpose–to support a family and God's greater agenda for life. We all have to understand that the time we take away from our businesses to be with our families is time well spent. It is a true measure of our love for our family that we not only support them through our work, but that we nurture them with our time, energy, and wisdom.

5) Sometimes we are escaping. The pressures of leading a family can cause a man to want to escape into his business or ministry. It is interesting to me that a person who is facing work problems rarely escapes into family activities. It's usually golfing, fishing, or worse yet, another woman. Alcoholism and drug addiction are very often the evidence of a man's attempts to escape the pressures and pains of life. A man who is somehow shackled and unable to solve his problems will tend to escape his frustration or fear of failure through some mind-numbing activity. Men are generally uncomfortable facing their fears or vulnerabilities. They don't like to talk about them to their wives or others by seeking counsel. When they do decide to share with others and don't find immediate solutions, they feel insecure or weak. David said, "When I am afraid, I will put my trust in thee" (Psalms 56:3 NAS). Men have to learn to trust God and go to Him with their problems and responsibilities. Being friends with the Lord gives a man a new sense of security, the wisdom and guidance he needs as a steward, and the opportunity to become known as a person like Daniel, who "was faithful, and no negligence or corruption was to be found in him" (Daniel 6:4 NAS).

Use Reasonable Judgment

Reasonable judgment is the logical product of a person's wisdom and common sense. It supports the concepts of equity and justice in a civil society because a great part of our law hinges on the principle of what a reasonable person would say or do in a given situation. If someone is going to judge our work or make decisions that affect our personal life, we ideally want them to be diligent, logical, and analytical in the pursuit of facts. Then we expect them to be rational, prudent, and discerning in the analysis of those facts. As they sift through the options available to them, we hope that they will be consistent and sensible. And finally, we want their judgment to be wise, judicious, and fair. In short, what we are expecting is that they will deliberate faithfully, with intellectual integrity and moral conscience, in arriving at a reasonable judgment.

Alexis DeTouqueville, in his landmark book, *Democracy in America*, recognized that the strength of America's democracy was related to its goodness and that its goodness was related to "mores" or moral conscience found in expressions of personal faith. He pointed out that if these important fibers in the fabric of public life were to deteriorate, that democracy itself would fail. As Solomon had said centuries before, "The good influence of godly citizens causes a city to prosper, but the moral decay of the wicked drives it downhill" (Proverbs 11:11 TLB). Our concept of a civil society has deteriorated along with its loss of intellectual integrity and moral conscience. As a result, we can no longer depend upon our leaders to produce reasonable judgments.

I learned a great lesson in Russia about what happens to a civil society when their ability to make reasonable judgments degrades. Russia suffers from the effects of what I call a "moral holocaust." Intellectual integrity, moral conscience, and faithfulness in personal actions were systematically extinguished by the policies of the Soviet era. The moral and economic abuses of the Czars, coupled with their selfish misuse of Russia's resources, not only crippled the economy, but presented socialists with both the rationale and opportunity for revolution. The Leninist socialists intended to prevent such future social and economic indulgences as those which occurred under the Czars. To accomplish their goals, they secularized society, eliminated individual responsibility, and replaced the social and moral values provided by faith in God with humanistic values. It was a futile attempt to achieve goodness without God. The result is a society that lacks the ability to make reasonable judgments and conduct business fairly. When you intentionally extinguish a system of values that is rooted in Biblical wisdom, "you shut off the kingdom of heaven from men" (Matthew 23:13 NAS).

Whether it is at home or at work, a man must make reasonable judgments to carry out his responsibilities before God. I pray for wisdom in my daily life more than anything else because of the consequences to other people that my actions may bring. The dictionary describes wisdom as "knowledge of what is true or right coupled with good judgment." Deciding what is true or right in a business proposal, a hiring decision, a performance review, the analysis of a major purchase, which appointment to cancel, who has given a correct explanation, whom to discipline, what counsel you should give, when you should speak or stay silent, where to trim a budget, or any number of decisions we must make in a day require wisdom. Fortunately, Proverbs 8:12 (TLB) tells us that "wisdom and good judgment live together, for wisdom knows where to discover knowledge and understanding."

The most difficult decisions we make are surely about people. People decisions can be complex and confusing. And they often carry with them consequences that can bring our own motives and intentions into question. If you are a person responsible for employees, volunteers, students, congregants, or a wife and kids, you have had to make countless judgments of people. Sometimes the painful memories of past mistakes or conflicts with people make it more difficult to judge reasonably. And there are times when avoiding judgment altogether becomes a way of avoiding new troubles. But a godly man has no choice but to search for the facts in each situation and fulfill his obligation to make reasonable judgments where he has responsibility.

"Do not love" (1 John 2:15 NAS) and "Do not Judge" (Matthew 7:1 NAS). I have deliberately misstated the Scriptures here to emphasize how easily the intended meaning of a Scripture can be modified by quoting it out of its intended context. Do you know which Scripture I have misquoted? It is obvious that "Do not love" could not be an accurate quote from the Bible because we know that there are so many Scriptures actually commanding us *to* love. In 1 John 2:15 (NAS) we are told, "Do not love the world nor the things in the world." Verse 16 goes on to describe what is meant by "the world"—"the lust of the flesh and the lust of the eyes and the boastful pride of life." This passage of Scripture sits in the middle of a wonderful dissertation on loving God and one another. So to quote this Scripture in a way that infers that it literally means "do not love," would dramatically change its intent, and if we obey it, undermine our ability to follow Christ.

You may be surprised to learn that I misquoted both Scriptures. Matthew 7:1 does not simply say "do not judge" any more than 1 John 2:15 says "do not love." But you may have heard it misquoted so much that you have come to accept it in this way. The strategic importance of this passage cannot be overstated. In it Jesus is actually warning us to be careful about how we make our judgments. He was not saying that we should not judge anyone at anytime for any reason, as it is sometimes taught. There are too many times in life that reasonable judgment is required and there are too many Scriptures throughout the Bible which support the idea of a man making accurate judgments about people and their behaviors. In fact, if we do not practice making reasonable judgments, we are being unfaithful in our walk with Christ. Hebrews 5:14 (NAS) tells us that, "solid food is for the mature, who because of practice have their senses trained to discern [or judge] good and evil."

In Matthew 7:12 (NAS) Jesus said, "Therefore whatever you want others to do for you, do so for them, for this is the Law and the Prophets." Someone once told me that when you see the word "therefore," always go back and see what it is "there for." What has become known as the "golden rule" is referring to the previous eleven verses. Jesus is teaching in this passage about how we should treat or "judge" people and that we should do so to them in the manner that we want them to do to us. So let's review Matthew 7:1-11 in this light.

Matthew 7:1-2 (NAS), "Do not judge, lest you be judged. For in the way you judge, you shall be judged; and by your standard of measure, it will be measured to you." This passage is consistent with Jesus' wrap-up in verse 12. The way we judge and the standard of measure we use, is exactly the way we will be judged; probably by other people, as well as by Him. So if our method or standard of measure for judging is wrong, it is better that we do not judge.

Matthew 7:3-5 (NAS), "And why do you look at the speck in your brother's eye, but do not notice the log that is in your own eye? Or how can you say to your brother, 'Let me take the speck out of your eye,' and behold, the log is in your own eye? You hypocrite, first take the log out of your own eye, and then you will see clearly enough to take the speck out of your brother's eye." It is a problem, particularly with men, that we do not spend enough of our energy working with the Lord to correct what is wrong in our own lives. Our first line of responsibility for reasonable judgment is to look intently at ourselves and rightly judge ourselves before Him. If we have spent time before Christ in confession and repentance, it will cause us to be humble and understanding, then we can see clearly to help others who might have a need. In fact, what we might have considered to be a log in someone's eye yesterday may look more like a harmless speck today.

Matthew 7:6 (NAS), "Do not give what is holy to dogs, and do not throw your pearls before swine, lest they trample them under their feet, and turn and tear you to pieces." It is important that we know when and with whom we should share our judgments. This Scripture implies that we can be careless with our judging and that we can be torn to pieces as a result. Besides the obvious conflict with people that offering judgments can cause, we should also be acutely aware of the mercy we have received from the Lord and not carelessly throw it away to indulge in improper judging. "He who despises his neighbor lacks sense, but a man of understanding keeps silent" (Proverbs 11:12 NAS).

Matthew 7:7-11 (NAS), "Ask, and it shall be given to you; seek, and you shall find; knock, and it shall be opened. For every one who asks receives, and he who seeks finds, and to him who knocks it shall be opened. Or what man is there among you, when his son shall ask him for a loaf, will give him a stone? Or if he shall ask for a fish, he will not give him a snake, will he? If you then, being evil, know how to give good gifts to your children, how much more shall your Father who is in heaven give what is good to those who ask Him!" Every man who wants to be faithful in his responsibilities will be required to make judgments about people and will need God's wisdom to do so. Proverbs 9:10 (NAS) tells us that the "fear of the Lord is the beginning of wisdom" and verses 1-6 of Matthew 7 should put the fear of the Lord in anybody. In fact, it is usually so effective that men would rather give up on judging anything at all, rather than ask God for the wisdom to carefully judge what is true and right. But if a man is going to mature in Christ, he must practice making reasonable judgments. Here's how:

1) Be determined to make reasonable judgments and ask God for wisdom. "If any of you lacks wisdom, let him ask of God, who gives to all men generously and without reproach, and it will be given to him" (James 1:5 NAS).

2) Make reasonable judgments with a right attitude. You will know when you have received God's wisdom because "the wisdom from above is first pure, then peaceable, gentle, reasonable, full of mercy and good fruits, unwavering, without hypocrisy " (James 3:17 NAS).

3) Act with wisdom. Proverbs 9:12 (NAS) tells us that "if you are wise, you are wise for yourself, and if you scoff, you alone will bear it." Act on your own judgments and keep your own counsel. Speak judgments only where you have authority and responsibility, and only when it is required. Keep in mind that the responsibility to make judgments carries with it the mandate to be merciful. "So speak and so act, as those who are to be judged by the law of liberty. For judgment will be merciless to one who has shown no mercy; mercy triumphs over judgment" (James 2: 12-13 NAS).

3

MORAL PURITY:
A MEASURE OF OUR CLEANSING AND
RESTORATION FROM SIN

Pavel was an elite member of the Russian mafia. He was a highly educated economist who had entered the business world during the restructuring in 1989 and battled his way into prosperity. His holdings included exclusive retail outlets, banking, timber, and other asset-rich businesses, and he had surrounded himself with bright young men to manage his interests. Although he was an articulate, impeccably dressed gentleman in every sense of the word, he was also a tough-minded strategist who knew how to take what he wanted and defend what he had. His private security force of three hundred loyal, experienced warriors provided him with a threatening advantage over anyone who might want to challenge his rights. He was the epitome of the "Godfather" with powerful men from around the world seeking his favor.

Through a series of providential events we met and instantly became friends, meeting for dinner almost every time I visited St. Petersburg. We often talked for hours and I had many opportunities to share my personal testimony. He was an avowed atheist but was not offended by my faith. In fact, he was eager to know more about the motivations that enabled me to switch back and forth between my work in the U.S. and my humanitarian endeavors. We also discussed the problems he was facing in his legitimate businesses and the strategies he was developing to solve them. Our conversations invariably turned to faith, and the Lord had urged me to stay in the relationship, freely sharing my insights and politely refusing anything in return but dinner and fellowship.

Money and power can be very seductive, and Pavel had plenty of both, but over time he became bored with his lifestyle. As he began to accept the existence of a living God who loved him, he also began to develop a moral conscience. He became concerned about the poor and actually created businesses to employ them. He also provided support for widows and orphans and others who had needs. And he had begun to pray. Pavel soon discovered that he had a serious problem. He loved learning about God, however, the more he believed in Him, the more aware he became of his own immorality. He could see that his growing faith was on a collision course with his whole philosophy of life, but did he dare make a complete commitment to faith in Christ? Could he? These were questions that wrenched his soul.

I challenged Pavel to test the Lord in some practical way. I knew that he needed to be certain he was dealing with a powerful God that he could trust and rely upon before he could yield to Him. It would be difficult for any man in his position to believe that a life of moral purity was better than his own, so I encouraged him to ask God for help that no one else could provide.

On one of my visits he greeted me with a big smile and said, "I did it! I made a deal with God!" He had two businesses he had been trying to sell, but none of his prospects had both the money and specialized knowledge needed to become serious buyers. He said he had just about decided to write them off as losses when an interesting idea came to him. Why not test God in the matter. He would ask God to bring him cash buyers. The market conditions made this humanly impossible, so in Pavel's mind, this would be a reasonable test. In his prayer, he promised to contribute every ruble from the sale to a group of pensioners who had been guaranteed dividends in one of his earlier ventures. The amount he would clear would equal what was owed. God was ready and waiting. He received cash deals for both businesses in only two weeks!

The Lord had met Pavel at his point of faith. He had mercifully presented His credentials as the only true God in a way Pavel could see and understand. When Pavel paid off his debtors with the proceeds of the sale, he was acknowledging God's superiority, but this was only the minimum qualification to continue the relationship. It then became his responsibility to believe and obey all of God's commands, not just the ones he thought he liked. To some degree, this is the way we all begin our life with the Lord as He reaches out to us in mercy to help us understand His will. We must then be prepared to completely surrender our will to Him, knowing that He is a jealous God who expects to be obeyed.

Moral purity is a measure of our cleansing and restoration from sin. It is relative to each person's obedience to the Lord and the measure of grace God has given him. Although we may be well aware of impure behaviors in our life, changing or eliminating the motivation behind them requires some effort. There are often sinful causes hidden away in our hearts that have to be uncovered and revealed to us by the Holy Spirit. Once we see them clearly, we must be ready to repent, forgive anyone associated with our sin, and reject the behavior from our lives.

The success we achieve in reaching moral purity is related to our determination to explore the truth about ourselves. As we examine the areas of our life that have been held captive by sin and yield them to the Holy Spirit, we will face obstacles. But to a follower of Christ, the challenges of this kind of spiritual journey are only indicators of the great rewards at its end. As the Apostle Paul said in Philippians 2:12-16,

> Continue to work out your salvation with fear and trembling, for it is God who works in you to will and to act according to his good purpose. Do everything without complaining or arguing, so that you may become blameless and pure, children of God without fault in a crooked and depraved generation, in which you shine like stars in the universe as you hold out the word of life.

In Matthew 18:3-4 Jesus said, "I tell you the truth, unless you change and become like little children, you will never enter the kingdom of heaven. Therefore, whoever humbles himself like this child is the greatest in the kingdom of heaven." For a long time, this Scripture was perplexing to me. I could not figure out how to be humble and childlike, and still maintain the toughness I thought I needed to carry out my responsibilities at home and at work. With other Scriptures calling me to maturity, I was confused about how to obey what the Lord was saying. Then I found 1 Corinthians 14:20, which says, "Brothers, stop thinking like children. In regard to evil be infants, but in your thinking be adults." And Matthew 10:16 (NAS) which says, "Behold, I send you out as sheep in the midst of wolves; therefore be shrewd as serpents, and innocent as doves." The balance of what He's asking us to do finally became clear to me. As children of God, we are to pursue moral purity until we attain the powerful combination of childlike innocence and humility along with mature thinking. We are not to be ignorant, but innocent and unyielding to sin. That means we can enjoy our life and work without having to experience the tormenting thoughts, mental images, or guilt associated with impurity. We can be prosperous without being greedy, enjoy sex without being lustful, and have a successful career without being a power seeker or hurting others.

We live in a crooked and depraved generation, where one person's purity is considered by another as fanaticism. But for the man who wants to please the Lord, seeking moral purity is not an option. The only question is how much each man will sacrifice to pursue it. Like the pioneers who crossed the American frontier, traveling across the western plains only to wearily face the imposing mountains of the continental divide, everyone must make a decision—will he settle or push on. The answer to that question depends upon a man's evaluation of what is important in his life. There will always be men who will settle east of the mountains, satisfied that they don't use profanity or steal from their boss. But others will push up and over the mountain, fighting for every inch of ground. They will find freedom—a childlike innocence and the favor of God they could never have imagined or even thought possible. "With men it is impossible, but not with God; for all things are possible with God" (Mark 10:27 NAS).

The journey to moral purity is a pilgrimage to healing and wholeness. It begins as we implement spiritual disciplines into our daily lives and eliminate the oppression that is produced when our appetites are unrestrained. To properly evaluate the purity of our life, we must compare ourselves with the Word of God and subject our behaviors to the conviction of the Holy Spirit. 2 Corinthians 10:12 (NAS) says that when people "measure themselves by themselves, and compare themselves with themselves, they are without understanding." Determining what needs to be changed and how much, is the Lord's choice. Then we must exercise our will to obey, realizing that it is "by grace you have been saved through faith; and that not of yourselves, it is the gift of God; not as a result of works, that no one should boast" (Ephesians 2:8-9 NAS).

The Apostle Paul makes the relationship between grace and obedience very clear. In Romans 6:1-4 (NAS), he says,

> What shall we say then? Are we to continue in sin that grace might increase? May it never be! How shall we who died to sin still live in it? Or do you not know that all of us who have been baptized into Christ Jesus have been baptized into His death? Therefore we have been buried with Him through baptism into death, in order that as Christ was raised from the dead through the glory of the Father, so we too might walk in newness of life.

I have especially enjoyed being a part of baptismal services over the years because of the opportunity it gives a new believer to obey the Lord in something so simple, yet profound. When we are baptized we identify with Christ in His death, setting our will against sin; His burial, allowing us to put away our old life by faith; and His resurrection, being raised in the power of His Spirit to do things differently. It is one of many steps of faith that a believer must take in following Christ. Because it is so simple, its importance is often missed by men whose concepts of power are worldly.

In 2 Kings 5:1-17, the story of Naaman demonstrates how easily man's misplaced perceptions can complicate things and cause us to overlook the power of simple obedience.

> Naaman was commander of the army of the king of Aram. He was a great man in the sight of his master and highly regarded, because through him the Lord had given victory to Aram. He was a valiant soldier, but he had leprosy. Now bands from Aram had gone out and had taken captive a young girl from Israel, and she served Naaman's wife. She said to her mistress, "If only my master would see the prophet who is in Samaria! He would cure him of his leprosy." Naaman went to his master and told him what the girl from Israel had said. "By all means, go," the king of Aram replied. "I will send a letter to the king of Israel." So Naaman left, taking with him ten talents of silver, six thousand shekels of gold and ten sets of clothing. The letter that he took to the king of Israel read: "With this letter I am sending my servant Naaman to you so that you may cure him of his leprosy." As soon as the king of Israel read the letter, he tore his robes and said, "Am I God? Can I kill and bring back to life? Why does this fellow send someone to me to be cured of his leprosy? See how he is trying to pick a quarrel with me!" When Elisha the man of God heard that the king of Israel had torn his robes, he sent him this message: "Why have you torn your robes? Have the man come to me and he will know that there is a prophet in Israel" (vss. 1-8).

This is a typical mistake made by men. We often try to acquire God's power or favor in our lives by using formal channels of contact or influence, instead of pursuing the Lord directly and on His own terms. Or we think of it as only a business deal. God wants something and we want something, so we exchange what He wants for what we want—nice, clean, business-like, and no relationship required. Here, Naaman was focused only on getting what he wanted through the means he was accustomed to using. It could have been a dead end, had the Lord not caused Elisha to hear of his problem.

> So Naaman went with his horses and chariots and stopped at the door of Elisha's house. Elisha sent a messenger to say to him, "Go, wash yourself seven times in the Jordan, and your flesh will be restored and you will be cleansed." But Naaman went away angry and said, "I thought that he would surely come out to me and stand and call on the name of the Lord his God, wave his hand over the spot and cure me of my leprosy. Are not Abana and Pharpar, the rivers of Damascus, better than any of the waters of Israel? Couldn't I wash in them and be cleansed?" So he turned and went off in a rage (vss. 9-12).

Strike two. Naaman again misses the point. Receiving God's blessings and grace is dependent on our doing what He expects, not on His doing what we might expect. Elisha did not bring attention to himself as God's prophet, but properly fulfilled his duty by sending Naaman a simple directive from the Lord that required faith and obedience.

> Naaman's servants went to him and said, "My father, if the prophet had told you to do some great thing, would you not have done it? How much more, then, when he tells you, 'Wash and be cleansed'!" So he went down and dipped himself in the Jordan seven times, as the man of God had told him, and his flesh was restored and became clean like that of a young boy (vss. 13-14).

When Naaman obeyed the simple command of the Lord, he received a miracle. I have seen this principle work time and time again as God deals with men's pride and draws them to Himself in simple obedience. When we do things by faith, in obedience to the Word of God, depending only on His grace, things happen.

> Then Naaman and all his attendants went back to
> the man of God. He stood before him and said,
> "Now I know that there is no God in all the world
> except in Israel. Please accept now a gift from your
> servant." The prophet answered, "As surely as the
> Lord lives, whom I serve, I will not accept a thing."
> And even though Naaman urged him, he refused
> (vss. 15-16).

Elisha wisely refused to confirm or reinforce Naaman's worldly perceptions of power, even in Naaman's sincere excitement about his healing. His refusal left Naaman in the position of not being able to relate any story but one of his obedience to the Word of the Lord. He did Naaman a great favor, because like most men, Naaman wrongly perceived that God might appreciate a sacrifice of some kind, when what He really wanted was further obedience.

> "If you will not," said Naaman, "please let me, your
> servant, be given as much earth as a pair of mules
> can carry, for your servant will never again make
> burnt offerings and sacrifices to any other god but
> the Lord" (vs. 17).

Naaman had a hard time accepting the concept of simple obedience, but he got one thing right. It was time to stop sacrificing to "any other god." When we are raised in "newness of life," it is time to get rid of any behavior that directly or indirectly offers a sacrifice of our will to other gods such as money, sex, or power. This is where our cooperation is important. If we are willing to seek the Lord through the Scriptures and prayer, He will begin to reveal to us those areas of our life that are impure. Once we have a revelation of our sin, our only obligation is to take simple spiritual steps of faith, so that God can cleanse and restore us by His grace. We can then add to our testimony the words of David who said, "He restores my soul. He guides me in paths of righteousness for his name's sake" (Psalm 23:3).

Purge Corrupt Imaginations

It is troubling to many men that they are not able to conform to the values they want to live by. I have talked to dozens of men over the years that had prayed with sincere remorse about sins in their life, but were unable to be free of the continuing torment of temptation. Eventually they had given up their good intentions, concluding that the standard they had set for themselves was unreachable. They returned to their sin, condemned in their heart by the knowledge that once "they have escaped the corruption of the world by knowing our Lord and Savior Jesus Christ and are again entangled in it and overcome, they are worse off at the end than they were at the beginning" (2 Peter 2:20). When the values we establish for ourselves become legalistic standards that are not supported by reasonable strategies, they fail. "Such regulations indeed have an appearance of wisdom, with their self-imposed worship, their false humility and harsh treatment of the body, but they lack any value in restraining sensual indulgence" (Colossians 2:23).

The problem with rules, or laws, is that they do nothing about the inner man. Proverbs 23:7 (NAS) says that as a man "thinks within himself, so he is." When we establish new values for our lives, they must be followed by reasonable strategies for changing how we think. What we really believe about the sinfulness or innocence of our behaviors, and how we consider thoughts, ideas, or temptations has everything to do with our ability to resist sin and obey the Lord. God's mercy always includes forgiveness for our sins, but He doesn't want us to continue in spiritual bondage, unable to obey Him. Instead, He wants to enable us to overcome evil temptations by changing the way we think.

When Jesus prayed for His disciples in John 17:15, He said, "My prayer is not that you take them out of the world but that you protect them from the evil one." If we are willing to establish the values of the Word of God in our life and implement scriptural strategies to support them, we can experience "protection from the evil one." Remember,

> For though we walk in the flesh, we do not war
> after the flesh: (For the weapons of our warfare are

not carnal, but mighty through God to the pulling
down of strong holds;) Casting down imaginations,
and every high thing that exalteth itself against the
knowledge of God, and bringing into captivity every
thought to the obedience of Christ.

2 Corinthians 10:3-5 KJV

If we are going to attain moral purity in our lives, we must begin to identify the thoughts we have that are in conflict with the Word of God. This is really not too difficult. For the most part a man can begin with the obvious, those sinful things about money, sex, and power which more typically occupy his mind. As we identify and reject them, the more subtle imaginations–the one's that disguise themselves as wisdom or spirituality–will begin to surface. The thoughts and ideas that occupy our minds and prevent us from obeying God are strongholds for the devil. When he knows we have sinned in a certain way before, and have not rejected the underlying argument that supports the behavior, he is able to easily tempt us to repeat our sins.

If a man has an addiction to food, drugs, sex, or intellectualism, it is an indicator of a greater inner need, possibly from feelings of insecurity or inadequacy. The addictive behavior sedates the uncomfortable feelings. If we repent only of the addiction, without repenting from our justification of the addiction, and forgiving anyone associated with it, we leave ourselves vulnerable to the devil's temptation. A person could be tempted directly to eat or drink and have some success resisting. But the temptation will be much more subtle and indirect. First, you can expect to be rejected or disappointed and experience feelings of inadequacy. Then, you will be tempted to eat, drink, etc. The devil knows how to play this game and he works hard to establish strongholds.

Therefore, prepare your minds for action; be self
controlled; set your hope fully on the grace to be
given you when Jesus Christ is revealed. As obedient
children, do not conform to the evil desires you had
when you lived in ignorance.

1 Peter 1:13-14

The following are some of the most common types of corrupt imaginations which entrap men. They are almost always connected with feelings of inadequacy and rooted in events that have caused us to feel insecure or rejected.

1) Greed. These imaginations are about money. They are directed toward the material things we want to possess or have in greater amounts. When we are expecting a promotion or working on a business transaction that will benefit us, we become fixated on that issue or event, fearful that it will not happen as we want it to. Fully expressed, these imaginations include the grasping, seizing, and predatory pursuit of our own desires.

2) Lust. These imaginations are about sex. They are directed toward causing us to experiment with and test the limits of sexual satisfaction. In particular, they cause us to defile the temple of the Holy Spirit and rebel against the normal order of creation. When a person is being driven by these imaginations he will find himself seeking new and more sensual expressions of sex.

3) Vengeance. These are imaginations about power. They focus on what we would like to do, or see done by someone else, when things do not go the way we want them. This is especially the case when we believe something is unfair or unjust. These imaginations include thoughts of reprisal, retaliation, punishment, and intense expressions of the need to see justice dispensed.

4) Intellectualism. These are imaginations about truth. They help us justify and defend our inadequacies, explain away our sins, and keep God comfortably at a distance so that we are not confronted with the realities of our life. These imaginations cause us to have an inordinate interest in philosophy and useless arguments that disguise the perverted nature of the desires that rage within us.

The bottom line is this, "Those who live according to the sinful nature have their minds set on what that nature desires; but those who live in accordance with the Spirit have their minds set on what the Spirit desires" (Romans 8:5). When you seriously consider doing what you might have only previously imagined, and then act upon it, you have created a stronghold in your mind. If the idea is of God, it will be a stronghold for Him. If not, it will become a stronghold for sin placed inside the borders of what is supposed to be secure territory. For this reason alone, we should spend whatever time is necessary to identify, renounce, and purge corrupt imaginations. 1 Corinthians 2:10-12 says:

> The Spirit searches all things, even the deep things of God. For who among men knows the thoughts of a man except the man's spirit within him? In the same way no one knows the thoughts of God except the Spirit of God. We have not received the spirit of the world but the Spirit who is from God, that we may understand what God has freely given us.

The secret channel that is created to our mind when we receive the Holy Spirit is of extreme strategic importance. God has always had access to our thoughts, but through this secret channel, we then have a secure way of receiving His. The Lord can help us evaluate ideas in the context of His Word, discern between good and evil, provide us with strategic or tactical guidance, and release wisdom to us as we need it in the secrecy and security of our mind. Then we can operate peacefully and with confidence, knowing that we have this advantage. In Colossians 1:9, the Apostle Paul emphasizes the importance of these private communications by saying, "we have not stopped praying for you and asking God to fill you with the knowledge of his will through all spiritual wisdom and understanding."

Not only can another human being not penetrate this spiritual barrier, neither can the devil. In Daniel 2, there is a defining example of the strategic advantage we have with the Lord in this regard. King Nebuchadnezzar had some dreams which bothered him and that he wanted interpreted. "So the king summoned the magicians, enchanters, sorcerers and astrologers to tell him what he had dreamed" (vs. 2). The king did not trust them to interpret the dreams unless they could tell him what they were about, so he threatened to have them cut into pieces and turn their houses into piles of rubble if they failed, and receive gifts, rewards and great honor if they succeeded (vs. 5-6). Not only did that give them all of the human motivation they needed, they were the devil's first-line troops in a high stakes challenge. Their answer?

There is not a man on earth who can do what the king asks! No king, however great and mighty, has ever asked such a thing of any magician or enchanter or astrologer. What the king asks is too difficult. No one can reveal it to the king except the gods, and they do not live among men.

Daniel 2:10-11

The king was furious and ordered their execution, but when Daniel heard of it, he asked the king for the opportunity to seek the Lord about his dreams. When Daniel prayed, the Lord told him what the dreams were and what they meant, which Daniel then explained accurately to the king. If the devil were capable of reading the king's mind, or Daniel's, he certainly would have done so and saved his influence in the king's court, by providing the information to the magicians and sorcerers; but he did not. Daniel was able to stand confidently before the king with the Word of the Lord. This is an important lesson. Our mind can become a secure, peaceful place to hold and evaluate information in the Lord's presence until we are sure of its value, and until it is time to act upon it. The only way anyone will know our thoughts or private communications with the Lord is if we reveal them. This is one reason why Proverbs 11:12 says, "A man of understanding holds his tongue." Keeping silent about our thoughts and plans allows us to maintain our strategic advantage in spiritual warfare.

So I tell you this, and insist on it in the Lord, that you must no longer live as the Gentiles do, in the futility of their thinking. They are darkened in their understanding and separated from the life of God because of the ignorance that is in them due to the hardening of their hearts. Having lost all sensitivity, they have given themselves over to sensuality so as to indulge in every kind of impurity, with a continual lust for more. You, however, did not come to know Christ that way. Surely you heard of him and were taught in him in accordance with the truth that is in Jesus. You were taught, with regard to your former way of life, to put off your old self, which is being corrupted by its deceitful desires; to be made new in the attitude of your minds; and to put on the new self, created to be like God in true righteousness and holiness.

Ephesians 4:17-24

Resist the Power of Temptation

As we purge corrupt imaginations from our mind, we should be able to yield more of our life to the Holy Spirit. But sometimes the strongholds have become so well established that they perceptibly oppose being evicted. The arguments we have made defending our behaviors may have become hardened by our pride, leaving us aware of the Lord's conviction, but unable to wholeheartedly receive it and respond in obedience. When we yield to sinful behaviors, it is not unusual for strongholds to become colonized outposts for the devil, that provide access for demonic concepts to be implanted, and a place for evil spirits to express their personality.

After I became a serious disciple of Christ, I had an experience which helped me more fully understand the power a demonic spirit can have to press us toward evil behaviors. I had become convicted of a particularly sinful behavior and was in the process of purging it from my life. I had prayed and repented only to find myself repeating the behavior the very next day. I prayed and repented again, this time enthusiastically rejecting the sin in the presence of the Lord. Again, the very next day, the urge to repeat the behavior returned with unusual strength. I began to pray and ask the Lord for wisdom about my situation and while I was praying, I had a daydream.

In my dream I was operating a backhoe, trying to dig a long ditch. The Lord was directing me in a straight line and encouraging me to follow His directions. Standing on each side of the ditch were faceless beings trying to interfere with my progress, tempting me with arguments for disobeying, waving red flags to distract me, shouting directions to turn this way or that, and generally trying to turn my attention away from the Lord who was moving quietly ahead, expecting me to follow Him. I had both my hands on the steering wheel and as the pestering beings continued their interference, I struggled to stay focused only on the Lord, carefully following Him as He moved me through and around various obstacles.

Then I became aware of another set of hands pulling at the steering wheel and subtle, yet aggressive, arguments flooding my mind, trying to get me to give up resisting and respond to the beings along the ditch. I began to fight for control of the wheel realizing that the beings on the outside were being assisted by a force from within my soul to cause me to sin. Something more than my own sinful nature was involved and it was terrifying. Demonic spirits had become part of a coordinated effort to cause me to sin.

I knew that the dream helped explain the temptations I was fighting. Sometimes it really felt like there was another set of hands on the steering wheel of my will. There were times that it was so strong that I felt like there was another person inside me, fighting against my will to obey the Lord. I shared my experience with some friends who explained that most Christians believe demons exist, but our discussions often became sidetracked in debates about whether or not demons are in us, upon us, or around us trying to entangle us in sin. I noticed that the more a person argued against the possibility that a demon could be in them, the less likely they were to focus their energy on combating sins. It made me wonder if creating this debate might not be part of the devil's strategy to disguise how he works and distract us from pursuing purity. All I knew for sure was that I wanted to be delivered from my sin and from any evil spirits which were working to keep me in bondage. From both my personal experience and the indications of my dream, it was clear that something within me was driving me to respond to temptation. Whatever it was, it was also combating my attempts to rid myself of it.

I realized that if the devil's power to tempt me could be kept outside my soul, resisting it should not be nearly as difficult as what I was experiencing. So the way to reduce my struggle with temptation was to break the links between myself and temptation by eliminating the strongholds of sin within my soul. In James 1:14-15 we are told that a man is "tempted when, by his own evil desire, he is dragged away and enticed. Then, after desire has conceived, it gives birth to sin; and sin, when it is full-grown, gives birth to death." There are two important points here: First, the potential to sin begins within us as our own "evil desire is dragged away and enticed," or tempted. Second, desire joins itself with temptation to conceive and give birth to sin. This means that we had to actively yield our will to temptation before sin could be conceived. So to free ourselves from the strongholds of sin, we have to take full responsibility for our actions and not try to blame our sins on anyone else, including the devil.

No matter how clever the devil's scheme, nor how many demons or people were involved enticing, provoking, or tempting us, *we* yielded our will to sin. This brings us back to the fundamentals of repenting of our sins and forgiving the people who have been associated with them. Full repentance would also include rejecting any arguments we have made defending our sins. Anything we have said to diminish the evil nature of our sins or to excuse them away, gives demonic strongholds a place in our life. This is important to remember because the Holy Spirit will sometimes bring to our memory past sins and circumstances so that we can fully cleanse ourselves of defensive arguments. When this happens, it is a gift from the Lord, and we should take full advantage of the opportunity to renounce them.

Strongholds that continue to respond to temptation and conceive sin, require the deep cleansing and discipline of the Lord. And in His mercy, the Lord will create situations to force our sins out into the open so that we can take responsibility for them, strongly resist them, and learn new behaviors. It is a part of the routine discipline of the Lord to help us retrain our will so that we do not conceive sin, but resist temptation and obey His Word. In Hebrews 12:5-11 (NAS) we are told,

> My son, do not regard lightly the discipline of the Lord, nor faint when you are reproved by Him; For those whom the Lord loves He disciplines, and He scourges every son whom He receives. It is for discipline that you endure; God deals with you as with sons; for what son is there whom his father

does not discipline? But if you are without discipline, of which all have become partakers, then you are illegitimate children and not sons. Furthermore, we had earthly fathers to discipline us, and we respected them; shall we not much rather be subject to the Father of spirits, and live? For they disciplined us for a short time as seemed best to them, but He disciplines us for our good, that we may share His holiness. All discipline for the moment seems not to be joyful, but sorrowful; yet to those who have been trained by it, afterwards it yields the peaceful fruit of righteousness.

The discipline of the Lord does not lend itself to quick fixes, although our deliverance may come suddenly and miraculously as we follow His prescription for purity. How long it takes before we are set completely free from a stronghold and how much work may be involved on our part, is all in the hands of the Lord. But as the Lord said to Cain, "If you do what is right, will you not be accepted? But if you do not do what is right, sin is crouching at your door; it desires to have you, but you must master it" (Genesis 4:7).

When we obey the Lord, submit each area of our life to His will, and purify ourselves, we can have victory over any demonic scheme. It is a simple matter of submitting more of ourselves to the Lord and leveraging His unlimited power against the limited power of the devil. One of the ways we can deepen our submission to the Lord is by fasting. When we give up food as an act of faith, we weaken our flesh, silence our soul, and strengthen our spirit. This increases our ability to yield to the Holy Spirit and fellowship with the Lord. Fasting is an act of dependence upon the strength of the Lord and not our own. It is amazing how much more focused on the Lord we become, and how much easier it is to receive conviction and wisdom from Him. "'Even now,' declares the Lord, 'return to me with all your heart, with fasting and weeping and mourning.' Rend your heart and not your garments. Return to the Lord your God, for he is gracious and compassionate, slow to anger and abounding in love, and he relents from sending calamity" (Joel 2:12-13). When temptations persist, fasting helps us draw closer to the Lord and deepens the revelation of our sin. The more we know about how and why we sin, the easier it is to fully repent and break the devil's link to our soul.

Like other spiritual disciplines, fasting is not meant to be a way for us to get what we want from God, but for us to conform to what He wants. There is no question that fasting benefits us greatly and brings His blessings upon us, as long as we do not equate starving ourselves with getting our own way. In Isaiah 58:1-4, the Lord rebukes Israel for this mentality.

> Declare to my people their rebellion and to the house of Jacob their sins. For day after day they seek me out; they seem eager to know my ways, as if they were a nation that does what is right and has not forsaken the commands of its God. They ask me for just decisions and seem eager for God to come near them. 'Why have we fasted,' they say, 'and you have not seen it? Why have we humbled ourselves, and you have not noticed?' Yet on the day of your fasting, you do as you please and exploit all your workers. Your fasting ends in quarreling and strife, and in striking each other with wicked fists. You cannot fast as you do today and expect your voice to be heard on high.

Fasting is not just a religious exercise which is supposed to impress God and get Him to choose in our favor. He expects us to fast as a way to "rend our hearts" and stop sinning. Verse 6 says, "Is not this the kind of fasting I have chosen: to loose the chains of injustice and untie the cords of the yoke, to set the oppressed free and break every yoke?" The purpose of fasting is to break the yoke of sin in our lives. Fasting does not take the place of repentance. It should, however, help make full repentance much more likely.

In verse 7, the Lord continues describing the kind of fast He has chosen and it has some very surprising strategies. "Is it not to share your food with the hungry and to provide the poor wanderer with shelter–when you see the naked, to clothe him, and not to turn away from your own flesh and blood?" Some people need help to get control of their will and motives. These external gestures are "economic acts of faith" that can touch our heart and cause us to get our eyes off of our own needs and onto others. This may be exactly what is needed to eliminate the power of temptation within our lives and give more of ourselves to the Lord. When we do these things, His promise is clear. In verse 8 He says, "Then your light will break forth like the dawn, and your healing will quickly appear; then your righteousness will go before you, and the glory of the Lord will be your rear guard." What demonic stronghold could stand against that?

Throughout the remainder of Isaiah Chapter 58 and on into Chapter 59, the Lord describes the kinds of behaviors He expects from us before we can fully enjoy our walk with Him. All of them require us to deny our own will, our own way of doing things, and the arguments we have used to defend them. Giving up food is just one way of fasting and giving God our will. But if we have pride in our heart, we may find ourselves, like Naaman, complaining about what the Lord requires of us. The whole point of fasting is to obey the Lord by simple faith and come to the place where we can honestly say,

> My heart is not proud, O Lord, my eyes are not
> haughty; I do not concern myself with great matters
> or things too wonderful for me. But I have stilled
> and quieted my soul; like a weaned child with its
> mother, like a weaned child is my soul within me.
> Psalm 131:1-2

It is from this peaceful position of stilled submission to the Lord that we can find the real power to resist temptation and destroy the strongholds of the devil. To those who follow His ways:

> He gives us more grace. That is why Scripture says:
> "God opposes the proud but gives grace to the
> humble." Submit yourselves, then, to God. Resist

the devil, and he will flee from you. Come near to God and he will come near to you. Wash your hands, you sinners, and purify your hearts, you double-minded. Grieve, mourn and wail. Change your laughter to mourning and your joy to gloom. Humble yourselves before the Lord, and he will lift you up.

James 4:6-7

Take Control of Money

How we earn money and what we do with it are important indicators of a man's submission to God. A man is not really submitted to the Lord until the fruit of his labor is yielded. This is because a man's labor is such a big part of his life. Our relationship with our money is almost never neutral. Either we have control of our money or it has control of us. If money controls us, we will be primarily interested in obtaining money and the things it provides, especially pleasurable objects and experiences. If we control money, we are more likely to be interested in work itself, and how it fits into God's plans for our life. Then, money becomes merely what is needed to support our family and help others. King Solomon said, "There is nothing better for a man than to enjoy his work, because that is his lot" (Ecclesiastes 3:22). So for most men, a major test of submission to the Lord will be what we do with our money.

When I first became a follower of Christ, I noticed that our church placed a lot of emphasis on "tithing." The earliest record of tithing was when Abraham tithed to God's High Priest, Melchizedek, in Genesis 14:17-20. This was important to me because I had discovered that there was serious debate in the church about whether, as New Testament believers, we are still required to obey the "law" of tithing or are now under grace to give as we choose. But since Abraham's act of tithing had preceded the Mosaic Law, I realized that its validity could not be limited to a matter of law. In Hebrews 7, tithing is used as an example of how Christ's life transcends the law. It also says that Jesus is "a priest forever, in the order of Melchizedek" (vs. 17). So to a follower of Christ, tithing is a method of offering Him the first fruits of our labor as worship. It tests and expresses our will to love, trust, and obey Him.

One Sunday morning our pastor shared several Scriptures from the Old and New Testaments which described how the Lord would prosper us if we obeyed Him, how the New Testament saints gave offerings, and generally how giving to God was an important measure of our love for Him. There are too many of these Scriptures to list here, but a search of your concordance on these subjects will take you all over the Bible. Then he mentioned Malachi 3:8-11 (NAS). It says,

> "Will a man rob God? Yet you are robbing Me! But you say, 'How have we robbed Thee?' In tithes and contributions. You are cursed with a curse, for you are robbing Me, the whole nation of you! Bring the whole tithe into the storehouse, so that there may be food in My house, and test Me now in this," says the Lord of hosts, "if I will not open for you the windows of heaven, and pour out for you a blessing until there is no more needed. Then I will rebuke the devourer for you, so that it may not destroy the fruits of the ground; nor will your vine in the field cast its grapes" says the Lord of hosts.

Wow! Robbing God? That settled it for me. Besides, I could see that I needed someone to "rebuke the devourer for me." I had noticed that a lot of my money was being spent fixing things that should not have broken or on business and household expenses that seemed out of control. As the pastor had said, "It made a lot more sense to have ninety percent of my income with God's blessing, than it did to have all of it without His blessing."

I rushed home and pulled out my calculator. I found that I was already giving eight percent. I calculated how much the extra two percent would be, and it was a very small amount, especially compared to being labeled a thief. Then all kinds of thoughts and fears about money flooded my mind and confused me. What the Apostle Paul wrote about in Romans 7 was happening to me. It wasn't until I considered tithing as the law of God and something to be respected, that I understood my truly sinful nature and what was really in my heart. In verses 7-8 it says,

> What shall we say, then? Is the law sin? Certainly not! Indeed I would not have known what sin was except through the law. For I would not have known what coveting really was if the law had not said, "Do not covet." But sin, seizing the opportunity afforded by the commandment, produced in me every kind of covetous desire. For apart from law, sin is dead.

My confrontation with the law of tithing surfaced fears, insecurity, selfish motives, hidden desires, and unbelief that I did not know were in me. And left unchallenged, they would not only affect my giving habits, but could be used by the devil at every opportunity to tempt me to conceive sin.

The devil uses any number of schemes to entangle us in sin and inhibit our faith regarding money. I have identified seven of the most common ones which are: idolatry, pride, tradition, greed, fear, debt, and prosperity. Each of these can begin with subtle imaginations and temptations which can then build into potential strongholds.

1) Idolatry. When something enters into our heart and stands between God and ourselves, it is an idol. We do not even have to worship it overtly. Whether it's a car, sports, or a woman, we only have to allow it to be more important than obeying God. In Matthew 6:19-21, Jesus said,

> Do not store up for yourselves treasures on earth, where moth and rust destroy, and where thieves break in and steal. But store up for yourselves treasures in heaven, where moth and rust do not destroy, and where thieves do not break in and steal. For where your treasure is, there your heart will be also.

It is essential that our treasure be in Christ, not in money, things, relationships, or experiences that take us away from devotion to Him.

2) Pride. What men have to say about us and about the value of things we own, say, or do, can draw our heart away from the purity of obedience that the Lord expects. In Matthew 6:1-4, Jesus said,

> Be careful not to do your 'acts of righteousness' before men, to be seen by them. If you do, you will have no reward from your Father in heaven. So when you give to the needy, do not announce it with trumpets, as the hypocrites do in the synagogues and on the streets, to be honored by men. I tell you the truth, they have received their reward in full. But when you give to the needy, do not let your left hand know what your right hand is doing, so that your giving may be in secret. Then your Father, who sees what is done in secret, will reward you.

3) Tradition. Whether we give to be seen by men or just to stay in step with men's values, we may be allowing tradition to rule in our hearts. A good example of this is found in Matthew 15:3-9 where Jesus asked,

> Why do you break the command of God for the sake of your tradition? For God said, "Honor your father and mother" and "Anyone who curses his father or mother must be put to death." But you say that if a man says to his father or mother, "Whatever help you might otherwise have received from me is a gift devoted to God," he is not to "honor his father" with it. Thus you nullify the word of God for the sake of your tradition. You hypocrites! Isaiah was right when he prophesied about you. "These people honor me with their lips, but their hearts are far from me. They worship me in vain; their teachings are but rules taught by men."

4) Greed. We live in a world of materialism and greed where only what people touch or feel is real and success is measured by how many things we possess. The desires for what we want, or think we need, can overwhelm our ability to exercise restraint. Jesus said, "Watch out! Be on your guard against all kinds of greed; a man's life does not consist in the abundance of his possessions" (Luke 12:15). I had a good friend who grew up in great wealth. He was a successful businessman in his own right and made a very good living. He once told me that I would have more trouble with greed than he would because he had already tasted wealth and knew what it could and could not do. We often think wealth can do things for us that only a clean heart will accomplish.

> People who want to get rich fall into temptation and a trap and into many foolish and harmful desires that plunge men into ruin and destruction. For the love of money is a root of all kinds of evil. Some people, eager for money, have wandered from the faith and pierced themselves with many griefs. But you, man of God, flee from all this, and pursue righteousness, godliness, faith, love, endurance and gentleness.
>
> 1 Timothy 6:9-11

5) Fear. The pressures of raising a family or insecurity about our job or career can create fear about finances. When we have fear about money, shopping for food and clothes, especially for a young family, can be a test of faith. Sometimes we doubt in our heart about whether we will have enough if we give to the Lord. Jesus said in Matthew 6:31-33,

> Do not worry, saying, "What shall we eat?" or "What shall we drink?" or "What shall we wear?" For the pagans run after all these things, and your heavenly Father knows that you need them. But seek first his kingdom and his righteousness, and all these things will be given to you as well.

I learned that I was literally making a choice for righteousness when I gave my tithe to the Lord. I did so believing that God was more able than me and more dependable than any system. Hebrews 13:5 says, "Keep your lives free from the love of money and be content with what you have, because God has said, 'Never will I leave you; never will I forsake you.'"

6) Debt. The motivations for going into debt can be produced by idolatry, pride, tradition, greed, or fear. I remember hearing one man say that he hoped he died in debt. This was part of his financial plan to avoid high taxation. It may have been a good plan for dealing with taxes, but it ignored the wisdom of the Bible. Debt is often the result of our inability to restrain ourselves from the impulses of greed or fear. It can also be the result of self-willed pride when we ignore wisdom and borrow to get what we want instead of waiting and saving the money we need. Proverbs 22:7 says, "The rich rule over the poor, and the borrower is servant to the lender." Debt is something to be avoided, whenever possible. Romans 13:7-8 says,

> Give everyone what you owe him: If you owe taxes,
> pay taxes; if revenue, then revenue; if respect, then
> respect; if honor, then honor. Let no debt remain
> outstanding, except the continuing debt to love one
> another, for he who loves his fellowman has fulfilled
> the law.

A person who is in debt and unable to fulfill his obligations will know what it feels like to be the slave of several masters. When I faced this dilemma, I decided that my first debt was an obligation of faith to the Lord. I resisted the temptation not to give to the Lord first, and trusted Him to help me pay my bills and solve my financial problems. He did, and His help began in my heart as he brought conviction and cleansing to my motives.

7) Prosperity. Having a lot of money can be either a blessing or a curse depending upon what is in our heart. 3 John 1:2 (NAS) says, "Beloved, I pray that in all respects you may prosper and be in good health, just as your soul prospers." Some people pursue prosperity with so much effort that they lose sight of their real

purposes in life. When we focus on moral purity, our soul prospers and we are then able to handle more realistically the responsibilities associated with material prosperity. In Job 1:9-11 Satan accused Job of only obeying God in his prosperity.

> "Does Job fear God for nothing?" Satan replied. "Have you not put a hedge around him and his household and everything he has? You have blessed the work of his hands, so that his flocks and herds are spread throughout the land. But stretch out your hand and strike everything he has, and he will surely curse you to your face."

I suppose that Satan had confidence in his theory because he had used it so many times to attack people's faith in God, but he was wrong about Job. After Job had been attacked by the devil; lost virtually everything he had, including his family; was covered with sores; and was in excruciating pain; he said this,

> If I have put my trust in gold or said to pure gold, "You are my security," if I have rejoiced over my great wealth, the fortune my hands had gained, if I have regarded the sun in its radiance or the moon moving in splendor, so that my heart was secretly enticed and my hand offered them a kiss of homage, then these also would be sins to be judged, for I would have been unfaithful to God on high.
> Job 31:24-28

Job's words and deeds are an example of how we should remain faithfully devoted to God in times of both prosperity and adversity. When we do not, we put ourselves at risk of losing the grace of God. Deuteronomy 28:47-48 says,

> Because you did not serve the Lord your God joyfully and gladly in the time of prosperity, therefore in hunger and thirst, in nakedness and dire poverty,

you will serve the enemies the Lord sends against you. He will put an iron yoke on your neck until he has destroyed you.

This is a particularly ominous warning to people who take their prosperity for granted or who are living in false prosperity achieved by going into debt. Jesus said,

If anyone would come after me, he must deny himself and take up his cross daily and follow me. For whoever wants to save his life will lose it, but whoever loses his life for me will save it. What good is it for a man to gain the whole world, and yet lose or forfeit his very self.

Luke 9:23-25

The real choice that is set before us is not between prosperity and poverty but between obedience or yielding to impurity. As we purge impure thoughts and motives about money, we should remember that:

Whoever sows sparingly will also reap sparingly, and whoever sows generously will also reap generously. Each man should give what he has decided in his heart to give, not reluctantly or under compulsion, for God loves a cheerful giver. And God is able to make all grace abound to you, so that in all things at all times, having all that you need, you will abound in every good work

2 Corinthians 9:6-8

Abstain from Sexual Immorality

In Acts 15, there is an account of a visit to Jerusalem by Paul and Barnabas. They came from Antioch with other believers to meet with the apostles and elders to report to them about the conversion of the Gentiles under their ministry and to resolve a dispute about what should be required of the new Gentile believers.

Barnabas and Paul shared about the miraculous signs God had done among the Gentiles through them (vs. 12), and James confirmed that what had taken place in their ministry was "in agreement with the words of the Prophets" (vs. 15). Then he said,

> It is my judgment, therefore, that we should not make it difficult for the Gentiles who are turning to God. Instead we should write to them, telling them to abstain from food polluted by idols, from sexual immorality, from the meat of strangled animals and from blood.
>
> Acts 15:19-20

These were the necessary fundamentals that the apostles and elders felt should be required of these new believers until they could be more fully taught the ways of the Lord. Abstaining from sexual immorality is fundamental. Although both the secular world and the church have been influenced by declining moral values, God's Word regarding sexual immorality has not changed. So to find the grace of God that is required for moral purity, a follower of Christ must choose to live by a higher moral standard than both the secular world and some believers. This is a critically strategic issue for men who are struggling with impure thoughts and immoral sexual behaviors. In 1 Corinthians 6:15-20, the Apostle Paul challenges the church to sexual purity when he says,

> Do you not know that your bodies are members of Christ himself? Shall I then take the members of Christ and unite them with a prostitute? Never! Do you not know that he who unites himself with a prostitute is one with her in body? For it is said, "The two will become one flesh." But he who unites himself with the Lord is one with him in spirit. Flee from sexual immorality. All other sins a man commits are outside his body, but he who sins sexually sins against his own body. Do you not know that your body is a temple of the Holy Spirit, who

is in you, whom you have received from God? You are not your own; you were bought at a price. Therefore honor God with your body.

Many men find themselves confused and unable to resolve the conflict between the convicting standards of the Scriptures and the absence of the right strategies for healing and deliverance. To help resolve this dilemma, men first need to fully understand the Lord's expectations for sexual purity and the consequences of disobedience. Then, when the standards and strategies are clear, our motivations can miraculously shift, releasing God's grace for deliverance from sexual immorality. But anything less than an honest confrontation with the Scriptures will produce only a short term effect of remorse and relief. The Scriptures are very clear about God's standards for moral purity, especially regarding sex. Related subjects can be found throughout the Bible, and the Lord's expectations for sexual behavior are often accompanied with practical wisdom about their importance. 1 Thessalonians 4:3-8 says,

> It is God's will that you should be sanctified: that you should avoid sexual immorality; that each of you should learn to control his own body in a way that is holy and honorable, not in passionate lust like the heathen, who do not know God; and that in this matter no one should wrong his brother or take advantage of him. The Lord will punish men for all such sins, as we have already told you and warned you. For God did not call us to be impure, but to live a holy life. Therefore, he who rejects this instruction does not reject man but God, who gives you His Holy Spirit.

In Ephesians 5:3-7 the admonition is even stronger.

> But among you there must not be even a hint of sexual immorality, or of any kind of impurity, or of greed, because these are improper for God's holy people. Nor should there be obscenity, foolish talk

or coarse joking, which are out of place, but rather thanksgiving. For of this you can be sure: No immoral, impure or greedy person–such a man is an idolater–has any inheritance in the kingdom of Christ and of God. Let no one deceive you with empty words, for because of such things God's wrath comes on those who are disobedient. Therefore do not be partners with them.

Men who find rationalizations for sexual impurity are taking enormous risks. In Proverbs Chapters 5-7, the consequences of yielding to lust and sexual impurity for a man's body, soul, work, family, and finances are described in excruciating simplicity. Phrases like "being reduced to a loaf of bread" or "taking fire in his lap" are common. There are also many references to the perverse thinking and lack of wisdom that leads to sexual sin. When a man indulges immoral sexual desires, he is, among other things, making a very costly business decision. He is taking immediate gratification in trade for something of far greater value. Hebrews 12:16 says, "See that no one is sexually immoral, or is godless like Esau, who for a single meal sold his inheritance rights as the oldest son." When we yield the members of our body to the evil desires of our nature instead of to the Holy Spirit, we are literally trading our inheritance in the Kingdom of God for sexual pleasure.

Revelation 22:14-15 and 21:8 both emphasize the ultimate risks of indulging in sexual immorality and the kinds of company in which it puts us.

Blessed are those who wash their robes, that they may have the right to the tree of life and may go through the gates into the city. Outside are the dogs, those who practice magic arts, *the sexually immoral*, the murderers, the idolaters and everyone who loves and practices falsehood.

But the cowardly, the unbelieving, the vile, the murderers, *the sexually immoral*, those who practice

magic arts, the idolaters and all liars–their place will
be in the fiery lake of burning sulfur. This is the
second death.

Sexual immorality is most often associated with the need to be
accepted or to express power. It is usually rooted in an extreme of
either pride or insecurity resulting from past rejections. It deceives
us into believing that sexual gratification equates to love and
acceptance. When we have been wounded emotionally, we can
spend a lot of effort trying to equalize who and what we think we
are with who and what we think we should be. This is often where
the power of ambition is born. Ambition in and of itself is not
necessarily wrong, but "where you have envy and selfish ambition,
there you find disorder and every evil practice" (James 3:16). So a
person who wants to be completely free of sexual torment must
hate his sin enough to seek out and eliminate every cause of it from
his soul, including any of his wrongly targeted ambitions. Psalm
97:10 says, "Let those who love the Lord hate evil, for he guards the
lives of his faithful ones and delivers them from the hand of the
wicked."

Lust establishes itself in a man's soul through simple ideas and
images. Then it begins to broaden the boundaries of our behavior
and establish greater strongholds. So when we repent of our sins,
we must also repent of our *potential* to sin. That includes purging
sexual imaginations, the rationalizations for our sins, and any
immodest behaviors or language. Ephesians 5:11-12 says, "Have
nothing to do with the fruitless deeds of darkness, but rather expose
them. For it is shameful even to mention what the disobedient do
in secret."

When a man commits sexual sin, he sows evil leaven into his
body and soul. Then, with every immoral act it is kneaded more
deeply into his being, eventually producing bondage and depravity
he could not have imagined. For some, escaping the grip of sexual
immorality might be as simple as following Job's example. He said,
"I made a covenant with my eyes not to look lustfully at a girl" (Job
31:1). This simple strategy would keep a lot of men out of trouble.
But for others, the work of restoring their soul may depend on how
much they have yielded to *porn* and ignited evil desires.

There are four Greek words in the New Testament which are related to *porn*. They are listed in Strong's Concordance as #4202-#4205. These Greek words have been anglicized into what we now refer to in the published form in magazines or films etc. as pornography. But you will probably be surprised to learn that the Greek definitions include: harlotry, idolatry, adultery, incest, fornication, indulging in unlawful lust with either sex, whoredom, male prostitution for profit or bribery, debauchery, and sexual immorality in general.

The Hebrew equivalent is the word *zanah* (#2181). It is found in many Scriptures, an example of which is Ezekiel 20:30, "This is what the Sovereign Lord says: 'Will you defile yourselves the way your fathers did and lust (#2181) after their vile images?'" The translations of *zanah* emphasize that God's people are regarded as His spouse and that idolatry and sexual impurity are related sins. When we find examples of idolatry in the Bible, contemporary society, or in the church, there will also be manifestations of sexual immorality. This is one of the reasons for the disappointing number of sexual failures among church leaders. As a fellow minister once said to me as we were discussing the sexual failures of a well-known pastor whom we had both served, "He was vulnerable because he was awash on a sea of adulation." The pastor and his congregation had begun to take his unusually eloquent pulpit ministry too seriously, placing him above reasonable accountability and ignoring many signals regarding his moral frailties. Whether we are the idolized or the idolater, sexual temptation cannot be far behind.

There are several practical steps that can be taken to eliminate sexual immorality from our life and extinguish the torment of sexual temptation.

1) "Flee from sexual immorality" (1 Corinthians 6:18). The simplest way to prevent being seduced by the rationalizations and arguments of temptation is to flee from it. Keep a healthy distance between yourself and temptation. You know where it is, so don't go there. You know what it will say, so don't listen.

2) "Set your minds on things above, not on earthly things. For you died, and your life is now hidden with Christ in God" (Colossians 3:2-3). Hide out in God's Word and in prayer. Immerse

yourself in His presence and enjoy the peace that His hedge of protection provides.

3) "Put to death, therefore, whatever belongs to your earthly nature: sexual immorality, impurity, lust, evil desires and greed, which is idolatry. Because of these, the wrath of God is coming" (Colossians 3:5-6). Vigorously apply the strategies that will support moral purity in your life.

4) "Live by the Spirit, and you will not gratify the desires of the sinful nature. For the sinful nature desires what is contrary to the Spirit, and the Spirit what is contrary to the sinful nature. They are in conflict with each other, so that you do not do what you want" (Galatians 5:16-17). Yield to the Holy Spirit and resist the devil.

5) "Husbands, love your wives, just as Christ loved the church and gave himself up for her to make her holy, cleansing her by the washing with water through the word, and to present her to himself as a radiant church, without stain or wrinkle or any other blemish, but holy and blameless. In this same way, husbands ought to love their wives as their own bodies. He who loves his wife loves himself. After all, no one ever hated his own body, but he feeds and cares for it, just as Christ does the church–for we are members of his body" (Ephesians 5:25-30). A man who is busy loving his wife and ministering to her by the Word of God is not nearly so temptable. If there are conflicts between you and your wife, intercede for her in prayer. Bless her, forgive her sins, and confess your own sins both to God and her.

6) "Marriage should be honored by all, and the marriage bed kept pure, for God will judge the adulterer and all the sexually immoral" (Hebrews 13:4). Here the word for "marriage bed" is *koite* (#2845), from which we derive the word *coitus* commonly understood as being the natural sexual act. The word for sexually immoral is *pornos* (#4205). This is a declarative statement which means that the act of sex between a married couple is to be kept free from adultery *and* sexual immorality or *porn*. Lust causes a man to experiment to find new ways of increasing sexual satisfaction which, when looked at objectively, can cause us to demean both ourselves and our partner.

7) "The name of the Lord is a strong tower; the righteous run to it and are safe" (Proverbs 18:10). When we make Christ the Lord over our sexual life, we are making a fundamental strategic move that will release His power and favor in great measure. "His divine power has given us everything we need for life and godliness through our knowledge of him" . . . so that we . . . "may participate in the divine nature and escape the corruption in the world caused by evil desires" (2 Peter 1:3-4).

Follow the Path of God's Favor

There is a recurring theme in the Bible concerning God's favor. Simply stated it is this: When we follow the Lord's ways and obey Him, we receive His favor. In both the Old and New Testaments the words favor and grace are often used interchangeably. There are several Hebrew and Greek words that are translated either as favor, grace, kindness, or mercy; each indicating the range of God's responses when we follow His ways. The expanded definitions include: to be pleased with, to satisfy a debt, to bend or stoop in kindness, and to divinely influence the heart. There is no limit to what God might do in any one of these categories. He can work in our own heart or in the heart of someone else on our behalf. One of my favorite Scriptures regarding this is Proverbs 21:1 (NAS) which says, "The king's heart is like channels of water in the hand of the Lord; He turns it wherever He wishes." I have often taken comfort in the Lord's ability to turn a decision to my benefit, whether it was to bless me with what I wanted or to keep me from making a mistake by blocking my path.

God's favor is not produced by any great work we do, how much money we make, or anything that is measurable against another man's life. The power or prestige we gain in life may be impressive in the worldly sense, but they are neither indicators of our obedience to the Lord nor of His favor. There are too many cases where people with power, money, and worldly success have turned out to be deceivers, clearly not enjoying the favor of God.

> For everything in the world–the cravings of sinful
> man, the lust of his eyes and the boasting of what
> he has and does–comes not from the Father but from

the world. The world and its desires pass away, but
the man who does the will of God lives forever.
1 John 2:16-17

God's favor is produced by our obedience to His Word and to His specific plans for us. It is indicated by His presence with us. In Exodus 33, Moses is involved in a discussion with the Lord about the leadership responsibilities he has been given regarding Israel. He asked the Lord for two things so that he could lead effectively. First he asked, "If you are pleased with me, teach me your ways so I may know you and continue to find favor with you" (vs. 13). And second, "If your Presence does not go with us, do not send us up from here. How will anyone know that you are pleased with me and with your people unless you go with us? What else will distinguish me and your people from all the other people on the face of the earth?" (vs. 15 -16). In verse 17, the Lord said to Moses, "I will do the very thing you have asked, because I am pleased with you and I know you by name." God's Presence was indicated by a pillar of fire at night and a cloud by daytime. Under our new covenant, God lives within us. When we cooperate with Him, His Presence is indicated by the release of His nature in and through us.

The life that God has for a man may be one of high office and great wealth or of meager duties and provision. But whether we have been given intellectual abilities and skills that are great or small, we will be judged by how we have responded to the will of the Lord with what we have. James 4:17 (NAS) says, "Therefore, to one who knows the right thing to do, and does not do it, to him it is sin." But if you say, "We knew nothing about this, does not he who weighs the heart perceive it? Does not he who guards your life know it? Will he not repay each person according to what he has done?" (Proverbs 24:12). God deals mercifully with us as individuals, based upon the grace He has given each of us, and how well we follow Christ's example of obeying the will of the Father. When we "flee the evil desires of youth, and pursue righteousness, faith, love, and peace, along with those who call on the Lord out of a pure heart" (2 Timothy 2:22), we can expect the Lord to support our efforts.

Moral purity is the spiritual equivalent of the Promised Land. It is the fertile ground from which real peace and prosperity can flourish. Of course, this goes against the devil's plans and schemes, so at some point you can expect to be confronted by questions which are intended to turn you away from pursuing moral purity. One of them is "How much purity is enough?" You will have the option of a number of different opinions on this topic depending upon how many people you ask. But only one person's opinion really matters. What Christ says in your heart is the standard for moral purity. As long as you have a revelation of sinful behaviors, you are obligated to respond to the Holy Spirit and yield them to Him for cleansing. When you became a follower of Christ, you were choosing to "enter through the narrow gate. For wide is the gate and broad is the road that leads to destruction, and many enter through it. But small is the gate and narrow the road that leads to life and only a few find it" (Matthew 7:13-14).

The more we purge our lives of sinful behaviors, the closer our walk with the Lord becomes. We also become more effective for the Lord at home and at work. This is helpful to remember when trials and temptations surround us, because no matter how much you must battle "in your struggle against sin, you have not yet resisted to the point of shedding your blood" (Hebrews 12:4). Nothing we will ever endure will compare either to the sacrifice Christ has made on our behalf or the joy of walking in purity.

> Therefore, since Christ suffered in his body, arm yourselves also with the same attitude, because he who has suffered in his body is done with sin. As a result, he does not live the rest of his earthly life for evil human desires, but rather for the will of God. For you have spent enough time in the past doing what pagans choose to do–living in debauchery, lust, drunkenness, orgies, carousing and detestable idolatry.
>
> 1 Peter 4:1-3

After the death of Moses, the Lord spoke to Joshua about taking His people across the Jordan into the Promised Land. The words that the Lord spoke to him then are just as relevant today for any man who sees the strategic importance of moral purity and wants to lead his family into prosperity. The Lord said to Joshua,

> Be strong and courageous, because you will lead these people to inherit the land I swore to their forefathers to give them. Be strong and very courageous. Be careful to obey all the law my servant Moses gave you; do not turn from it to the right or to the left, that you may be successful wherever you go. Do not let this Book of the Law depart from your mouth; meditate on it day and night, so that you may be careful to do everything written in it. Then you will be prosperous and successful. Have I not commanded you? Be strong and courageous. Do not be terrified; do not be discouraged, for the Lord your God will be with you wherever you go.
> Joshua 1:6-9

In Joshua chapters 23 and 24, we find Joshua as an old man recounting to the elders and leaders of Israel everything God had done to bless and prosper them and hold them accountable for the sins that had crept into their lives. He repeated to them the same message as was given to him by the Lord before he crossed the Jordan. "Be very strong; be careful to obey all that is written in the Book of the Law of Moses, without turning aside to the right or left" (Joshua 23:6). He repeated the warnings of God to remain pure in their commitment to the Lord, and the consequences of disobedience. And he challenged them saying, "Yield your hearts to the Lord" (Joshua 24:22). Joshua had lived on both sides of the Jordan and knew that there was nothing better than serving the Lord. He also knew that the future of Israel was not in its corporate power or wealth, but in its obedience to the Lord and His commands. At the end of his life Joshua was still calling God's people to purity saying,

Now fear the Lord and serve him with all faithfulness. Throw away the gods your forefathers worshiped beyond the River and in Egypt, and serve the Lord. But if serving the Lord seems undesirable to you, then choose for yourselves this day whom you will serve, whether the gods your forefathers served beyond the River, or the gods of the Amorites, in whose land you are living. But as for me and my household, we will serve the Lord.

Joshua 24:14-15

The record of Joshua's exhortation for moral purity is not unique. All through the Bible, there are examples of kings, prophets, apostles, and Christ Himself repeating the message. It is a strategic theme because the primary conflict within a man's soul is one of moral purity. So the man who follows Christ should not consider it unusual to experience the regular prodding of the Holy Spirit to examine the nature of his behaviors. It is the favor, grace, kindness, and mercy of the Lord.

4

SPIRITUAL AUTHORITY:
A MEASURE OF THE POWER AND FAVOR OF
GOD IN OUR LIFE

There are sixteen old, run-down prisons scattered around St. Petersburg, Russia, and not one of them is a good place to live or work. The government's resources are spread thinly over many priorities and the lowest of them is the prisons. As one official told me, "When winter comes and you have to choose between heating a children's hospital or a prison, it's an easy decision." Inmates are also poorly fed and often depend upon relatives throwing food over the fences to them. Russian prisons are not encumbered by civil rights issues. If prisoners are miserable, so be it; they are there to be punished anyway. Even though tensions can run high, there are rarely protests or outbreaks of violence as we have in the west. Peace is kept by Special Weapons and Tactics (S.W.A.T.) teams that operate with impunity and shoot to kill when they find it necessary. This limits violence in the prisons to skirmishes between inmates, which prison officials routinely choose to ignore.

Diseases among inmates are at epidemic levels, with high rates of infection for tuberculosis, hepatitis, and HIV. Contaminated water supplies and limited sewage facilities create conditions that would not be tolerated elsewhere. A simple cut on the finger could become infected by invasive bacteria and result in death because inmates who do receive treatment are often greeted at prison clinics by doctors with no medicines or supplies.

I have volunteered and consulted in American prisons for about twenty years, and one of our board members was a prison warden who often traveled with me to Russia. David and I had prayed about the prisons and felt that the Lord wanted us to reach out to the wardens and physicians at each facility. We invited them to a luncheon at our headquarters and almost all of them attended, along with the head of the prison system, who had become a close friend to both David and me. After lunch we sent each of them home with small bags of non-prescription drugs for their families. Then David visited every prison to develop closer relationships with his colleagues.

The Lord began to provide us with medicines and supplies that were perfect for the prison hospital and clinics. Each delivery brought new hope to the prisons, and the staff and inmates were always thrilled to see us. But Mr. Kreshenko, a high government official who had heard about our visits to the prisons, had other ideas. He called me into his office and questioned me at length about my motives for giving medicine to prisoners. I answered all his questions as both a humanitarian and a follower of Christ, but he was not swayed in the least. He told me that I should stop taking medicines to the prisons and use them to help people who were more deserving.

His authority in the matter was unquestionable at the human level and I knew this could be the end of our outreach to the prisons. However, a special calm came over me. Before I realized what I was doing, I sat up in my chair and said firmly and respectfully, "Mr. Kreshenko, I am not sure you have the authority to stop the deliveries." He bristled and in classic Russian style said, "What? Are you questioning my authority?" I said, "Well, yes and no. May I explain my position?" He looked both angry and mystified but gave me permission to continue.

I quoted the parts of Matthew 25 which command us to visit the sick and those in prison. Then I said, "As you can see Sir, I have a very specific mandate from the Lord to do this work. But even more problematic is that I am sure He spoke to me during my prayer time and ordered me to use the medicines that He has provided in the prisons. As you can see, I am trapped between the two of you—I must obey Him and, of course, I must obey you. I would not presume to challenge your authority, but I am concerned that in ordering me to stop the deliveries that you will be opposing the Lord. This, I think, if I am correct, could be problematic for you, so I am only asking you to please reconsider your position."

I think at that moment we were both terrified. He stared intensely into my eyes and said, "You are sincere aren't you?" I said, "Yes, Sir, and I would appreciate your consideration of my predicament." He looked down at his papers and thought for a few moments and then said, "Well, let's just keep an eye on this situation and see how it proceeds. You may continue your deliveries for now, but I may have to reconsider the matter at a later date." We never heard from him again.

Spiritual authority is a measure of the power and favor of God in our life. It's purpose is to influence individual behavior and to empower the work of His servants. God's general agenda for men is outlined in the Scriptures. It emphasizes strategic issues such as developing moral character and spiritual awareness. As His power has its effect in us and we begin to grow in faith and practice, we discover that God has a plan for every part of our lives. God's plan always fits us perfectly, and when we are occupied with activities that fulfill it, we can sense His power intervening on our behalf, giving us favor with men, and sometimes affecting the natural order of things. As King David said,

> Better is one day in your courts than a thousand elsewhere; I would rather be a doorkeeper in the house of my God than dwell in the tents of the wicked. For the Lord God is a sun and shield; the Lord bestows favor and honor; no good thing does he withhold from those whose walk is blameless.
>
> Psalm 84:10-11

"There is no authority except from God" (Romans 13:1 NAS), and in the world there is both natural and spiritual authority. Natural authority is a combination of God's order for the world and its systems, along with the limited will of man. It is used to control assets and processes, and to command and restrain the actions of people. Natural authority is imposed through constitutions, laws, charters, corporations, contracts, and other instruments and can be granted by a person, or a legal or political entity. It is given so that the grantor can be served in specific ways. For example, the police receive authority from the government they serve to perform specific tasks of safety and law enforcement. A surgeon could receive authority from a hospital to direct medical personnel and use resources to perform specific medical tasks. Each person is given specific authority to take action and use the power and resources of the person or entity he serves within the boundaries of the specific tasks that are assigned to him. The policeman has no authority to direct the work in the operating room, while the surgeon has no authority to enforce laws.

In Luke 7:1-8, Jesus was asked by some Jewish leaders to visit the home of a Roman Centurion to heal his servant. He agreed to make the trip, but on the way they received word from the Centurion that he felt undeserving to have Jesus actually visit him. He explained that he believed there was no need for Jesus to come but that He only had to "say the word" (vs. 7) and the servant would be healed. The Centurion understood that Jesus could use His spiritual authority to heal his servant's illness the same way that the Centurion used natural authority over his troops. He said,

> For I myself am a man under authority, with soldiers under me. I tell this one, "Go," and he goes; and that one, "Come," and he comes. I say to my servant, "Do this," and he does it. When Jesus heard this, he was amazed at him, and turning to the crowd following him, he said, "I tell you, I have not found such great faith even in Israel." Then the men who had been sent returned to the house and found the servant well.
>
> Luke 7:8-10

The Centurion obviously understood the concept of delegated authority. He knew he had authority from the government he served for a specific agenda, and that he could delegate that authority to others who served him in that agenda. But he also recognized the limits of his authority and that it did not extend into the realm of the spiritual. He could not heal his servant because he had no authority in the Kingdom of God. However, he rightly concluded that Jesus was operating as a servant of the Kingdom of God, and he had faith that Jesus would use His authority to heal his servant. Later, when Jesus "called his twelve disciples to Him and gave them authority to drive out evil spirits and to heal every disease and sickness" (Matthew 10:1), He was delegating spiritual authority to them. After following Him around and seeing Him heal so many people, it must have shocked them when He said, "I tell you the truth, anyone who has faith in me will do what I have been doing" (John 14:12).

A man could easily find himself in a position where he might need both natural and spiritual authority to fulfill God's agenda for his life. If the agenda requires the control of systems or assets, then he will probably need some measure of natural authority like the Roman Centurion. If so, God will give His servant favor with man so he can obtain the natural authority he will require. The stories of Joseph and Nehemiah both point to this principle. Joseph survived a murder conspiracy by his brothers, who then sold him into slavery into Egypt. There, he was falsely accused and thrown into prison. Eventually though, according to God's plan, he was raised up in authority second only to Pharaoh. From this powerful position of natural authority, and with the wisdom and favor of God, he saved not only Egypt from a devastating famine, but ultimately the future of Israel (Genesis Chapters 37-50). Nehemiah served as the cupbearer to King Artaxerxes of Persia. From his trusted position, God gave him favor and he was able to obtain the authority and resources he needed to restore the walls of Jerusalem (Nehemiah Chapters 1-13).

Another interesting example is when Moses delegated the authority God had given him to judge the people of Israel. Jethro, Moses' father-in-law, observed Moses as he sat all day judging disputes between the people and said,

What you are doing is not good. You and these people who come to you will only wear yourselves out. The work is too heavy for you; you cannot handle it alone. Listen now to me and I will give you some advice, and may God be with you. You must be the people's representative before God and bring their disputes to him. Teach them the decrees and laws, and show them the way to live and the duties they are to perform. But select capable men from all the people—men who fear God, trustworthy men who hate dishonest gain—and appoint them as officials over thousands, hundreds, fifties and tens. Have them serve as judges for the people at all times, but have them bring every difficult case to you; the simple cases they can decide themselves. That will make your load lighter, because they will share it with you. If you do this and God so commands, you will be able to stand the strain, and all these people will go home satisfied.

Exodus 18:17-23

Moses organized and delegated authority through a structure that was typical of natural authority. There is nothing inherently good or evil about the processes of natural authority or the organizational structures that are created by it, they are merely the tools of organization and management. What turns them toward good or evil is the character of the men who fill the positions of responsibility, their vision, and whether or not they also have spiritual authority. Moses' plan was reliable because of the kind of men he chose to fulfill this great responsibility. He selected "capable men; men who fear God; trustworthy men who hate dishonest gain" (vs. 21). In Deuteronomy 1:13 they are described as "wise, understanding and respected" men. They were reliable men who would not misuse their authority.

God's authority moves with us from the general, to the specific, to the detail of His agenda for our lives, as we continue in obedience to His will. Jesus naturally fulfilled God's general agenda. He was first of all a Son to His Heavenly Father, just as we are expected to be. Jesus' specific agenda required Him to occupy Himself in practical activities which ultimately led to fulfilling the specific purposes of His Father; becoming the Word to us and offering Himself as a sacrifice for our sins on the cross of Calvary. To accomplish this, He became a man and entered into family life, living and working as any human being until the time for the fulfillment of His specific agenda came into focus. Like Jesus, our specific agenda is to occupy ourselves in the activities of our home and work life as we wait for the unveiling of God's ultimate purposes. Deciding things like how we should be educated, which job to take, who to marry, etc., are all part of His detailed agenda that positions us for service and shapes His will into our life.

Jesus had a simple solution for fulfilling His responsibility to His Father's agenda and remaining under His authority. "I tell you the truth," He said, "the Son can do nothing by himself; he can do only what he sees his Father doing, because whatever the Father does the Son also does" (John 5:19). It's almost as though He were saying to us, "No kidding guys. It is really this simple. I don't do anything I am not sure my Father wants Me doing. That's the secret to having His power and favor working in you." Jesus faithfully sought to know the will of His Father and then fully and completely obeyed Him. In return, Jesus was granted "all authority in heaven and on earth" (Matthew 28:18).

Fulfill the Calling of a Vocation

Work is an essential element of every man's life. From the beginning, it has been God's intention for man to work and establish a home. In Genesis 1:28, He said to Adam "Be fruitful and increase in number; fill the earth and subdue it. Rule over the fish of the sea and the birds of the air and over every living creature that moves on the ground." After Adam sinned, God intensified the agenda for man to one in which work was the priority. He told Adam, "By the sweat of your brow you will eat your food until you return to the ground, since from it you were taken; for dust you are and to dust you will return" (Genesis 3:19). All through the Scriptures a man's skills and talents, the work he does, and the outcome of his labors, are tied to God's plan for his life.

Work is one of the fundamental stewardship's of God's servant. King Solomon wrote about the importance of a man diligently occupying himself in his work. In Proverbs 18:9 he says, "One who is slack in his work is brother to one who destroys." In Proverbs 12:14, we are reminded that "from the fruit of his lips a man is filled with good things as surely as the work of his hands rewards him." Then, in Proverbs 14:23 we are told that "all hard work brings a profit." These are only a few of the many Scriptures that link the need to work with the micro-economy which the Lord provides for each of us.

Some men have become so captivated by the relationship between work and profit that they spend too much of their time working only for profit. At the other extreme are men who have pursued social and intellectual fulfillment to the detriment of their ability to provide for themselves. It is on this continuum of extremes that a man must find the balance God requires of him. He must carefully divide his energies between working for his family and the common good while he develops his life socially and spiritually. The Apostle Paul demonstrated this principle in the way he spent time in the direct work of the ministry God had given him while he worked as "a tentmaker" (Acts 18:3). He said, "I have not coveted anyone's silver or gold or clothing. You yourselves know that these hands of mine have supplied my own needs and the needs of my companions" (Acts 20:33-34).

> For you yourselves know how you ought to follow our example. We were not idle when we were with you, nor did we eat anyone's food without paying for it. On the contrary, we worked night and day, laboring and toiling so that we would not be a burden to any of you. We did this, not because we do not have the right to such help, but in order to make ourselves a model for you to follow. For even when we were with you, we gave you this rule: "If a man will not work, he shall not eat."
>
> 2 Thessalonians 3:7-10

Paul challenged men to follow the principles he modeled regarding work and left it to each man's conscience to "know how you ought to follow." There are a number of principles from God's general agenda for men that can guide us in making the right determinations about work. But we must also be aware of God's specific agenda for our life in order to properly apply the principles with wisdom. Work is essential. It must be balanced to meet our needs for living as we fulfill the plan of God. Our vocation provides us with the opportunity to identify and sharpen the talents that God has given us and then, in His time and purpose, to strategically apply them.

As a boy, I learned to enjoy hard work. I had my own lawn mowing business when I was twelve. I can still remember the deep satisfaction of going to the Western Auto store to purchase my own mower. I paid it off on the revolving credit plan in only a few weeks. Then, nearly everything I earned was mine to spend. I started working and never stopped. I worked all through high school, spending thirty hours per week at various jobs. I bought a car, paid my own way to a local community college and lived in a small rooming house until I was married. Then I began what I thought would be a career in aerospace, working in the Apollo program at Cape Kennedy, while I attended college part-time. But that idea was derailed by massive layoffs and I turned my attention to the business world.

From that time until I became a disciple of Christ, my work was all about supporting my wife and son. It never occurred to me there might be some higher purpose in what I had been learning at my various jobs and that God had a plan for my life. But I eventually realized the futility of constantly thinking about making and spending money. I became more aware of the needs of people around me and started volunteering at my church. When I volunteered I felt an especially clear presence of the Lord with me. I knew that God was with me at work, but when I ministered to people, His favor was even stronger. As I became less materialistic, I started to think of working full-time in some sort of ministry. I was sure that God was causing me to see and do things that were more important, so I wanted to completely immerse myself in what I hoped was His calling for me.

I did not yet know enough about the Kingdom of God to understand that He was first of all calling me to maturity. There was a lot about my character and spiritual accountability that God wanted to improve. I completely missed the significance of 1 Corinthians 7:24, which says "Brothers, each man, as responsible to God, should remain in the situation God called him to." I could only see two options. Working to make money or working for the Kingdom of God. Unfortunately, most of the counsel I received at that time was from people who were already in full-time ministry. They had a limited viewpoint and primarily interpreted what I was experiencing as a "call to the ministry." In their opinion, it was simply a matter for me to decide how and when. I have seen a lot of men mistakenly leave their jobs and go off to seminary or some kind of ministry when God was only calling them to a more mature walk with Him. Like me, many of them later discovered that all He wanted to accomplish could have been done right where they had worked and lived.

"Each man has his own gift from God; one has this gift, another has that" (1 Corinthians 7:7). And, "Each one should use whatever gift he has received to serve others, faithfully administering God's grace in its various forms. If anyone speaks, he should do it as one speaking the very words of God. If anyone serves, he should do it with the strength God provides, so that in all things God may be praised through Jesus Christ" (1 Peter 4:10-11). These scriptural admonitions imply that we should develop our gifts and use them, wherever we are, in a way that pleases God.

The key issue is about discipline and whether or not we have worked hard to learn and implement the rules and practices of our profession. "If the ax is dull and its edge unsharpened, more strength is needed; but skill will bring success" (Ecclesiastes 10:10). When a man sets out to discipline his gifts and become credentialed in his work, he can do so with the assurance that God will be there to give him grace. Proverbs 22:29 says, "Do you see a man skilled in his work? He will serve before kings; he will not serve before obscure men." A man who is skilled in his work can become very influential and can expect doors of opportunity to be opened for him. In this regard, one career is no better or worse than any other as long as it provides the activity we need to apply our gifts and talents. The real importance of our work is that it conforms to God's agenda and gives us opportunities to reach people for His Kingdom, not evangelistically, but as a living testimony of His grace. No matter what we do or where we go, the skill with which we use our talents is visible to everyone. And so is the spirit in which we perform our work. As the Lord said in Exodus 20:24, "Wherever I cause my name to be honored, I will come to you and bless you."

With all the effort we put into improving our skills and working hard at what we do, it is important to remember that our faith must remain in God, not in work. It is easy for a man to become so focused on his work, even when it is God's agenda, that he can forget about the Lord's place in his life. When a man puts work ahead of fellowship with God, it harms the man. And it will eventually undermine the agenda. Psalm 67:5-7 says, "May the peoples praise you, O God; may all the peoples praise you. Then the land will yield its harvest, and God, our God, will bless us. God will bless us, and all the ends of the earth will fear him."

Establish Order and Unity at Home

There is no place more essential for the Kingdom of God to be established than at home. While a man's work life is an important measure of how he is applying his natural gifts and talents to God's specific agenda, a man's home life is where the practice of the Word of God has critical long-term implications for his wife and children. "For the kingdom of God is not a matter of eating and drinking, but of righteousness, peace and joy in the Holy Spirit" (Romans 14:17). It is a man's responsibility to bring his family into proper alignment under the leadership of Christ and to provide them with a consistent example of obedience to His will. When men do not seriously make an effort to fulfill their role as a leader in the home, their marriage and family will suffer. In Mark 3:24-27 Jesus said, "If a kingdom is divided against itself, that kingdom cannot stand. If a house is divided against itself, that house cannot stand. And if Satan opposes himself and is divided, he cannot stand; his end has come. In fact, no one can enter a strong man's house and carry off his possessions unless he first ties up the strong man. Then he can rob his house." "But when a strong man, fully armed, guards his own house, his possessions are safe" (Luke 11:21).

When a man is "tied up" with sins, his life and home will become divided and will not stand. Satan can then enter his house and rob him. How? He will use whatever means is available to disrupt the unity in a household. He will bring strife, confusion, chaos, and disarray; trying to undermine a man's credibility and ignite rebellion against his leadership. He will enter through whatever access sin gives him to injure a man and his family. Just as Jesus is the door to the Kingdom of God, a man, under Christ, guards the door to his family. He can help block the door by living out the values and strategies of the Bible, but when a man yields to the indulgences of sin and irresponsibility, he causes his family to be vulnerable to attack.

When I came to Christ, I saw how my failure to serve Him had left my family virtually unprotected. But making a decision to follow Christ represented a dramatic shift away from being someone who was serving Satan's agenda unaware, to a man with the potential to break his grip on my family. Of course, I knew that I was not able to do the job alone, but I could rely on the fact that "God made Him who had no sin to be sin for us, so that in Him we might become the righteousness of God" (2 Corinthians 5:21). I had become righteous through Christ Jesus. Now all I needed to do was honestly to begin working my way through my problems and fulfilling the duties of managing my family for the Lord.

Dorothy and I had to find a way to restore God's order to our home. We lacked unity and were constantly experiencing the effects of our past conflicts. 1 Corinthians 11:3 provided us with a blueprint for how things should be organized. Paul said, "Now I want you to realize that the head of every man is Christ, and the head of the woman is man, and the head of Christ is God." The right organizational structure for our home would bring God's power and favor to bear on our problems. So we had to agree to His established order for operating as a family. First God the Father, then Christ, then the man, and then his wife. As Christ followed the lead of His Father, we would follow Him in an orderly and unified way. That seemed simple enough, but I knew it was not going to be easy.

My family had adjusted to two extremes of bad leadership. I tended to ignore my responsibilities and let things reach crisis levels before I paid much attention. Then, I would attack the problem, belligerently forcing things to a resolution. Now I had to figure out how to get my wife to cooperate and follow my leadership again, but this time it had to be from her heart and not under duress.

Our biggest problems were about trust and respect. My wife, like most women who have not received the kind of love and leadership they deserved, had worked out a lot of things for herself just to survive. She had made excuses for some of my problems, condemned me in her heart for others, and generally made a judgment that I was not worthy of exercising any authority in the household. Actually she was right about most of it. Although I had given my heart to the Lord, there were still lots of behaviors in my life that were ungodly and not indicators of someone who could be trusted. All of these factors led her to conclude that she did not really have to respect me. Anyone who knew all the facts could not blame her, least of all me. But her lack of trust still hurt and caused me to feel weak and impotent as a leader. Sometimes it provoked me to angry outbursts, which only made the problem worse.

One day, while I was praying and meditating about the situation, the Lord showed me a four-step plan that would, over time, solve our dilemma. It required the simple application of spiritual authority in our family and a comprehensive commitment to His Lordship. I was overjoyed because I knew that He was giving us an opportunity to see our relationship restored, but at the same time, I had the distinct impression that this was a serious situation that required my complete obedience. I had gone far enough in my relationship with the Lord that I not only respected Him, I wanted to please Him. So I felt secure in the knowledge that He was intervening in my family.

1) I had to bring myself completely under the authority of Christ as His disciple. I had to be willing to improve as a person at every level and become a reliable man. My values and strategies had to be consistent with God's Word and I had to learn to operate day to day in a way that was trustworthy. I knew that I could not be perfect and succeed in all of this every day. But the Lord was only

asking me to press toward these goals with sincerity. His grace and mercy would be sufficient to keep me going. Just to make sure, I prayed a comprehensive prayer of repentance and re-commitment to His plan. This is something I did quite often during the early days of my new leadership, and occasionally since then. I have also drawn a lot of encouragement from Scriptures like Philippians 4:13, which says, "I can do all things through Him who strengthens me" (NAS).

2) I had to pick up the scepter of His authority and rule my home. As sweet as my wife was about most things, I literally feared trying to explain that one to her. She had suffered a lot under my leadership and would not be eager to submit to me. But the Lord was persistent. He reminded me how His power and favor came over my life when I aligned myself under His authority. All He was asking me to do was extend the blessing of that authority to my wife and son. As they aligned themselves under the leadership of God, Christ, and me from their heart, they would also experience a new power and favor of God in their lives. He assured me that He would be faithful to confirm it. So in the fear of God, I prayed another prayer where I symbolically raised the scepter of authority in my right hand and pledged to Him to rule my home for His glory. I also asked for His wisdom to properly lead my family. Proverbs 8:33-36, says,

> Listen to my instruction and be wise; do not ignore it. Blessed is the man who listens to me, watching daily at my doors, waiting at my doorway. For whoever finds me finds life and receives favor from the Lord. But whoever fails to find me harms himself; all who hate me love death.

3) I had to practice my leadership openly. Ephesians 5:21 says, "Submit to one another out of reverence for Christ." This meant taking the time to describe to my wife what I thought God had shown me, listen to her viewpoint, answer any questions she had, confess my sins to her as they occurred, and fully explain what I was going to do to improve our situation. God was not asking me to do

this only once, but anytime I made a major decision, sinned, noticed any fractures in our relationships, or saw that we needed to review the plan He had given us. I had to hold myself and my family accountable to God's Word. Psalms 45:6 says, "a scepter of justice will be the scepter of your kingdom." I was under God's authority to lead our home and He was expecting all of us to respect that stewardship. I had to make sure I earned the credibility to exercise authority by bringing just decisions to our family processes. They had to be careful to listen for the voice of the Lord in what I said and did. It was a challenge that was intended to cause each person to be humble before the Lord and more aware of the results of his or her actions.

4) I had to love my wife as Christ loved the church. Ephesians 5:21-33 provided an overview of God's plan for us. Verses 21-24 restates God's structural order for the home. But the key to success is having the right structure along with the right spirit for leadership. A woman must be able to sense a man's love and integrity in what he is trying to accomplish. Verses 25-27 provides the most critical instruction for men who want to lead effectively at home.

> Husbands, love your wives, just as Christ loved the church and gave himself up for her to make her holy, cleansing her by the washing with water through the word, and to present her to himself as a radiant church, without stain or wrinkle or any other blemish, but holy and blameless.

This Scripture commands a man to become spiritually accountable for his wife. As scary as that sounds, if a man is prepared to become a priest to his family and apply the right strategies to his responsibilities, he can, by grace, fulfill this mandate.

Paul said in Romans 15:1, "We who are strong ought to bear with the failings of the weak and not to please ourselves." In a marriage each partner will have the opportunity to be strong when the other is weak. While it is good to be able to depend upon one another's strengths, we should be careful that in doing so, neither party does anything that changes their fundamental order under

Christ. Galatians 3:28 says, "There is neither Jew nor Greek, slave nor free, male nor female, for you are all one in Christ Jesus." But when a person confuses equality in Christ, or the relative strengths and weaknesses in a marriage, with his or her responsibility to maintain the proper order under Christ, he or she will bring disorder into the relationship.

A man, who is able to model the love, humility, and cooperation of a servant, and maintain his proper place of authority, can become a great blessing to his family. Proverbs 31:10-21 describes what is called "The Wife of Noble Character." It is the perfect description of a woman operating in her own gifts under the authority of her husband. This "Noble Woman" has been washed by the Word and encouraged by her husband to grow and prosper as a person. The result is that her husband "lacks nothing of value" (verse 11). A man whose home operates in God's order can expect many blessings for his wife and children, and a full and fruitful life together.

Extend the Church into the World

1 Peter 2:4-5 reminds us that as we "come to Him, the living Stone—rejected by men but chosen by God and precious to Him—you also, like living stones, are being built into a spiritual house to be a holy priesthood, offering spiritual sacrifices acceptable to God through Jesus Christ." Each of us who follows Christ becomes one of those living stones. We are called the "church." The Greek word which is translated as "church" (#1577) is more accurately translated as "the called out." We are "called out" as individuals and as a community to serve and represent Christ here on the earth. Many people have come to think of the church only as the organized entity which meets in a building and has services at a certain time and place. They often expect that entity to say and do the things on their behalf that Christ has actually called each of us to do personally as His servants. In Matthew 28:19-20, Jesus said,

> Go and make disciples of all nations, baptizing them in the name of the Father and of the Son and of the Holy Spirit, and teaching them to obey everything I have commanded you. And surely I am with you always, to the very end of the age.

He was not speaking these words to an entity or an organization, but to His disciples. He was commissioning all who would return to their homes, communities, and work to live their lives for Him and reach out to others for Christ. There are many practical ways that we can make disciples. Christ gives every man skills or talents that, when properly applied, will support him in his own economy and provide food and shelter for life. In the same way, He also provides each of us with the ability to influence others to believe in and obey the Lord.

> Just as each of us has one body with many members, and these members do not all have the same function, so in Christ we who are many form one body, and each member belongs to all the others. We have different gifts, according to the grace given us. If a man's gift is prophesying, let him use it in proportion to his faith. If it is serving, let him serve; if it is teaching, let him teach; if it is encouraging, let him encourage; if it is contributing to the needs of others, let him give generously; if it is leadership, let him govern diligently; if it is showing mercy, let him do it cheerfully.
>
> Romans 12:4-8

The mission of the church–living stones like you and me–is to fulfill the commission that Christ gave us. That can easily be done through the opportunities provided by our home and work life, or in helping to meet the needs of others. Everyone knows the story of the "Good Samaritan" whose acts of kindness saved a man who was beaten and left half dead after he fell into the hands of robbers along the road from Jerusalem to Jericho (Luke 10:30). This took place after a priest (verse 31) and a Levite (verse 32) passed by the man without helping him. In verse 36, Jesus asked, "Which of these three do you think was a neighbor to the man who fell into the hands of robbers?" It is a painful truth that the organized entity we call the local church often does not see or respond to the needs of people right in their own community. Just like the priest and the

Levite, they pass by opportunities to minister, often leaving the job for government agencies and secular groups.

There was a particular ministry to the poor that was regularly overlooked in a congregation I once attended. As I became more aware of how important it was and watched the need go unmet I became troubled about what I could do about it. I finally started to respond to the need myself, regularly taking time to directly engage in a ministry of mercy. Although the leaders at my church nodded approvingly when I told them what I was doing, they never spent a minute directly supporting my work or becoming involved themselves. During prayer one day, I began to complain to the Lord about their lack of interest and asked Him why our church did not respond to people's needs the way I thought He expected. His answer was immediate and startling as He spoke to my heart, "You are the church. I am blessing what you do. What do you want from them that I am not giving you?" The Lord had taken a personal interest in my ministry of mercy. He had provided what I needed, given me favor with everyone involved, and created a sense of satisfied obedience in me that was almost indescribable. I was ashamed when I realized that my complaining was the same as saying to God, "Your participation in this is not enough. I want these other people to take an interest." What the Lord was allowing me to do was precious in His sight and I was missing the significance of it.

Over the years I discovered that I had not been alone in my ignorance about how the Kingdom of God operates. I have met a lot of people who were ministering with full spiritual authority, yet felt that they were alone and unappreciated by their church. But as God led them, they could not have been more directly connected to His will than when they were doing the things Jesus described in Matthew 25:35-40. Jesus said,

> For I was hungry and you gave me something to eat, I was thirsty and you gave me something to drink, I was a stranger and you invited me in, I needed clothes and you clothed me, I was sick and you looked after me, I was in prison and you came

to visit me." Then the righteous will answer him, "Lord, when did we see you hungry and feed you, or thirsty and give you something to drink? When did we see you a stranger and invite you in, or needing clothes and clothe you? When did we see you sick or in prison and go to visit you?" The King will reply, "I tell you the truth, whatever you did for one of the least of these brothers of mine, you did for me."

In Luke 7:36-47 we find that:

One of the Pharisees invited Jesus to have dinner with him, so he went to the Pharisee's house and reclined at the table. When a woman who had lived a sinful life in that town learned that Jesus was eating at the Pharisee's house, she brought an alabaster jar of perfume, and as she stood behind him at his feet weeping, she began to wet his feet with her tears. Then she wiped them with her hair, kissed them and poured perfume on them. When the Pharisee who had invited him saw this, he said to himself, "If this man were a prophet, he would know who is touching him and what kind of woman she is—that she is a sinner." Jesus answered him, "Simon, I have something to tell you." "Tell me, teacher," he said. "Two men owed money to a certain moneylender. One owed him five hundred denarii, and the other fifty. Neither of them had the money to pay him back, so he canceled the debts of both. Now which of them will love him more?" Simon replied, "I suppose the one who had the bigger debt canceled." "You have judged correctly," Jesus said. Then he turned toward the woman and said to Simon, "Do you see this woman? I came into your house. You did not give me any water for my feet, but she wet my feet with her tears and wiped them with her hair. You did not give me a kiss, but this woman, from the time I entered, has not stopped kissing my feet. You did not put oil on my head, but she has poured perfume on my feet. Therefore, I tell you, her many sins have been forgiven—for she loved much. But he who has been forgiven little loves little."

The behaviors of this incredibly thankful woman show us that when someone gets his sins forgiven and comes to fully know Christ, he will naturally have a heart full of love and be ready to serve. In fact, when the Lord comes to live within us, it should be almost effortless to "let your light shine before men, that they may see your good deeds and praise your Father in heaven," as Jesus exhorts us to do in Matthew 5:16. When I meet a man who professes to know Christ and is not burning inside to serve the Lord in some practical way, I can guess that one of three things applies to him. He, 1) was never really saved, 2) has forgotten the value of his redemption and become entangled in sin again, or 3) has been subdued into lifeless conformance by an organized entity calling itself the church.

Too often, we spend our time and money preserving the infrastructure and economics of our institutions instead of extending ourselves, "the church," into the world around us. In a world of materialism and self indulgence, it is possible for the church to forget who we are and what we are doing. This is not just a problem of our own time, but one that the church has struggled with for centuries. In Philippians 2:20-21, Paul says of Timothy, "I have no one else like him, who takes a genuine interest in your welfare. For everyone looks out for his own interests, not those of Jesus Christ." This is a surprising perspective from a man who lived and worked with people who had observed first hand the events written about in the Gospels and the book of Acts.

When groups of believers come together in community, they very often try to conform to a single agenda. This is not unusual because it is a fundamental premise of management that a group or entity must have a common goal in order to fulfill its purposes effectively. But when the organized entity draws people away from their God-given agendas to bring unity to their corporate goals, it fails the purposes of the Kingdom, and takes on a life of its own. The church should be helping every man fulfill God's agenda for his life. It has no legitimate purpose other than supporting the mandates of Christ for each of us as individuals and reaching out to the lost. This is because *we* are the church. Every man must find and fulfill his own agenda in Christ for the body of Christ to function properly. As each of us fulfills the design and function God has given us, we can powerfully fulfill the commission of Christ at home, at work, and in our communities. When we fail to do so, we have "lost connection with the Head, from whom the whole body, supported and held together by its ligaments and sinews, grows as God causes it to grow" (Colossians 2:19).

Resolve Conflicts Peacefully

A few years ago I was on a ski vacation with my family when I met a young man named Vernon. He was the maintenance man where we were staying and came to our condo to see why we were not getting any hot water. I noticed immediately that Vernon was a no-nonsense type of guy. He was clean-cut, polite, and quickly went about his business. As he was checking out the water heater he asked me, "Are you some kind of preacher?" A little surprised, I answered, "Yes, sort of, I do a lot of volunteer work in prisons. Why do you ask?" He said that he had noticed our Bibles and tapes lying around and some literature that was stacked on the counter. I asked him if he was a follower of Christ. His response sounded like a plea for help. "I thought I was," he said. "I got saved in prison. But now I guess I am a backslider." His cheery voice had turned cynical and depressed. I sat down next to him and listened as he shared a glorious testimony of how God had delivered him from a life of alcoholism and violence. He had a gentle, sincere spirit and talked about the Lord with such genuine affection that I began to question him about his life. I wanted to know how and why he could have turned away from Christ after all he had experienced.

After his parole from prison he had rejoined his family in a small rural area where the local church played a significant role in the community. Several members of the church had reached out to him and provided a safety net of security which had helped him grow emotionally and spiritually. Their kindness and the peace he experienced when he was with church people had made it easy for him to adopt their routines. Until just a few days before we met, he had regularly studied his Bible, prayed, tithed his income, attended church meetings, volunteered to repair the building, and generally immersed himself in church life. He had been diligently trying to "put the things he had read and heard about God into practice."

Vernon told me how he had made Christ the first priority in his life, followed by his family and work. He had taken serious steps to heal and restore his marriage and was working hard to advance on his job and provide a good living for his family. Each time he had taken a practical step in this direction, he had felt the power and favor of God move on his behalf. God was blessing and prospering his path and he had felt sure that he was fulfilling Christ's agenda for his life.

The problem had arisen when he had decided he was spending too much time at his church's extracurricular activities such as the Saturday morning bake sales. He realized that he was not really needed at some of these events, and that his time could be better spent doing other things at home. But he had no idea that this simple decision to manage his time would bring his spirituality into question. After he had missed a few events, his pastor confronted him. He saw Vernon's absence as an indicator of his failure to recognize the importance of the church in his life. Vernon explained to him how he was only following what he thought was the leading of the Lord to fulfill his responsibilities to his family and that he had continued to attend Bible studies and worship services as before.

His pastor was not satisfied. He insisted that Vernon's failure to attend these events was evidence that he was moving away from his devotion to the church. Vernon protested. He told his pastor about how he had experienced the power and favor of God when he had made decisions to serve his family more consistently. He expected his pastor to understand that his devotion to his family was an expression of his devotion to Christ and that attending a bake sale was not as important as ministering to the needs of his family. But his pastor was adamant, insisting that Vernon should be at the church "every time the doors were open."

At this point Vernon realized that his pastor's attitude had changed from what had appeared to be loving concern about his well being, to boldly ordering him to do what he was told. He scolded Vernon for acting so independently and reminded him of his authority as a pastor to hold him accountable. But Vernon's heart would not let him easily concede. He had experienced God's miraculous protection too many times in prison to be intimidated by what might only be one man's misjudgments, but how could he be sure? His dilemma was heartbreaking because he had been so sure he was doing the right thing. Finally, his pastor told him that he was acting like a backslider and that he needed to obey the authority of the church (which, of course, was him) in the matter.

Vernon was stunned and disoriented. Only a few days later, with the issue still unresolved, he was sitting on the floor of my condominium spilling his heart. He turned to me and said, "Mr. Kennedy, I really love the Lord. I didn't think I was a backslider, but my pastor was so angry with me. Still, I just don't feel right about what he said. If serving the Lord means yielding the responsibility for my life to someone who orders me to go to bake sales, I guess I might be backsliding. I don't think I can do it."

I knew Vernon was no backslider and I spent some time reassuring him. But he felt hurt and betrayed by his pastor and was having trouble expressing himself and dealing with the anger that was growing in his heart. He had experienced a head-on collision with an "institutional man" whose actions had exceeded his spiritual authority. However, Vernon was not yet mature enough in Christ to know how to deal with his pastor's oppressive intrusion into his life. He wanted to preserve his relationship with the man and stay connected to the church. But at what cost? The problem of resolving conflicts in authority or agenda's is difficult for most men, not only at church but in all areas of their lives. Handling conflicts correctly strengthens a man and raises his confidence in Christ. When we fail to do so, it can be destructive to both ourselves and others.

There are generally four ways that a man will respond to conflicts. He will, 1) yield to the other person, 2) avoid and escape the conflict, 3) aggressively confront the issue, or 4) peacefully seek understanding and resolution.

1) Yielding to the other person can be an act of wisdom and humility, especially if a man discovers that he is in error. There is certainly no better way to settle a dispute than to give up the hair-splitting agony of debating the details, confess our mistake, ask forgiveness, and go on with our life. It keeps the peace, preserves relationships, and avoids the risks of doing or saying something much worse. It also makes sense for a man to yield, at least temporarily, when he finds himself at a strategic disadvantage of power or timing. Waiting for a better time, place, or conditions to press an issue could help everyone involved. But when a man routinely yields to unrighteousness, he is not only encouraging more and greater sins on the part of his oppressor, he damages his own soul. Proverbs 25:26 says, "Like a muddied spring or a polluted well is a righteous man who gives way to the wicked."

2) Avoiding and escaping conflict can also be an act of wisdom and humility, but again, only as a short term solution until a better time or place can be found. When a man can reduce the tension between himself and an oppressor by avoiding certain situations or topics, he is probably wise to do so. He should pray for his oppressor and delay serious confrontation until a discussion can be reasonably expected to lead to resolution. But when avoidance becomes the primary method of dealing with conflict, it has the same effect as yielding to wickedness. A man cannot ignore oppression and expect it to just go away. Withdrawing from relationships or changing wives, jobs, or churches to isolate ourselves from the hard work of resolving conflicts only complicates matters. It leaves the old wounds unhealed and ready for exploitation by the next oppressor. "A man who isolates himself seeks his own desire; he rages against all wise judgment" (Proverbs 18:1 NKJ).

3) Aggressive confrontation rarely brings resolution to a dispute. It usually leaves the parties without real understanding of each other's issues because someone ends up yielding to superior power, intellect, or strategic advantage. The person who yields remains angry and unconvinced and the other is unsatisfied. In 1 Peter 2:16-19, we are directed to:

> Live as free men, but do not use your freedom as a cover-up for evil; live as servants of God. Show proper respect to everyone: Love the brotherhood of believers, fear God, honor the king. Slaves, submit yourselves to your masters with all respect, not only to those who are good and considerate, but also to those who are harsh. For it is commendable if a man bears up under the pain of unjust suffering because he is conscious of God.

Not only that, if someone's "purpose or activity is of human origin, it will fail. But if it is from God, you will not be able to stop [it]; you will only find yourselves fighting against God" (Acts 5:38-39).

4) Every believer can identify to some degree with the story of Vernon and his pastor. We will all experience conflict between ourselves and another believer at some time. The spiritual authority we believe we have to fulfill God's agenda for our own life will inevitably come into conflict with what another person thinks is a superior agenda with greater spiritual authority. When this happens, it is important that the sanctity of each person's priesthood with Christ is not violated. For some reason, Vernon's pastor did not use reasonable judgment in his assessment of the facts and stepped across the line of his rightful authority. He was judging Vernon as though he was his own servant and not the Lord's. He may have forgotten for a moment that:

> To his own master he stands or falls. And he will stand, for the Lord is able to make him stand. One man considers one day more sacred than another; another man considers every day alike. Each one should be fully convinced in his own mind.
> Romans 14:4-5

The church is made up of individuals, all responsible to hear from the Lord. Our individual authority is dependent upon our personal relationship with God and how well we are hearing and obeying Him. Vernon's pastor should have been encouraging him to continue his growth in the Lord. Instead, he became too aggressive about his own agenda. He was not hearing from the Lord and came dangerously close to where he could be held responsible by God for causing Vernon to stumble. Hebrews 13:17-18 says,

> Obey your leaders and submit to their authority. They keep watch over you as men who must give an account. Obey them so that their work will be a joy, not a burden, for that would be of no advantage to you. Pray for us. We are sure that we have a clear conscience and desire to live honorably in every way.

This Scripture surely was not intended to give men the authority to set the agenda for another man's life, nor does it give either party the option of ignoring their personal vulnerability before the Lord. Rather, it places a burden on both Vernon and his pastor to avoid the risks of staying in conflict.

Romans 12:18 provides a simple mandate for people who find themselves in a situation such as this. It says, "If it is possible, as far as it depends on you, live at peace with everyone." When you ask people about how they settle conflicts, they are more likely to describe their peacemaking skills in very limited ways such as yielding or avoidance. I believe it is because most people are trying to attain peace and quiet for the moment, not real and lasting peace. They almost never describe a reasoned, truthful process leading to peaceful reconciliation. They commonly lament the need for a counselor, arbiter, or some reliable process which was not available to them. Fortunately, the Scriptures outline just such a process. Although it has often been overlooked, it provides the steps for two or more people to hold themselves and each other accountable. It puts the parties of a conflict into a search for the truth, forcing each person to honestly reassess his position and seek a resolution in Christ, and the agreed-upon outcome is binding on the participants. Properly applied, it provides a practical model for conflict resolution and the opportunity to develop the skills of a peacemaker. In Matthew 18:15-20 Jesus said,

If your brother sins against you, go and show him his fault, just between the two of you. If he listens to you, you have won your brother over. But if he will not listen, take one or two others along, so that every matter may be established by the testimony of two or three witnesses. If he refuses to listen to them, tell it to the church; and if he refuses to listen even to the church, treat him as you would a pagan or a tax collector. I tell you the truth, whatever you bind on earth will be bound in heaven, and whatever you loose on earth will be loosed in heaven. Again, I tell you that if two of you on earth agree about anything you ask for, it will be done for you by my Father in heaven. For where two or three come together in my name, there am I with them.

Vernon had a right to due process. But like many people, he did not realize that Matthew 18 provided a level playing field for believers to settle their conflicts. Either he or his pastor could have initiated the process simply by saying, "I think we need to follow the steps of Matthew 18 to resolve our differences." Knowing that both of their actions were going to come under the scrutiny of other believers might have been enough for Vernon's pastor to rethink his position. It might also have helped Vernon to decide how comfortable he was with the facts as he saw them and whether or not his story would remain unchanged before one or two witnesses as they came together in the presence of the Lord. This scriptural process is not intended to give someone the ability to make another person conform to his own perceptions. It is intended to help all the parties honestly review their own perceptions and make whatever adjustments or admissions that will bring real peace. Repentance and forgiveness would have definitely been in order for one of these men and maybe for both.

Too many men have disconnected from the body of Christ, or are thinking about it, because of the failure to properly resolve conflicts. Some of them may even be backsliders. But many of them are probably like Vernon, needing encouragement and the support of due process to find a peaceful resolution. Of course, Matthew 18 does not always bring resolution. When it does not, the fault can often be laid at the feet of people who lacked the proper respect for the Lord and one another. Or it can be because one or two skilled peacemakers were not available to assist them. Men who have learned humility and have become peacemakers by resolving their own conflicts are extremely valuable to the Kingdom of God. They are essential to the success of reconciliation, especially when the conflicted parties lack the maturity or wisdom to settle the issues between them. "Peacemakers who sow in peace raise a harvest of righteousness" (James 3:18). They help bring real peace by requiring each person to see their conflict from the perspective of God's Word.

Each man is ultimately responsible before God to properly discern his own thoughts and behaviors. Whether or not he does so will have a direct affect on the power and favor of God in his life, and whether or not he has spiritual authority to continue in the path he has chosen. Jesus said,

> Blessed are the peacemakers, for they will be called sons of God. Blessed are those who are persecuted because of righteousness, for theirs is the kingdom of heaven. Blessed are you when people insult you, persecute you and falsely say all kinds of evil against you because of me. Rejoice and be glad, because great is your reward in heaven, for in the same way they persecuted the prophets who were before you.
> Matthew 5:9-12

This Scripture provides hope for the person who has failed to find reconciliation through no fault of his own, but for someone who has ignorantly defended his own perspective, it is a call to repentance. Proverbs 28:1 tells us that, "the wicked man flees though no one pursues, but the righteous are as bold as a lion." It is every man's responsibility to be sure that his boldness is in Christ and not just in the power of his own soul.

Live by Faith and Principle

Philippians 2:3-7 says,

> Do nothing out of selfish ambition or vain conceit, but in humility consider others better than yourselves. Each of you should look not only to your own interests, but also to the interests of others. Your attitude should be the same as that of Christ Jesus: Who, being in very nature God, did not consider equality with God something to be grasped, but made himself nothing, taking the very nature of a servant.

In this exhortation we are encouraged not to take ourselves or our own agenda so seriously that we become unaware of its possible detriment to others. What we want or what we are trying to accomplish may not always be in our own best interests or of the people around us. Because a man can be "led astray by his own great folly" (Proverbs 5:23), he should be prepared to pray and question himself to be sure that his motives are established in faith and principle.

The Kingdom of God operates on reliable principles that are described in the Scriptures. Our ability to function effectively in the Kingdom is dependent upon our ability to apply God's principles to our life through our faith in Christ. Faith is an expression of our confidence or trust in God as a person and in His principles. When we live by faith, we believe and act in accordance with principles that often go counter to the world around us. Jesus explained this to His disciples in Matthew 20:25-28:

> Jesus called them together and said, "You know that the rulers of the Gentiles lord it over them, and their high officials exercise authority over them. Not so with you. Instead, whoever wants to become great among you must be your servant, and whoever wants to be first must be your slave – just as the Son of Man did not come to be served, but to serve, and to give his life as a ransom for many."

Here the Lord explains the principle of what is often called "servant leadership." When a follower of Christ reads this Scripture, he must make a decision to fully open his heart and mind to believe it and then act in accordance with it. To do so means that at home he will serve his family, instead of lording it over them. At work he will find ways to serve the interests of his customers and superiors, instead of spending his time and energy reaching for positions of prominence. When he does so, he will be depending on methods and motives that are much different than the world around him. And as he has chosen to trust the Lord with the results of his life at home and at work, he can expect to receive His help. God's power and favor will sustain a man living by faith and principle.

Another example of faith and principle is found in Luke 4:9-12, when Jesus was being tempted by the devil.

> The devil led him to Jerusalem and had him stand on the highest point of the temple. "If you are the Son of God," he said, "throw yourself down from here. For it is written: 'He will command his angels concerning you to guard you carefully; they will lift you up in their hands, so that you will not strike your foot against a stone.'" Jesus answered, "It says: 'Do not put the Lord your God to the test.'"

Jesus trusted His Father to protect him. Because He was secure in His Father's love, He provides us with an important example of not frivolously applying our faith. He could have surely taken a dive from the temple, defying gravity, and landing safely, if it was His Father's plan. But He was here on earth to become an example for us. He responded to the devil's attempt to cause Him to act imprudently by acting in accordance with a higher principle. Jesus did not need to prove anything to the devil or any one else about His faith, and neither do we. Our faith is in God and His Word and all we are required to do is to use our faith in reasonable ways as we respond to His plan for us.

From time to time, I counsel with men who are about to do something at home or at work which is comparable to a leap from the roof of the temple. They have usually been deceived by the devil into demonstrating the intensity of their commitment to God in some unreasonable way. Instead of living out each day by faith and principle, they concoct an aggressive act of faith to please God, or impress someone else in their life. This kind of behavior is almost always the result of a person's need for acceptance or recognition he has not received. It is frightening to see a man come to the point of leaping, because it is very difficult to turn him away from his ill-conceived idea. By then he has rationalized the risks to his family or business, and has overlooked or rejected the Biblical principles that would direct him to a safe, productive strategy. He has ignored diligence and chosen a desperate course of action, expecting God to "honor" his leap of faith. "It is fine to be zealous, provided the purpose is good" (Galatians 4:18). But sometimes our acts of faith are the moral equivalent of telling God what we want to happen or a foolish attempt to force Him outside the borders of faith and principle. "This is what the Lord says–the Holy One of Israel, and it's Maker: Concerning things to come, do you question me about my children, or give me orders about the work of my hands?" (Isaiah 45:11).

This is not to say that there is never a time for bold or forceful action. The most vivid example can be found in one of Jesus' visits to the Temple in Jerusalem.

> He found men selling cattle, sheep and doves, and others sitting at tables exchanging money. So he made a whip out of cords, and drove all from the temple area, both sheep and cattle; he scattered the coins of the money changers and overturned their tables. To those who sold doves he said, "Get these out of here! How dare you turn my Father's house into a market!" His disciples remembered that it is written: "Zeal for your house will consume me." Then the Jews demanded of him, "What miraculous sign can you show us to prove your authority to do all this?" Jesus answered "Destroy this temple and I will raise it again in three days."
>
> John 2:14-19

135

His authority to take this action was unquestionable; He was God, and after He was crucified He rose from the dead to prove it. But the mandate for this kind of aggressive action is rare and should not be carelessly mimicked. Each picture of faith and action that we read about in Scripture must be carefully compared with the principles that come to bear on the subject. When we fail to do so, we can create rules to live by that are based on narrow and unrealistic interpretations of what God intends for us.

For example, when they came to arrest Jesus to crucify Him, and His "followers saw what was going to happen, they said, 'Lord, should we strike with our swords?' And one of them struck the servant of the high priest, cutting off his right ear. But Jesus answered, 'No more of this!' And he touched the man's ear and healed him" (Luke 22:49-51). "Put your sword back in its place," Jesus said to him, "for all who draw the sword will die by the sword. Do you think I cannot call on my Father, and he will at once put at my disposal more than twelve legions of angels?" (Matthew 26:52-53).

Peter (John 18:10) made a mistake that any man could make in a similar situation. He might have misinterpreted a single instance of Jesus' aggressive actions in the temple as something other than a rarity. After all, Jesus Himself had told them, "If you don't have a sword, sell your cloak and buy one" (Luke 22:36). When Peter and the other disciples realized they were in a situation which might call for a strong response, they asked the Lord what to do. Then Peter took the kind of action he thought was justified without waiting to hear what Jesus had to say. When a man does not have a full grasp of the situation he is in, does not understand the principles that apply, or does not wait to hear from the Lord, he may very well be committing a sin of presumption instead of an act of faith. "Faith is being sure of what we hope for and certain of what we do not see" (Hebrews 11:1), and "everything that does not come from faith is sin" (Romans 14:23).

Our home and work life should be centered upon our faith in the Lord and the principles He has given us to live by. We will make mistakes. But like anything we try to do, we can learn from them and grow. Proverbs 24:32 says, "I applied my heart to what I observed and learned a lesson from what I saw." The Kingdom of God is not for the casual observer but for the active participant who is as eager to learn from his trials, tribulations, and mistakes, as he is from what comes easily. When we don't get the lesson right, He patiently sustains us. "If the Lord delights in a man's way, he makes his steps firm; though he stumble, he will not fall, for the Lord upholds him with his hand" (Psalms 37:23-24).

I have walked with the Lord long enough to have experienced His intervention on my behalf many times in many situations. The Lord is so kind and faithful that He is able to take almost any event and from it teach us faith and principle. Even the things that are painful and do not make sense to us at the moment can become healing events with wonderful lessons that cause us to trust Him more. When my wife and I lost our newborn baby boy after only one week, we were devastated. Still in shock and reeling from the spiritual battle to which I had given all my strength, I wandered through the halls of my home praying and thinking, trying to find some reason or explanation for our loss. As I entered the nursery we had prepared, I was overwhelmed by the glaring closeness of our pain. At the same moment I recognized the unusual Presence of the Lord. It felt as if He had moved nearer to me and in a very fatherly way put His arm around my shoulders.

I was startled because both the Lord and I knew what was in my heart at that very instant. There was confusion, doubt, despair, and some anger. Just as I crossed the threshold into the room I had come to the point of questioning Him about the inconsistencies I saw and how they were affecting my faith. As clearly as you might hear a father whisper his comfort and in a direct answer to my unspoken thoughts, He said, "You trust me more than that, don't you?" My heart nearly stopped as I answered with a simple "yes." There was a pause as seemingly thousands of things flashed through my mind reminding me of His faithfulness and how I had grown to love and trust Him through many previous trials. I was relieved to be reminded that I really did trust Him in spite of what had been going through my mind. Then He said, "And you know I am a merciful God, don't you?" In an instant, His peace flooded my soul as I yielded to the truth of these two principles. I did know that I could trust Him in whatever situation I found myself, and I knew that He is a merciful God and Father.

This was a time of faith and principle. It was not a time to leap from the roof of the temple either in presumptive faith or self-indulgent despair. The devil often tries to take advantage of our honest questioning and turn it into unbelieving doubt, but the Lord is always faithful to bring to our memory what we need to keep faith with Him. He can also use these events to shake us free from doctrines and beliefs that are unrealistic or unbalanced. Although we have received no specific explanation for the loss of our son, we have continued to learn many things about the reality of our faith, the principles we live by, and how the Lord ultimately reigns in sovereignty. As we are told in Jeremiah 6:16, "Stand at the crossroads and look; ask for the ancient paths, ask where the good way is, and walk in it, and you will find rest for your souls."

PART 11

THE FOUR FOUNDATIONAL VALUES
OF SPIRITUAL GROWTH

5
KINGDOM IDENTITY:
A MEASURE OF OUR PARTICIPATION IN GENUINE CHURCH LIFE

Nikolai was a man with a well-established identity. He was a child of God, a member of the body of Christ, and a citizen of His Kingdom. Everything about his life, talents, work, and family were expressions of his identity in Christ, and a testimony to the incredible durability of his faith. He had grown up in St. Petersburg, Russia under some of the most brutal leaders of the Soviet regime. Until he began attending the university, he and his mother, Anna, both marked as criminals because of their faith, had lived alone in a four-foot by six-foot storage closet at the end of a musty hallway in an old apartment building. They were outcasts, being pressured by the cruel circumstances in which they were forced to live, to recant their faith and embrace Soviet ideals. The severity of their lives was intended to be an exhibit against faith, sufficient to extinguish the good intentions of any observer.

Anna had survived the Stalin purges only to endure evil treatment at the hands of party officials who had selected her to suffer public humiliation instead of death. But the more they tortured and tried to brainwash her, the stronger she became in Christ. She was determined to provide for Nikolai and had turned her harsh cubicle into a warm, cozy nest. She scavenged for necessities and occasionally found favor with neighbors who would secretly leave a piece of bread, a warm slice of cooked meat, or used clothing outside her door.

Anyone caught helping her would be guilty of treason, so the things she received came at great risk. Eventually, after several years of complete rejection, she was allowed to work, earning a few rubles each week doing the lowest and dirtiest jobs, and she was permitted to plug a tiny hotplate into a hallway light fixture to cook or make hot tea.

Nikolai's education began on his mother's knee as she told him stories from the Bible she had once owned. She explained to him that God had a plan for his life and trained him to embrace the sufferings they endured as a privilege. By the time he was of school age, he was strongly grounded in the Scriptures although he had not read a single line from the Bible. Anna boldly pressed the Soviets to allow her son to attend school. It was unprecedented, but Nikolai showed promise as an academic, so they relented. He excelled in his studies, even though he had to endure oppressive classroom drills designed to undermine his identity in Christ. And he had to attend occasional meetings with the headmaster in which he would be threatened with dismissal if he did not deny his faith. But as he passed each course level, the Lord gave him favor, and he kept studying until he had earned a doctorate in physics.

Anna and Nikolai had always enjoyed wonderful fellowship with Christ. Even during the worst parts of their ordeal they never felt completely alone because they dedicated each day to the Lord, and He was always with them. And from time to time another exile would nod to them in the train station or stop for a brief moment of fellowship at the market. These deeply satisfying contacts with fellow believers sometimes developed into secret meetings that took place on park benches, and in the darkened corners of museums or libraries, where they encouraged one another and shared small scraps of Scripture pulled from one of Stalin's fires. Anna and Nikolai's church life was genuine, and they knew what was real and necessary in their walk with Christ. When Nikolai married, it was to a wonderful young lady who had faced her own struggle for the faith and they established an extended family of powerful believers.

As far back as he could remember, the deepest desires in Nikolai's heart had been to study the Bible and teach. During his childhood there were no opportunities for such things because most of the

Bibles and cathedrals had either been confiscated or destroyed. Thousands of priests had been murdered by the Soviets during the Stalin era and their activities had primarily been limited to maintaining archives, which were kept by monks and older priests who had survived the purges. But not long after Nikolai had completed his doctoral studies, the Russian Orthodox seminaries had been allowed to reopen and enroll students. He had long hoped that he could be part of a renewal of faith in Russia, and he was willing to sacrifice the comfortable standard of living he had gained through academics, so he enrolled in seminary, eventually becoming a priest and professor. It was at the Seminary that I first met Nikolai.

It was a great blessing to be Nikolai's friend and to enjoy times of fellowship with him at the Seminary or in my office. But my most special memories are my visits with his family at their apartment. Anna was truly a saint, and her daughter-in-law and grandchildren were a tremendous witness to their love and care for one another. A meal with them was a visit to a New Testament church meeting, as they prayed, sang, recited Scriptures and told wonderful stories of faith. It was common for us to be laughing and crying at the same time as someone recounted one of the heart-rending absurdities of Soviet life and how the Lord had routinely baffled their opponents. I always left their home encouraged and revitalized, and my problems always seemed smaller than my faith after spending an evening with these battle-tested brothers and sisters in Christ. It was what I thought church life ought to be like, although I had rarely experienced it since my earliest days in the faith. Like many of my friends, my experiences with the church had been very disappointing, and we had allowed it to extinguish our joy.

One of the things that intrigued me about Nikolai was how he had remained so free and alive in Christ through all of his seminary training and formal ministry. But to my surprise, he shared with me how he was almost as much of an outcast within the institutions of the church as he had been to the Soviets. From his very first day in seminary, they had unsuccessfully tried to turn his faithfulness to Christ into loyalty to their programs. Later he was shunned and isolated from some ministries because he had pointed out inconsistencies and corruption among his colleagues. They had even tried to discredit him by producing phony evidence that he was personally unreliable, but his confidence had been established in the fact that he was a citizen of the Kingdom of God, not the Russian Orthodox Church. Because he knew who he was, his life had been one of many living testimonies against the Soviet state, and it had also become a testimony against the bureaucracies of the church. He had withstood the conforming pressures of two of the most powerful institutions in history by clinging to the most fundamental truth. They had not given him his faith and they could not take it away.

Kingdom identity is a measure of our participation in genuine church life. God has a plan for every person that includes how, when, and where we fit into the body of Christ for each part of our life. It is a dynamic plan that requires freedom of movement within the Kingdom and active participation by each believer in worship, training, fellowship, and service. God wants us to experience a variety of ministry gifts and relationships that are intended to teach us how to become functioning parts of His family, "until we all reach unity in the faith and in the knowledge of the Son of God and become mature, attaining to the whole measure of the fullness of Christ" (Ephesians 4:13).

The basic organizational unit of the Kingdom of God is relationship. It is by the power of our Spirit-born relationship with God through Jesus Christ, that the "called out" (*ekklesia*, #1577) escape a life of sin and death. And as each of us "called out" brothers and sisters "walk in the light, as He is in the light, we have fellowship with one another, and the blood of Jesus, His Son, purifies us from all sin" (1 John 1:7). This is the nature of our relationship with God and one another, and it is not dependent upon any other relationship, power, charter, creed, or institution. When the Soviets demeaned Nikolai and Anna, trying to get them to renounce their faith, they were oppressing God's "called out." When the institutional church shunned and ridiculed Nikolai for refusing to conform to their standards, they were oppressing God's "called out." When we "walk in the light" alone, as two, or with many, we are the "called out." It is upon the foundation of this unshakable identity that all other tenets of the faith are built.

God's "called out" people picked up the nickname *Christians* during the first century. In Acts 11:26 Luke writes that, "for a whole year Barnabas and Saul met with the church (called out, #1557) and taught great numbers of people. The disciples were called Christians (followers of Christ, #5546) first at Antioch." For at least ten centuries following Antioch, those people who professed a relationship with God through Jesus Christ were known as the "called out" or simply Christians. Then, because of various changes in language and culture, the word "church" was coined. So each time you see the word "church" in the New Testament, it literally means the "called out" people who profess to have a relationship with God through Jesus Christ. When we refer to "church life," we are referring to the kind of life to be lived by the "called out." *When we refer to the "institutional church," we are referring to the man-made religious institutions, which have been used to organize the "called out" people of God.*

And just as language has evolved and sometimes confused our identity, so have the rules and regulations men have tried to invoke in an effort to hold together their particular sect or denomination. It's obvious that in the process of congregating people, developing infrastructures, and figuring out how to manage and finance them, men have sometimes forgotten that "the Lord is God," and that, "we are his people, the sheep of his pasture" (Psalms 100:3). It is necessary to debunk some of those rules and philosophies so that we can be free to serve the Lord both as individuals and as functioning members of the body of Christ. To the many men and their families who have begun their walk with Christ deeply desiring a genuine church life, only to be oppressed or exiled from fellowship because of their inability to conform to a man-made religious system, we offer some practical alternatives.

Meet with the Church at Home and in Public

Over the centuries the word "church" has become synonymous with the buildings in which we meet. In fact, Sunday morning meetings in a church-owned building have become the focal point of church life. What we do when we meet together has changed dramatically from New Testament times, but not just because of church buildings. During the period 312-325 A.D. the Roman Emperor, Constantine, created one of the first and most widely-copied institutional churches, with buildings, corporate authority, and a more refined form of public worship with professional ministers. (See Appendix). Since then, the vitality and power of the church have progressively diminished, as impersonal public meetings and religious bureaucracy have slowly replaced a relational church life.

In Acts 20:20 (NAS) the Apostle Paul said, "I did not shrink from declaring to you anything that was profitable, and teaching you publicly and from house to house." There is evidence in both Scripture and history to support the viewpoint that the church met in homes and in public places. But the New Testament pattern for church life was primarily based upon a small-group, participant form of worship and fellowship that took place in homes, not public meetings. It was a lifestyle in which God could set the lonely in families (Psalms 68:6) and the "called out" ministered to one another's needs. Jesus said, "By this all men will know that you are my disciples, if you love one another" (John 13:35); and the identity of the church became a loving and caring community. The broad meaning of the Greek word *koinonia* (#2842) is "the share we have or the part we play by participating in community, fellowship, communion, or a gift jointly contributed." This gives great significance to 1 John 1:7, which says, "if we walk in the light, as he is in the light, we have fellowship (*koinonia*) with one another."

The mutual and reciprocal nature of ministry between the "called out" is highlighted in the term "one another." It is used in John 13:35 when Jesus said, "If you love one another" and in 1 John 1:7, "we have fellowship with one another." These words "one another" indicate active participation in ministry as opposed to just being a member of an audience. Then in Hebrews 10:24-25 we are urged to "consider how we may spur one another on toward love and good deeds. Let us not give up meeting together, as some are in the habit of doing, but let us encourage one another." You might be more familiar with a portion of the King James Version of verse 25, "Not forsaking the assembling of ourselves together," which is widely misquoted to make you afraid to miss Sunday morning services at an institutional church. But do those kinds of public services really fulfill God's purposes for ministry to "one another?" Standing together to sing a hymn or greeting your neighbor as you're being seated is usually the closest thing to mutual participation that a public meeting has to offer, unless there is an altar call or prayer circle where the believers pray for one another.

I became a follower of Christ on a Monday night in my brother-in-law's office in a private school. Then on Wednesday night, I attended a meeting at an institutional church. On Saturday night I attended my first home meeting, which was not affiliated with any local church. It was a house-to-house meeting of the "called out" who attended several different institutional churches in town. On Sunday morning I was back in the institutional church. I soon began to realize, as many men have, that there were things about the public services which often left me dulled in my spirit instead of stimulated to "love and good deeds." But I almost never left a home meeting without being encouraged in my faith. Sometimes what I needed to see, hear, say, or experience took place during a meal together, or during our discussions about the Bible, or prayer times, or as we sang and worshiped together. Or it might have been during a lingering conversation in the driveway or as we worked together to help someone in need.

The public meetings primarily helped me to realize that we were only a small part of the Kingdom of God, which caused me to enjoy my meetings with individuals and small groups even more. I did appreciate the corporate sense of praise and worship the public meetings provided, but too often the interests of the pastors were not the same as ours. Their focus wasn't so much on helping us draw near to the Lord as it was on the various projects or programs they were advocating to perpetuate their institution. One thing is certain, there were not many opportunities to participate and grow in faith during the public meetings.

Men have tried and failed to fit into the lifestyle of the institutional church for centuries. They often describe it as dull or monotonous, with dry, sometimes manipulative, sermons that have no relevance to their daily grind. Many are put off by the repeated emphasis on money, building programs, and membership, which draw our attention away from the Lord to the institution's purposes. Some leave quietly; while others depart in anger because of inconsistencies that church leaders could not reasonably explain. These men join the many millions who are trapped between their desires for something real and lasting in Christ and their refusal to continue in a religious system that has failed them. The solution to this dilemma includes recognizing three important facts:

First, the institutional church's programs, infrastructure, and Sunday morning meetings have become synonymous with the biblical mandate for God's people to "gather." But neither Scripture, history, nor archeology confirms them as the New Testament model.

Second, home meetings are a priority of church life. They should be a primary activity of the "called out," not an afterthought or a tool for managing church growth as the institutional church has made them.

Third, believers have a legitimate biblical need for meeting both in small groups and in public for worship and fellowship, but they are free in Christ to exercise their creativity about when, where, and how to meet.

There are three questions that, for most believers, have framed the dilemma regarding these facts:

First, if it's true that the public meetings of the typical institutional church do not properly represent the New Testament pattern, why have they remained so unchangeable?

Second, if it's true that home meetings should be a higher priority than public meetings, why has the institutional church's activities always centered on the Sunday morning public meeting?

Third, if everyone is free to choose which public and home meetings they want to attend, including the institutional church, why has the institutional church remained so dominant?

These are troubling questions since there is no record in the New Testament of church-owned buildings, nor professional "pastors" giving lectures each Sunday to a denominationally-segregated section of the body of Christ. Both history and archeology indicate that the church met in small groups, from house to house, and occasionally at some public place where more than one home meeting could gather together. The primary ministry activities were non-professional, requiring each person to contribute his or her gift or talent to the success of the meeting and to participate as an active learner and maturing member of the "called out." So why has the institutional church's rigid format remained intact and become the most prevalent representative of the church to the world? It is because of the self-preserving nature of religious institutions and their power to entice or condemn their followers into conformance.

An institution is defined as "a significant practice, relationship, or organization in a society or culture." To institutionalize means, "to incorporate into a structured and often highly formalized system." As each member of the "called out" is incorporated into the systems of the institutional church, it becomes more difficult to make a distinction between the institution and the people who sustain it. *Thus, when we mention the institutional church we are referring to both the corporate structure and the people who organize and operate its systems.* Every person who has tried to bring change to an institution has learned from experience that institutions don't reform or change in practical ways very easily, if at all. They usually only make slight adjustments to their doctrines and practices to settle divisions among their membership or to attract the next generation of supporters as the demographics of a society change. Institutions realize that when the marketplace changes, they must develop new marketing techniques to remain viable. But the values that define an institution almost always remain the same.

Religious institutions are unusually resistant to change because of the way their members become emotionally and spiritually entangled in their traditions. Guided by misplaced zeal, their leaders often defend unscriptural practices by quoting false doctrines that may have been misinterpreted and legitimized for generations by people they have been taught to revere. In many cases, they have unwittingly "rejected the law of the Lord and have not kept His statutes; their lies also have led them astray, those after which their fathers walked" (Amos 2:4 NAS). Confronting a religious institution about the error of one of its rules or regulations often arouses powerful emotions that can be intensified by pride, politics, and economics. Institutional leaders may also fear they will open a floodgate of unanswerable questions if they admit to a significant error. So they can become a compelling force of rejection to anyone who questions the validity of their institution's policies, especially when it has been presumed that they speak on behalf of God.

A typical conversation with someone about his or her problems with the institutional church usually includes a statement similar to this: "I would like to leave, but I don't know how to solve the problem of not forsaking the assembly." This reference to Hebrews 10:25 demonstrates the power to condemn that a mistakenly-applied Scripture can have, especially when the institutional church has become synonymous with the "called out," or with public meetings. Jesus made a simple but powerful promise to each of us who follow Him. In Matthew 18:20 He said, "Where two or three come together in my name, there am I with them." You can attend an institutional church if you want, but it is not mandated. You are the "called out," the church; and God has a divine purpose for you when you meet with other believers. And His purpose is more likely to be realized in a small group.

My wife and I have a few close friends with whom we often go to dinner or share an evening in some way. Although we usually have a lot of fun together, our evenings are also sprinkled with serious discussions about our work, kids, relationships, and church life. One night as we enjoyed fellowship with a couple at our favorite yogurt shop, we talked seriously about how most of the people we knew were longing for something more than what the institutional church offers. We had spent about three hours together discussing one another's ideas and problems when I thought to ask this question. "Do you believe the spiritual experience we've had tonight is equal to, less than, or greater than what normally takes place in a public meeting of the institutional church?" Everyone answered simultaneously, "greater, much greater."

So I continued to probe: "Do you believe the Lord has met with us and has given us wisdom tonight?" Again they answered, "Yes, of course." "And has our sharing of the Scriptures been as relevant, less relevant, or more relevant to our lives than what takes place in a typical service at the institutional church? Is our knowledge of how to pray for one another more specific, less specific, or equal to what we could have learned about each other in the hallway after Sunday services? Are we more likely, less likely, or equally as likely to take these lessons home and actually live them out?" As we answered each of these questions we realized that the best experiences that most public meetings have to offer are only occasionally equal to, and rarely greater than, what takes place in small groups where we can share intimately about our lives with people we trust. It's not the size or venue of the meeting or its institutional authority that should concern us, but the ministry to "one another" that we must be careful "not to forsake."

Teach and Admonish One Another

A "disciple" is a "learner" (#3101) and learning is a process "to gain knowledge, understanding, or skill by study, instruction, or experience." Almost no one would disagree with these definitions even though the primary educational method of the institutional church has been the Sunday morning sermon. A sermon is a Christian speech given by pastors who are separated by a wide variety of personality types and delivery styles, but connected by one common handicap—they are attempting to deliver critical spiritual information by a method that is extremely ineffective. Sermons are usually conveyed without discussion, questions, or any legitimate instructional feedback from the learners. Every educator knows that these fundamentals of interaction are essential for learning to take place and that their consistent absence indicates a failure to seriously consider the objectives of learning.

As do many things that don't make sense about the institutional church, the practice of gathering into a "church" building to hear a pulpit-delivered sermon from the same man week after week, without educational interaction, dates back to Emperor Constantine. When he made the Christian church an official religion of the state, he was careful to provide for it in a manner equal to the other state-funded religion, which was "sun worship." The Emperor appointed the church hierarchy and they exercised executive powers over the members of their congregations on his behalf. In return for these simple yet profound compromises, this institutionalized church was provided the comforts and resources of an official state religion, with a politically-empowered organizational infrastructure and the guarantee of protection from persecution. (See Appendix.)

The benefit to Constantine's government was a manageable society of cooperative believers. And like any institution, the partisans of the institutional church soon became accustomed to the level of order and control their new authority gave them. Before long they had established "the ministry" as a profession with their own criteria for accepting other men into what by then had become an industry. For the next twelve hundred years there were many developments including an established order of worship and seminary training for those who desired to enter "service." Like all traditions and institutions, each passing generation declared the previous generation's religious advances (or mistakes) as holy and built upon them. By the time Martin Luther came along in 1517, only the priests could read, study, or teach the Bible. (See Appendix.)

Luther, a Roman Catholic priest, became disillusioned by the way his superiors abused their authority and with many of the institutional church's perverted and sometimes occult practices. Everything was for sale, including forgiveness of sins, as men bargained and battled for the title of Bishop just as they would for the authority any political or commercial franchise brings. Although Luther sincerely tried to bring reform, the Roman Catholic Church summarily rejected him. He was excommunicated, along with many disgruntled priests and members who left with him. In short, they then proceeded to establish another institutional church with a modified order of worship and an increased emphasis on Greco-Roman rhetoric, or speech making, which we now call "preaching." Luther was also instrumental in the development of a pastoral "job description" that has evolved into the modern day pastor-teacher-CEO, and for which there is no basis in Scripture. (See Appendix.)

Luther's efforts proved one thing beyond any doubt: Religious institutions do not easily reform. They sometimes achieve measurable change but usually fail to get to the heart of the matter, only further dividing the church. With all of the historical weight theologians have given Luther's effort, there is one revealing fact that defines the level of success of the reform movement. On October 31, 1999, four hundred and eighty-two years after the "protestant reform" began, the Roman Catholic Church finally agreed to officially recognize that "salvation is by faith" (lutheranworld.org). But little, if anything, has changed inside the Roman Catholic Church. In fact, Martin Luther's work, although significant for its renewal of individual faith in God, primarily resulted in a proliferation of protestant denominations, each with its own institutional distinction. It is from these traditions that the educational methods of the modern institutional church sprang forth.

In Colossians 3:16, the Apostle Paul wrote these instructions about what should take place when the "called out" meet together: "Let the word of Christ dwell in you richly as you teach and admonish one another with all wisdom, and as you sing psalms, hymns and spiritual songs with gratitude in your hearts to God." Here again is the emphasis on "one another." Unfortunately, institutionalized people prefer the Constantine and Luther forms of meeting together because they require little or no preparation by believers who want to sit in an audience. But it is the very pressure of being responsible to learn and then teach, first at home, and then when the "called out" meet together, that helps create spiritual growth and maturity. No one learns like someone preparing to teach and be held accountable for what he says. This is why Paul calls for "reliable men who will also be qualified to teach others" (2 Timothy 2:2).

When you recall some of the examples the institutional church has provided as teachers, it's easy to see why a man might think twice about trying to teach the Bible even in a small group. If he believes that he is expected to make dynamic Christian speeches like the professional pastors do on Sunday, he has the wrong idea altogether. And for the most part, so do the professional pastors. Too much of what I have seen is akin to theater, not ministry. I was asked to attend a meeting of secular foundation executives a few years ago that took place during one of our "televangelist" scandals. I had been invited specifically because I was a "person of faith" and they wanted to hear my perspective on some of the issues with which they were grappling. Their most riveting question was this one: "How do you know who is real and who is not when you see these guys on television." It was one of those hushed moments when everyone was listening and I knew the Lord did not want me to give them a "know your Bible" answer. So I pondered for a moment until this thought came to me. "Try to imagine Jesus saying and doing the things that you see these people saying and doing on T.V. with all of their affectations and theatrics. If you don't feel a sense of embarrassment, it's probably O.K." They looked stunned, and then very sincerely said, "Thank you, we've always wondered."

A lot of men don't know whether or not to reject some of the teaching models we have seen, but their common sense tells them they don't want to copy their styles. They would rightly feel embarrassed, not necessarily by what they say (although it can get pretty strange) but more so by how they say it. Once the ministry became a profession, it naturally produced all kinds of aberrations from the extremely "pious" to the extremely ridiculous. Besides the fact that we are not making a very good impression on the world by letting these guys represent us, they have a tendency to either quench the spirit in most men or drive them away from the church altogether. I wonder how many men have wrongly thought they could not teach or lead because they were unable to feel comfortable strutting in front of a large crowd at a public meeting, or thought they must be slick, eloquent, or highly educated to do the Lord's work.

Ephesians 4:11 describes some of the ministries the Lord has provided for His work to be accomplished. There are two common interpretations of this passage, depending on the setting in which it is taught. The most prevalent lists five ministries—apostles, prophets, evangelists, pastors, and teachers. This view is sometimes advocated by the people who have become aware of the limitations of listening to one man teach every Sunday. It gives them what they believe is a scriptural option to have someone other than their pastor, preferably a "teacher," do some of the teaching. The second, and I think the more accurate interpretation, lists four ministries—apostles, prophets, evangelists, and pastor-teachers. This interpretation, unfortunately, strengthens the argument of the Constantine-Luther followers who think the pastor is "the" teacher. But either way, there are at least two problems with the way this Scripture is applied by the institutional church.

154

First, whether you believe Ephesians 4:11 actually describes four or five ministries, one thing is clear: Each of them should fulfill much more than their traditionally understood roles because each performs a teaching function. Evangelists often say important things not directly related to an altar call for the lost. And prophets have a lot more to say than what can be reasonably shouted out during a pause in the worship service. The teaching function of apostles is beyond doubt. What remain are pastors and teachers or pastor-teachers. But all of these ministries have an instructional purpose that is better understood by reading this passage in its context.

> It was he [the Lord] who gave some to be apostles, some to be prophets, some to be evangelists, and some to be pastors and teachers, *to prepare God's people for works of service, so that the body of Christ may be built up until we all reach unity in the faith and in the knowledge of the Son of God and become mature, attaining to the whole measure of the fullness of Christ.*
>
> Ephesians 4:11-13

Second, where are the ministries other than pastor-teacher supposed to fit into God's plan and provide their instruction? If you are a Constantine-Luther institutional church member, you believe they are either away at seminary preparing to fit into the pastor-teacher mold that awaits them, volunteering in the Sunday School or visitation ministry, or have been "sent out" as a missionary or "para-church ministry" to reach the lost and poor. Coincidentally, you also believe that the tithe belongs to the institutional church and that the other three or four ministries are supposed to forage among the body of Christ for whatever "contributions" are available after the tithe has gone to the "local church." Any way you look at it, the institutional church has invested heavily in its pastor-teacher model and has a tight grip on who does ministry.

But what if most of the people who are supposed to fulfill the four teaching or instructional ministries described in Ephesians 4:11 are truck drivers, tradesmen, pharmacists, office workers, teachers, salesmen, and managers—just normal people who make their living at a job while they maintain their responsibilities at home? What if God has intended for them to share about their life in a small group, discuss the Scriptures with one another, and teach those who are younger or less experienced? What if the institutional church has emphasized their professional pastor-teacher model so much that they have virtually eliminated the place of these other ministries and their various ways to be supported. The answer might be found in a more literal translation of pastor-teacher, which is "herdsman-teacher" or "shepherd-teacher," and a more realistic understanding of the scriptural model for learning.

The most common model for teaching described in the New Testament is dialogue or discussion. Although in some verses the Greek word *dialegomai* (#1256) is erroneously translated as "preaching," it is more accurately translated as "discussing" or "reasoning." It is not merely a speech, nor is it a conversation without purpose. It often begins with the teacher saying thoroughly what he wants to present followed by a discussion. However, the teacher's lesson could be interspersed throughout a discussion, with questions, answers, and arguments becoming a part of the learning process. In many respects, it is very similar to what might happen at a family meeting or around a dinner table, with the father giving instructions about how something should be done, moderating a discussion, or settling a dispute. Another more commonly used Greek word is *didasko* (#1321) which is translated as "teach" or literally "to hold discourse with others in order to instruct them." When you think about it logically, it's the kind of thing a shepherd-teacher would do.

In Acts 17:17, we are told that Paul "reasoned (#1256) in the synagogue with the Jews and the God fearing Greeks, as well as in the marketplace day by day with those who happened to be there." In Acts 19:9, "he took the disciples with him and had discussions (#1256) daily in the lecture hall of Tyrannus." And in Acts 5:42, we are told that the disciples continued "day after day, in the temple courts and from house to house, they never stopped teaching (#1321) and proclaiming the good news that Jesus is the Christ." A meeting of the "called out" is described in Acts 20:7-11 which clearly shows the interactive shepherd-teacher nature of Paul's ministry.

On the first day of the week *we came together to break bread.* Paul *spoke* (#1256) to the people and, because he intended to leave the next day, kept on talking until midnight. There were many lamps in the upstairs room where we were meeting. Seated in a window was a young man named Eutychus, who was sinking into a deep sleep as Paul *talked* (#1256) on and on. When he was sound asleep, he fell to the ground from the third story and was picked up dead. Paul went down, threw himself on the young man and put his arms around him. "Don't be alarmed," he said. "He's alive!" Then he went upstairs again and *broke bread and ate.* After *talking* (#3656) until daylight, he left.

Acts 20:7-11

There are several things here to be emphasized. For instance, they obviously came together on the first day of the week (vs. 7) to break bread and eat (vs. 7 and 11) and have a discussion or reason together (vs. 7 and 9). This doesn't sound like anything the typical institutional church would do, even occasionally, for Sunday services. But to get a further idea how the usage of words change and evolve, in verse eleven the Greek word *homileo* (#3656) is translated as "talking." This is the word which the Constantine-Luther institutional churches and their seminaries have institutionalized into "homiletics" or "preaching." Essentially, it has become part of the speech-making doctrine of the institutional church even though the original word really means, "to be in company with, to converse, or to commune." That's what shepherd-teachers do. They fellowship and teach one-on-one, in small groups, from house to house, and in public. It's something that a lot of men are capable of doing very well.

In Matthew 16:7, 12 Jesus said to His disciples, "Be on your guard against the yeast of the Pharisees and Sadducees." After some discussion, His disciples understood that "He was not telling them to guard against the yeast used in bread, but against the teaching of the Pharisees and Sadducees," the New Testament equivalent of the institutional church. The challenge for every man is whether he

157

will be active or passive in his walk with Christ. If you are actively following Christ, the "teaching" that you will be required to do, at home or in a small group of the "called out," will come to you very naturally. But if you are passively sitting in an audience absorbing and following the doctrines of the institutional church, you will never learn to teach and lead.

Minister the Gifts of the Holy Spirit

There are many advantages to meeting in a home, not the least of which is the increased willingness of most people to confess their sins or use their spiritual gifts. One of my earliest recollections of Spirit-led ministry was a visit to a man's home to counsel with him about his intense problem with anger. He was a fairly successful businessman, and otherwise very kind, but he sometimes erupted into a cursing tirade over simple disagreements with his customers. He had become a follower of Christ and was deeply convicted about his behavior. As we sat and prayed with him, we asked the Lord to show us what was hindering his ability to fully repent and be free. When I closed my eyes I could see the head and shoulders of a man dressed in a white Ku Klux Klan hood. It was one of my first experiences in receiving a word of knowledge and I hesitated to mention it to the man. Finally I said, "Do you know anything about the KKK?" The color drained from his face, then he admitted he had been very involved with the KKK prior to his coming to Christ and no one in his family knew about it, not even his wife. The power of secret sin had taken its toll, but was no match for the power of repentance. He was like a new man after he renounced the various aspects of this gripping demonic covenant.

The man who teamed with me to pray that night was a postal worker. Another partner who often prayed with me was a merger-acquisitions analyst for a large company. One night a painting contractor and I prayed for his mother. Another time a schoolteacher and I prayed for his son. A retired military officer was also a regular team member. We came from all walks of life and were all "amateurs." Whenever we met in home church meetings, the results were stirring as people confessed their sins and were set free from torment. One night a couple brought their son, a drug-addicted

Navy seaman who had received a weekend pass from a federal drug treatment center. It was a sovereignly arranged meeting as we asked the Lord to lead us to the roots of his addiction. When he gave his heart to the Lord, and renounced his addictive lifestyle, he was wonderfully delivered from drugs. He became a tremendous witness in the Navy and later a missionary. This kind of New Testament ministry was commonplace in our meetings, and people were often miraculously healed and filled with the Holy Spirit.

In a large building with a crowd, the people who are most likely to speak or minister are the extroverts and, of course, important people like "Queen Elizabeth" who showed up in a service I once attended and demanded to be recognized. As with most troubled people who attend the public meetings of the institutional church, the ushers quickly escorted "the Queen" out through a side door. The probability of her receiving any real ministry was virtually nonexistent. In an institutional church setting there are usually very few people who have been "approved" to minister, and then only in limited ways. Even in "Spirit-filled" meetings, the institutional church's concerns about keeping order and limiting legal liability often restrict the "called out" from providing genuine Spirit-led ministry to those who might need it.

One of the things the institutional church says it is trying to accomplish by putting limits on whom it will allow to minister, is to obey the admonition "to know them which labor among you" given by the Apostle Paul in 1Thessalonians 5:12-13 (KJV). The Greek word here translated as "know" literally means "to perceive, notice, or discover; or with eyes wide open, to discern clearly" (#1492). But keep in mind that this Scripture was not written to an institutionalized church. It was written to the "called out." I am certain that my prayer partners were better known to me (because of our time together in a home church) than the institutional church typically knows anyone who has filled out a form and attended personal-ministry training. Even pastors who are "under the authority" of a denominational board are rarely as well-known as they should be before they are licensed to minister. The institutional church has a poor record of "keeping the ministry pure," as evidenced by the number of local and national scandals. Even when they succeed, their process often shuts off ministry by the "called out."

Another thing the institutional church emphasizes in its effort to control the ministry activities that take place is its concern that "everything should be done in a fitting and orderly way" (1 Corinthians 14:40). While this Scripture is actually speaking of the orderly use of the gifts of the Spirit, they mistake it to mean that their Constantine-Luther order of worship should be done in an orderly way, with no interruptions except to occasionally say "Amen" during the sermon. Ironically, most of their concerns about order are created by the very nature of their meetings. Since there are rarely any discussions about the sermon or active participation in Spirit-led ministry by the "called out," they have produced an arena that is ripe for striving by both frustrated members and the strange visitors that sometimes show up. It's hard to imagine that the institutional church's vision for ministry is what the Lord had in mind, because of the way it has extinguished ministry by the "called out." The following are a few scriptural perspectives about how each of us should be ministering the gifts of the Holy Spirit.

> Just as each of us has one body with many members, and these members do not all have the same function, so in Christ we who are many form one body, and each member belongs to all the others. We have different gifts, according to the grace given us. If a man's gift is prophesying, let him use it in proportion to his faith. If it is serving, let him serve; if it is teaching, let him teach; if it is encouraging, let him encourage; if it is contributing to the needs of others, let him give generously; if it is leadership, let him govern diligently; if it is showing mercy, let him do it cheerfully.
>
> Romans 12:4-8

> There are different kinds of gifts, but the same Spirit. There are different kinds of service, but the same Lord. There are different kinds of working, but the same God works all of them in all men. Now to each one the manifestation of the Spirit is given for

the common good. To one there is given through the Spirit the message of wisdom, to another the message of knowledge by means of the same Spirit, to another faith by the same Spirit, to another gifts of healing by that one Spirit, to another miraculous powers, to another prophecy, to another distinguishing between spirits, to another speaking in different kinds of tongues, and to still another the interpretation of tongues. All these are the work of one and the same Spirit, and he gives them to each one, just as he determines.

1 Corinthians 12:4-11

[1]Follow the way of love and eagerly desire spiritual gifts, especially the gift of prophecy.
[12]So it is with you. Since you are eager to have spiritual gifts, try to excel in gifts that build up the church.
[26]What then shall we say, brothers? When you come together, everyone has a hymn, or a word of instruction, a revelation, a tongue or an interpretation. All of these must be done for the strengthening of the church.
[39]Therefore, my brothers, be eager to prophesy, and do not forbid speaking in tongues.
[40]But everything should be done in a fitting and orderly way.

1 Corinthians 14:1, 12, 26, 39, 40

A reasonable person reading these Scriptures with an open mind can easily see that some of the doctrinal positions various segments of the institutional church have developed are unbiblical. For example, some say that there are no miracles or healing today. Some say that there are neither living prophets nor prophetic utterances. Some admonish us neither to seek nor forbid speaking in tongues and other spiritual gifts. And nearly all tell us to leave the ministry to the professionals. Each such conclusion requires a very twisted application of the Scriptures. Equally as difficult to comprehend is how all of the ministry gifts described in these Scriptures could possibly find expression through the institutional church's Constantine-Luther model of the pastor-teacher as he conducts a public meeting on Sunday mornings.

As you sort out all of the modern issues, you can also identify how the institutional church has become so concerned about protecting its assets and income from the lawsuits that might occur as a result of some ministry activities, that in some cases it has virtually shut them down. It's true that an institution that has no solid scriptural basis for its model of ministry, is operated by flashy professional staff with expensive buildings and deep tax-free pockets of income, and has failed to retain the public confidence, is a juicy legal target. But an un-credentialed volunteer, who is not being compensated, is not representing an institutional church, and is invited into a person's home to minister to a family member, is almost free from liability. As you can see, the ministry plan that was used in New Testament times is still relevant today.

When I first began to counsel and pray with men and their families, I was shocked to discover how many "church" people were trapped in tormenting sin. The people I counseled had regularly attended public services (often three times a week) and sometimes attended "approved" fellowship groups, yet without relief. They were completely sincere people who were serving the Lord the way they had been taught. But the institutional church's agenda had left them struggling with life as the confused victims of their own sins in a powerless spiritual environment. I found myself routinely giving counsel or ministry that set people free from sin and at the same time put them at variance with the things they had learned on Sunday mornings from their inexperienced pastor. The irony was that their pastors had usually been "in the ministry" for many years and I was just a young businessman, but I was not intimidated by my lack of credentials. My confidence was in the Scriptures and the personal healing and deliverance I had received from the Lord. I also had many irrefutable experiences in ministering the gifts of the Holy Spirit to others.

One of those life-shaping experiences came on a short mission trip to a Caribbean Island. It was a thoroughly evangelized place where the Baptist missionary comes through on Monday, the Presbyterians on Tuesday, the Pentecostals on Wednesday, and then the various witchcraft cults and covens the rest of the week. It was not unusual for people to attend both church and witchcraft services. So almost everyone you met had heard the "gospel" as well as the doctrines of the various witchcraft religions, whose priests attracted many people with their powerful demonstrations and rituals. We held several meetings and spent most of our time praying for the sick and oppressed, helping them discover the pure power of fellowship with God. At the end of one of our more dramatic meetings, a "deacon" from a local church and his wife invited me to their home the next day for lunch and to pray for their daughter. I immediately felt the Lord nudge me to accept their invitation and agreed to visit them.

Their home was nicely kept and a little upscale for the area in which they lived. As I entered the front gate I could hear a lot of noise coming from behind the house and an eerie howling sound, very much like a coyote. There were about ten children playing outside and twenty to thirty adults standing around. When they saw me they all stopped what they were doing and gathered around a small wooden hut behind the house that was about eight feet square. It was built on stilts about three feet above the ground and had no windows, only two double Dutch doors. The tops of both doors were opened but the bottoms were closed and bolted on the outside. As I got closer, I could hear howling, hissing, and thrashing sounds coming from the hut. I knew that it could be a cockfight or some other strange diversion which was common to the islands, so I braced myself and peered carefully through the doorway. There, inside the bare walls and floor of what I then realized was a "cage," was a little three year old girl literally bouncing off the walls. It was she who was making all the noise.

Her parents turned to me and asked, "Can you help?" I stood there for a moment almost in shock, thinking and praying, wondering what the Lord would have me do. Then I simply replied, "I'll try." As soon as I said those words, a godly confidence began to rise inside me. I reached over, unbolted the door, stepped inside the cage, and closed the door behind me in what felt like a single motion. The little girl turned and looked at me with a demonic glare that sent chills up my back. Then she went totally wild, running around and around the hut, slamming against the walls, and screaming, "No! No!" in a loud ear-piercing shriek. It was not the voice or the strength of a little girl. The whole hut shook from the force of her pounding. The Lord whispered to me, "Sit down in the middle of the hut." So I sat down and crossed my legs, pivoting only slightly to the right or left to keep eye contact with her as she circled around me.

As she continued to howl and scream, I very quietly started repeating the name of Jesus. "Jesus . . . Jesus . . . Jesus." Then very gently, "Jesus is Lord . . . Jesus is Lord." As I did, the little girl began to focus as though she were listening to me. In about ten minutes she came to a complete stop, sitting in a corner looking directly at me. I kept up the vigil, always looking directly into her eyes, "Jesus . . . Jesus . . . Jesus is Lord." Then "Jesus loves you . . . Jesus loves you." She suddenly got up from the corner, walked over to me and sat down in my lap leaning up against my chest. Then I whispered in her ear, "Let her go in Jesus' name. I rebuke you in the name of Jesus. Let her go, in Jesus' name." Her little back and arms stiffened like rods and then she let out a deep, long sigh and slumped into my arms, asleep. She was free.

As I sat there holding her, I silently asked the Lord, "How could a demon have such complete control of a three year old girl?" His response was stunning. "This little girl was conceived during an Obi ritual." (Obi was a witchcraft religion widely practiced on the island and her mother had an adulterous relationship with one of its priests.) He also said, "Her mother has been afraid to confess her sin to her husband. Tell her to confess and I will forgive her and remove the curses from their family." I got up and headed for the house, handing the little girl to another lady. The little girl's mother looked at me as though she knew what was coming. I took her and her husband into the kitchen and privately repeated all that the Lord had shown me. The lady completely repented and asked God (and her husband) to forgive her. Then I left the two of them to talk and pray alone.

I remember the Scripture that was given to me by the evangelist who had invited me to come to the island. It was Acts 10:37-38:

You know what has happened throughout Judea, beginning in Galilee after the baptism that John preached–how God anointed Jesus of Nazareth with the Holy Spirit and power, and how he went around doing good and healing all who were under the power of the devil, because God was with him.

When I asked him what he wanted me to do on the trip, he encouraged me to do whatever Jesus would have done had He visited the island. No man who has experienced such an event could ever again be satisfied with the limitations of the institutional church. That was God's plan. He had to take me outside of what, for me, were the normal perimeters of church life and ministry to let me see how much more there was to the Kingdom of God than I had experienced before.

Practice Generosity and Benevolence

When the Son of Man comes in his glory, and all the angels with him, he will sit on his throne in heavenly glory. All the nations will be gathered before him, and he will separate the people one from another as a shepherd separates the sheep from the goats. He will put the sheep on his right and the goats on his left. Then the King will say to those on his right, "Come, you who are blessed by my Father; take your inheritance, the kingdom prepared for you since the creation of the world. For I was hungry and you gave me something to eat, I was thirsty and you gave me something to drink, I was a stranger and you invited me in, I needed clothes and you clothed me, I was sick and you looked after me, I was in prison and you came to visit me." Then the righteous will answer him, "Lord, when did we see you hungry and feed you, or thirsty and give you something to drink? When did we see you a stranger and invite you in, or needing clothes and clothe you? When did we see you sick or in prison and go to visit you?" The King will reply, "I tell you the truth, whatever you did for one of the least of these brothers of mine, you did for me." Then he will say to those on his left, "Depart from me, you who are cursed, into the eternal fire prepared for the devil and his angels. For I was hungry and you gave me nothing to eat, I was thirsty and you gave me nothing to drink, I was a stranger and you did not invite me in, I needed clothes and you did not clothe me, I was sick and in prison and you did not look after me." They also will answer, "Lord, when did we see you hungry or thirsty or a stranger or needing clothes or sick or in prison, and did not help you?" He will reply, "I tell you the truth, whatever you did not do for one of the least of these, you did not do for me." Then they will go away to eternal punishment, but the righteous to eternal life.

Matthew 25:31-46

The "called out" have a consistent testimony of wanting to help the poor and extend mercy to a wide variety of social and moral needs. But when you think of the institutional church, generosity and benevolence are not the first things you would associate with its activities. In fact, many of the people who have turned away from the institutional church point to its lack of concern for the poor as one of the foremost reasons they left. The reluctance of pastors to commit significant money to the poor and destitute, or even people with needs within their own congregations is relatively common, although they might regularly preach about it in their sermons. They usually have to be prodded by some fervent soul to spend "the church's money" on benevolent actions. Ask anyone who has started a "Matthew 25 ministry" and that person will consistently describe how difficult it is to convert the enthusiastic support of the pastor into reliable finances.

Actually, I had some good experiences related to benevolence and ministry to the poor when I served as an associate pastor of an institutional church. With over six thousand people attending each

Sunday, we had a fairly generous budget for helping the needy, both from our congregation and from the community. Although there was not much flexibility in our procedures, we were able to get real needs met in a timely fashion and without humiliating the recipients in the process. In one instance, I learned that a fellow-member who had asked for help with his rent and electricity was experiencing a downturn in his small construction business. As we talked I discovered that he had a simple two-to-three day project that would provide him with a profit of about four times the money he needed from us. But he no longer had credit from his suppliers so he could not buy the materials to start the job.

While he waited, I went to the church administrator and made a case for investing in the man's life, instead of only being benevolent. I obtained a variance from our procedures so we could write a single check to him personally, instead of separate checks to the electric company and the landlord. With our full knowledge and consent, he could use the money to buy the supplies he needed to start his project. I will never forget the look on his face when I explained that we wanted to express our confidence in him. He received an instant infusion of hope that accomplished much more than benevolence alone ever could have. Of course, it was not a blind investment. I knew him. And the results were fantastic. By the end of the week, he finished his project, paid his bills and had enough cash to finance the next two jobs.

We have also had some heart-breaking disappointments attempting to help people. It's shocking the lies some people are willing to tell in order to get money they know would not be given to them any other way. And no matter how experienced you become, there is some risk that you will give money where you shouldn't, or that you might not handle things as sensitively as you wanted. Plus, there are people who will make you feel used by their lack of appreciation or the attitude of entitlement that is now widespread in society. But all in all, it's very simple. Benevolence is part of the work of the "called out" and we need to remind ourselves that when we do these things we are serving the Lord, Himself. Even with all of our mistakes and frailties, when we give, He receives it. This attitude has made the majority of our contacts with people in need a wonderfully satisfying and rewarding part of our service to Christ.

People from all walks of life share a natural affinity for acts of generosity especially when children or the elderly are involved. Most of us can recall a time when our family or someone we knew faced a serious financial crisis and the tremendous mental pressures it created. It was just that kind of personal empathy that motivated some friends of ours to start a ministry to "street people." Gary and Beth did not fit the profile of the typical street ministry leaders. They were white, upper-middle-class entrepreneurs whose only ministry experience was serving as an usher or hostess at various church events. Gary was a "salt-of-the-earth" guy who had built a profitable business brokerage with honesty and hard work. He was quiet, cooperative, and always ready to help a neighbor or friend. The only visible indulgence of his success was his shiny new truck, which he kept filled with the latest fishing tackle. But behind his peaceful exterior was a heart that agonized over the plight of the homeless.

Gary and Beth had made a practice of praying over each business deal and had depended upon the Lord to provide the financing and guide them through every closing. They had prospered greatly and often spent time asking God how they should help others. Their giving had always exceeded a tithe and had been done quietly and without fanfare, although they were known to be generous supporters of the ministries of their church. After one particularly profitable sale, they sat down to figure the tithe and offerings they wanted to give. It came to a healthy sum and to their surprise, when they prayed about what to do with it, they felt reluctant to give it to their church. Since the church was in the middle of a difficult building program and was having trouble meeting its financial goals, they had thought the Lord might have them add the new contributions to their already significant pledge. But God had other plans. He wanted Gary and Beth to start a part-time ministry to the homeless and fund it themselves.

They were absolutely delirious with joy because what God was asking them to do aligned perfectly with the deep motives of their hearts. Before long, several friends from church volunteered to help, and their plans literally began to fall into place, moved along by the sovereignty of the Lord. It was the way they had always thought the body of Christ should operate, with someone receiving a vision for service from the Lord and the people and resources being pulled together as the Holy Spirit nudged each person into his or her part of the plan.

When I met with them to discuss their vision, I was immediately struck by the grace of God on their plans, so I was not at all surprised to see their ideas so enthusiastically supported by their friends. But just as they had started to gain momentum, they hit a major roadblock. They had a meeting with their pastor and he had strongly discouraged them from attempting their new ministry. He pointed out that there were other ministries in the city working with the poor and that their lack of experience would limit their success. He also encouraged them to stay focused on the ministries of their church and help them fulfill the vision for the new building. When I next saw them the sparkle was gone from their eyes. They were sincerely confused about how they could have been so wrong about God's purposes and why there had apparently been so much grace on their progress. If they were wrong, why didn't all their friends see it? If they were right, why didn't their pastor support them?

As we sat in their home discussing their dilemma, I was reminded of how many other ministries I had seen the institutional church snuff out in their infancy. I had consulted with many men and their families over the years who had been given almost exactly the same counsel as Gary and Beth from this and other churches around town. Not only that, I knew of one instance where a young entrepreneur, misguided by presumptuous faith and trying to gain favor with his church's leaders, actually paid his pledge to a building program, instead of paying an equal debt to the IRS. The church, knowing what he was doing, accepted the money and stood by quietly as he went bankrupt. The young man and his family moved out of state and had to live out of their car until he could find work. It took him several years to recover from the financial and emotional mess his poorly counseled decision had caused.

Fortunately, Gary and Beth realized the subjective nature of their pastor's counsel and chose to reject it in favor of the consistently positive insights of other close friends and advisors. They believed the Lord could give them wisdom in doing this work of service just like He had always done in their business. Thousands of meals, showers, changes of clothing, and changed lives later, we rejoiced with them for God's sustaining grace. We knew with certainty that their obedience to the Lord had reached hundreds of people for Christ whom the institutional church would never have touched.

The institutional church is characteristically unable to be selfless and turn its energy and resources to serving people the way they really need to be served. Its finances are usually tied to its own agenda, which is almost always dominated by buildings, pastoral salaries, and a few programs primarily designed to continue the institution. As it is with any economic entity, the size of the budget "nut" that must be cracked each month has a dramatic effect on its vision. The necessities of the organization come first and what's left is applied to missions, benevolence, and other acts of mercy. This means that a lot of important ministries that are mentioned from the pulpit never get any real attention. Typically, volunteers making special contributions of their time or money do most of the work that touches people's lives. Behind this inconsistency is a centuries-old conflict about how to finance the ministries outlined in Matthew 25. The solution can be found in the answers to two very simple questions.

First, to whom were the mandates of Matthew 25:31-46 directed? Again, it's hard to imagine that the Lord is going to be separating the institutional church's denominations into sheep and goat categories. Nor is it reasonable to think that it's only pastors who will be judged this way. These Scriptures obviously apply to every member of the "called out." There is no provision in Scripture for anyone to abandon his responsibility to perform these acts of mercy or to hire someone to do all of them on his behalf. So each of us must find the Lord's will regarding our giving.

Second, how are these mandates supposed to be financed? Malachi 3:10 says, "Bring the whole tithe into the storehouse, that there may be food in my house." You often hear pastors stating in a very matter-of-fact tone that this scripture means, "the tithe belongs to the local church." They believe that the institutional churches are "the" branch banks of the Kingdom of God. In fact, they essentially tell us to deposit our tithe with them so that they can do the work of ministry and decide who eats from the storehouse. But unfortunately, the money is used primarily to fund their role as a Constantine-Luther pastor-teacher. So their priorities are quite obvious.

Usually, no more than ten to twenty percent of the budget of the institutional church gets applied to activities not associated with supporting Sunday services. In some smaller congregations even less is available after the infrastructure and staff are funded. It's not unusual for the institutional church to spend five to ten times as much to preserve its Constantine-Luther infrastructure as it does to spread the Gospel or minister to the poor. Imagine being able to increase the impact of your tithes and contributions by five hundred to one thousand percent simply by choosing not to support that agenda. Five families could have the same impact in a community as twenty five to fifty families in the institutional church.

The Lord clearly wants the "called out" to support a wider variety of ministries and acts of mercy than those the institutional church has traditionally helped. To do so, the branch banks of the Kingdom of God's storehouse have to be wherever God tells you they are. Contrary to what the institutional church has taught, you are and always have been free to deposit your tithes and offerings in a street ministry, or to a widow down the street, or to someone who is out of work, or to a missionary, or to the single mom who can't pay her rent, or to help with someone's hospital bill, or to the hungry, thirsty, or poorly clothed person the Lord sends across your path, or to anyone, anywhere that the Lord presses on your heart, even to the institutional church. Remember, even if the institutional church were able to efficiently and effectively perform the ministries of Matthew 25, and limit its other expenditures to reasonable infrastructure and salaries (which it rarely does), it still could not relieve you of your individual responsibility to give, nor call itself "the storehouse." At best, it is only one of many depositories authorized by the Lord.

A very practical place to learn benevolence is in a home church. By keeping your own private ledger of what your tithe should be and setting it aside, ready to be distributed, you can enjoy participating in a wide variety of fulfilling ministry opportunities. When someone knows of a need, you can talk about it together and wisely determine what the need is and how it should be met. Then each person or family can decide what part, if any, the Lord wants them to contribute. For everyone who's concerned about his tax deductions, there are a number of simple options for combining funds in one shared account or keeping separate ledgers within one account. You can also keep your tithe in your own checking account until the Lord directs you to give. Just ask the person who does your taxes or a friendly accountant for advice. But even without the tax deduction, when people are free to follow the Lord's prompting, innovate, serve one another, and reach out to the lost, wonderful things can happen.

Celebrate Truth and Faithfulness

One of the foundational principles of the institutional church is loyalty. It is a highly valued attribute that must be clearly demonstrated before full acceptance and participation in organizational life is granted. Passing the loyalty test has become a "rite of passage" not only into leadership but often just to participate in routine acts of service or fellowship. Even when it is not spoken about, loyalty to the pastor, denomination, doctrines, creeds, and policies is expected. If you express an idea or attitude that is perceived as disloyal or non-conforming, it can produce the chill of condemnation or rejection. The organizational and relational expectations for loyalty are so universally accepted that they feel natural to most people, except when they realize they have been forced to ignore or rationalize sin, deny truth, or keep silent about simple facts.

When you think about what loyalty requires, you can't imagine Jesus and His disciples expecting it of one another, especially since all through the Scriptures God is described as faithful, not loyal. I was sharing my thoughts about loyalty at a friend's home one evening and he looked at me in horror, as though I was speaking a heresy. He had been a longtime adherent of the institutional church and I could see that the discussion was making him feel very insecure. So I asked him this question: "Do you think I have been loyal to you?" He stopped for a minute, thinking back about all the ways I had served him, asking nothing in return. We had been friends for many years and since he was "in the ministry," I had helped him with an assortment of business and personal issues. "I have been sure of your loyalty, at least until now," he said. "I am sorry to disappoint you," I said, "but I don't believe in loyalty, because it is based upon fear and control. And I don't trust relationships that are not mutually accountable. The difference between a loyal slave and a faithful friend is an honest, truthful relationship."

My friend was a Hebrew scholar and seminary professor so his next thought was to begin checking different Scriptures to see what the Hebrew word really meant. He thought that I might be just splitting hairs over something insignificant, but what I had discovered was much more than that. We got on the computer together and as he rattled off Scripture addresses, I pulled up the original words and definitions from the Bible software. "What about Hosea 6:4-6?" he asked. This is one of the Scriptures most commonly referred to by pastors whose goal is to exhort people to be loyal to the institutional church and its programs. It says:

> What shall I do with you, O Ephraim? What shall I do with you, O Judah? For your *loyalty* (#2617) is like a morning cloud, and like the dew which goes away early. Therefore I have hewn them in pieces by the prophets; I have slain them by the words of My mouth; and the judgments on you are like the light that goes forth. For I delight in *loyalty* (#2617) rather than sacrifice, and in the knowledge of God rather than burnt offerings.
> Hosea 6:4-6 NAS

This Scripture can be very misleading and condemning if you believe it requires loyalty because the Lord is apparently thrashing His people via the words of His prophets for their disobedience (just like the pastors frequently do). But the Hebrew word "checed" (#2617) is interchangeably translated as "mercy, kindness, goodness or faithfulness," throughout the Old Testament. It is not correct to translate it as loyalty. In Matthew 9:13, and again in Matthew 12:7, Jesus repeats these important words, "I desire *mercy* (#1656), not sacrifice." This Greek word has virtually the same meaning. It is translated as "mercy, kindness, or goodness." So God was rebuking His people for not being merciful, kind, good, and faithful, not for lacking loyalty. And He obviously desires these attributes more than any sacrifice.

"Checed" is the same word used in Exodus 34:6 (NAS) where God meets with Moses on Mt. Sinai and describes His own nature to him. It says, "The Lord, the Lord God, compassionate and gracious, slow to anger, and abounding in *loving kindness* (#2617) and *truth* (#571)." The word translated here as "truth" is also accurately translated as "certainty, trustworthy, reliable, or faithful, as to facts." This is very important because all through the Scriptures God links mercy, goodness, kindness, faithfulness, and truth together. It is fair to say that there are two fundamental aspects to the faithfulness of God, and all dependable relationships. One is to be kind and merciful, and the other is to be true to the facts. This is the intent of the exhortation in Hosea 6, and the real mandate for every follower of Christ.

So how has the concept of loyalty worked its way so thoroughly into the fabric of the institutional church? Again, we can look back to Constantine to get an idea. When he established his institutional church, he appointed himself as the primary authority. He also placed icons of himself and the twelve original apostles in the first church building, thus elevating his spiritual stature. Then he appointed bishops to exercise a top-down style of authority that mirrored the power of the emperor. The final authority on all issues of church life, including the order of worship and finances rested with the bishop. (See Appendix.) It is this framework of authority to which Luther later attached his pastoral job description and which has evolved into the modern pastor-teacher-CEO. In the process, truth, mercy, and mutual accountability were stripped away and what's left is loyalty.

After searching through several translations of the Bible and discovering that every location where the word loyal or loyalty is used was actually "checed" or some other equivalent of mercy or truth, my friend was prepared to accept the fact that loyalty is not a legitimate Kingdom concept. Instead what the Bible consistently requires of men is truth, faithfulness, and the reasonable accountability that relationships enable. No one is exempt, not pastors or bishops or popes, or any member of the "called out." We must be willing to absorb the pain of confrontation in order to help a friend find truth or to receive it from him. Zechariah 7:9 tells us to "administer true justice; show mercy and compassion to one another." Proverbs 27:6 (NAS) says "the wounds of a friend" are "faithful" (like a parent or nurse who is supportive, #539).

Just like being a parent, the responsibilities that accompany truth and faithfulness in our relationships are not always pleasant. But they are worth the effort, even when they require long hours of late night discussions or intense debates about the facts. Anyone who has caught one of their children in an act of disobedience, only to see them stand defiantly and deny their guilt, knows how frustrating it can be to explain to someone who is entangled in sin, that the accountability you represent is an extension of God's love to them. That's why most men want to avoid the work involved in correcting mistakes or misunderstandings, especially in the institutional church. But when we do not love people enough to correct them, they only go on to greater sins.

That was certainly the case with Mr. J. T. Park. Even though he had been in the institutional church since before I was born, he didn't quite fit my concept of a church elder. He was in his sixties and had been very successful in business and politics. But he often sounded evasive when he answered a question and rarely had much to say that reflected any spiritual depth. He almost never looked at you when he spoke, always shifting his glance away or seeming to be somehow preoccupied. There was something about him that made me feel uncomfortable, even though he acted like a harmless older man busy with church life. Mr. Park was chairman of the building committee, which met regularly with the pastor to discuss the plans for our future as a congregation. Together, they had developed an impressive master plan for our expansion, which had been presented to the church as "God's vision," and was widely supported.

When rumors began to surface that Mr. Park might be connected to some kind of illegal business deal, the pastor quickly dismissed them as "politics." "After all," he said, "Mr. Park was essential to our building program. He was regularly in negotiations with city and county officials and we should expect the devil to be attacking us, trying to undermine his credibility and sidetrack our plans." The men who best knew Mr. Park and had done business with him strongly agreed with the pastor. But I had an uneasy feeling so I asked the pastor what, if anything, had been done to check out the rumors. His face turned blood red. He was obviously angry; but before he could respond, some of the men in the room came to his defense, arguing that we needed to trust these things to his leadership. The meeting broke into confusion and ended with several men speaking at once, arguing for or against the reasonableness of my question.

I had become increasingly troubled at how many times I was finding myself "out of step" with the elders of the church, and I knew that this incident would bring with it more of the cool relations that came with expressing any kind of disunity. A few nights later, as I was putting down newspaper to train our new puppy, my eyes fell on an interesting headline tucked away in a back section of the paper, "Local Businessman on Trial in Atlanta Federal Court for Money Laundering." I knew instantly that it somehow involved Mr. Park, and sure enough, the article mentioned his name as having given testimony. I decided to do my own research and find out what one of our elders could possibly have to do with this case, which involved another prominent citizen accused of laundering money from drug trafficking. I contacted the clerk of the court and ordered a copy of his testimony.

Several months later, I found myself sitting across the table from Mr. Park at a local restaurant, with a manila envelope at my side containing his testimony. I thanked him for meeting with me and then proceeded to ask him some very specific questions to which he very calmly and convincingly responded with lies. Finally, he boldly asked me if I was satisfied with his answers, or did I have any others to ask. I answered very directly, as I laid the envelope on the table, "No, Mr. Park, I am not satisfied, because all the things that you have told me today are in direct conflict with this transcript of the testimony that you gave under oath." He exploded with rage. The calm assurance he had projected disappeared as he launched into a vulgar, cursing tirade. "Who the (expletive deleted) do you think you are talking to me like that? No one in the church has talked to me like that in fifty years. You have no authority to be involved in this."

I had all of the authority I needed. I was his brother in Christ and a fellow-elder, either of which carried with it both the authority and responsibility to get to the truth. But the most revealing part of this exchange was that apparently no one had ever taken the time to research the facts and question him about this or who knows what else that had happened over fifty years. He had learned from experience that if you busy yourself in church business and are loyal to the leadership, it's unlikely that anyone will seriously check out your story. I leaned across the table and looked straight into his tormented face. "I apologize to you Mr. Park, on behalf of the church, because we have obviously failed you to allow you to have gotten this far off course and not know it."

When we think and speak truthfully from our heart, and expect truth to be the minimum requirement in our relationships, we are building a strong spiritual foundation. And just as importantly, we must test the reliability of any important fact or perception. It is every man's right and responsibility to become "morally persuaded of the truth." In fact that is the definition of "faith" (#4102). When there's a question about the facts, we should take the time to sift through them until we are fully persuaded. In a practical sense, the man who has not made truth and the pursuit of reliable facts his first priority is destined to a life of disappointment and confusion. Why? Because our family, friends, colleagues, and customers will suffer the consequences of our unnecessary mistakes.

If Mr. Park had continued to be a faithful truth-seeker, he would have never entered into an even potentially-illegal arrangement. Or if he had been faithfully participating in a home church, his inconsistent life would probably have been discovered and challenged long before it became so bizarre. But like a lot of men in the institutional church, his concerns about integrity had probably been diminished by the many years he had participated in church politics. With all the pressure to be loyal, I can also understand how easy it was for my colleagues to rationalize the rumors about him or to push them aside as someone else's responsibility. The institutional church does not celebrate truth and faithfulness. But if I had ignored my convictions, and shirked my duty to seek the truth, I not only would have been disobeying the Lord, I could have been placed in the very embarrassing position that eventually confronted some of my fellow elders. More importantly though, the episode strengthened my faith about the significance of following my conscience. As King David said:

> I have chosen the way of truth; I have set my heart on your laws. I hold fast to your statutes, O Lord; do not let me be put to shame. I run in the path of your commands, for you have set my heart free. Teach me, O Lord, to follow your decrees; then I will keep them to the end. Give me understanding, and I will keep your law and obey it with all my heart. Direct me in the path of your commands, for there I find delight. Turn my heart toward your statutes and not toward selfish gain. Turn my eyes away from worthless things; preserve my life according to your word.
>
> Psalm 119:30-37

6
SPIRITUAL ACCOUNTABILITY:
A MEASURE OF OUR PRACTICE OF
SPIRITUAL DISCIPLINES

The middle-aged man walking down the hall toward me looked friendly. He was wearing a simple black clerical robe and carried a file of papers under his arm. He walked directly to me and said, "His Holiness will see you now." As he peeked into the file, I recognized the documents I had sent ahead to brief his boss, the Patriarch of the Russian Orthodox Church. We walked down the hall together toward the office of Alexy II as the man explained the protocol for our meeting. "This will be a very unusual audience in that you will meet alone to discuss these sensitive matters. You should feel free to speak candidly on the issues because the information you forwarded has been carefully reviewed. You may use your own translator, and your colleague (David, a board member of our foundation) may attend. You can expect the meeting to last ten to fifteen minutes. Anything longer will be at his option."

The most significant aspect of this meeting was that it should have been completely unnecessary. We had been working on an important project with one of the church's most respected priests, and had discovered his attempt to convert designated assets to his own purposes. We had remodeled an old building into a warehouse and training facility with fortress-like security that was intended to receive and distribute humanitarian medicines and train medical personnel from across the city. But the priest had secretly been using our eighteen-wheel truck and trailer to make commercial deliveries and had been keeping two sets of books. Our routine audits, which no one expected to be made of such a revered man's work, fortunately had exposed the infraction in time for us to preserve the assets. His actions were so clearly wrong that when we met with the bookkeepers, one of them—an honest woman who respected our mission—handed us a stack of papers she had prepared with all the information we needed.

When we confronted the priest, we explained that we were coming as brothers in Christ and fellow ministers, not as legal adversaries, even though his actions had betrayed our trust, his vows, and the law. We wanted to settle the matter amicably and work out a plan to restore his moral authority, but to our surprise, he demonstrated virtually no conscience about his deeds and denied the validity of our charges. We had no choice but to limit his activities and begin the arduous process of trying to hold him accountable through the church's hierarchy. It took months to work through the various procedures of the Diocese, without result. The man's only response was to instigate a slanderous campaign against both our project and me. He never expected us to persevere to the highest levels and was depending upon religious politics to protect him.

The Patriarch greeted us warmly and I quickly outlined our problem and asked him to exercise his authority in the matter. We engaged in a thorough debate for almost an hour, not as opponents, but as colleagues seeking a common purpose. This was a man whose institutional authority was unmatched in Russia, but his ability to bring reconciliation was limited to the priest's willingness to be truthful. It was quite a dilemma because he clearly wanted to preserve our working relationship, even though there were political risks for him in ruling against one of the church's well-known leaders. The highly structured religious institution he led had pockets of corruption and he knew it. His authority only worked when a man feared the Lord or the Russian Orthodox Church. In this case the misguided priest apparently feared neither.

We were able to work out a business-like arrangement and I returned to St. Petersburg with an official order handwritten in my presence by the Patriarch. Although we had preserved the project and maneuvered the errant priest safely out of authority into a politically correct position, what our process had proven was that only a man who fears the Lord can truly be held accountable. If the priest had practiced spiritual accountability, he would never have committed the initial act of dishonesty. Or at the very least, he would have repented and reconciled himself to the truth at some point in our discussions. Sadly, the only thing institutional authority was able to do was provide him with organized opportunities to accept correction. But a man whose heart is truly set on obeying the Lord will have little need for such formalities.

1 Peter 2:9 reminds us that the followers of Jesus Christ are a "chosen people, a royal priesthood, a holy nation, a people belonging to God." That means every person can come before God as a priest, offering prayers, and receiving the wisdom required for each day. But to fully benefit from our "priesthood," we must have an obedient heart, and be easily governed by the conviction of the Holy Spirit. When we depend on external rules and institutions to guide us, we may find ourselves just going through the motions of obedience. Instead we should become like Caleb who was spoken of by God as one who "has a different spirit and follows Me wholeheartedly" (Numbers 14:24).

Spiritual accountability is a measure of our practice of spiritual disciplines. With all the demands on us, at home and at work, we need to choose wisely between competing agendas and bring our responsibilities into harmony with the Scriptures. To do so, we must seek the Lord's will in every part of our life; and as the caretaker of our family, prayerfully "represent them in matters related to God" (Hebrews 5:1). Fulfilling these duties effectively will require that we become proficient in:

1) Reading and studying the Bible, so that we can apply it accurately and understand the will of God in life's many circumstances.

2) Praying prayers of repentance and forgiveness, so that we can cleanse our souls of sin-guilt and use our faith for His purposes.

3) Being filled with the Holy Spirit, so that we can learn to hear His voice, sense Him nudging us toward His will, and yield our behaviors to Him.

4) Using God's authority to bless others, intercede for them in prayer, and engage in spiritual warfare against the powers of evil.

I have seen far too many men trying to lead at home and at work without putting these fundamentals solidly in place. They busy themselves in other things and neglect spending the time to develop the spiritual disciplines they really need. Without intending to, they are rejecting the call of the Lord to properly steward their responsibilities. In Jeremiah 32:33 God says, "They turned their backs to me and not their faces; though I taught them again and again, they would not listen or respond to discipline."

For some men, bearing the weight of life's expectations feels like too much to manage. The pressures of work, family, or personal problems can overwhelm us and cause us to want to avoid them. Even the things we normally love to do can begin to irritate us. Mistakes and conflicts can stimulate feelings of hopelessness and anger to the point that we find ourselves avoiding our responsibilities. Even if we have not said it, what man has not thought at least once, "My inheritance has become to me like a lion in the forest; she has roared against me; therefore I have come to hate her" (Jeremiah 12:8).

Tortured feelings can be lodged so deeply in our soul that we almost forget we have them and become spiritually paralyzed, unable to fully give ourselves to the Lord. We can begin to rationalize our ineffectiveness, allowing our relationship with God to take the form of partial obedience with church meetings and religious activities becoming a substitute for our spiritual disciplines. But as Samuel asked King Saul, "Does the Lord delight in burnt offerings and sacrifices as much as in obeying the voice of the Lord? To obey is better than sacrifice, and to heed is better than the fat of rams" (1 Samuel 15:22).

The week before I became a follower of Christ I signed a contract to represent a major insurance company. Although I had a solid background in insurance sales, I was a little nervous about balancing the requirements of my new contract with my other interests. I had made a very large production commitment for the first six months of our arrangement and was concerned that I might have made an unreasonable obligation. But I kept telling myself it could be done.

The deal had been sweetened with some unusual perks, and if I reached my goal, I would gain recognition that would help me negotiate an even better contract.

On Monday, the first day of my new contract, I began making telephone calls to a list of prospects I had developed from my previous business contacts. Actually some of the names on the list were people I would call, without a referral, to ask if they were satisfied with their insurance services. To my surprise, on the very first call the man I spoke with started asking questions about the product I wanted to discuss. Within a few hours I had visited his office and left with a sizeable application. I was energized. I got back on the phone and started making calls. Before the end of the day I had made several appointments, and the first customer called back to double his order. It was one of those amazing weeks when everything worked. By Friday afternoon I had delivered applications and checks to the insurance company's regional office that exceeded my six month's obligation, and established records that lasted for many years.

When I returned home to tell my wife about my success, she was standing at the kitchen sink washing lettuce. I told her that I had just accomplished something that had never been done before. I had broken records and made a bundle of money in the first week of my new contract. But for some reason, I had an empty feeling inside. She seemed unmoved as she turned to me with a cool, "That's nice, I am very happy for you." Little did I know that as she had been preparing dinner she was contemplating divorce. I had met my obligations at work, but not at home, and I had no idea how badly I was failing. A man can be deceived by the importance of the efforts he is making in one area of his life while another may be slipping out of control. That empty feeling I had was the mercy of the Lord calling me to realize that some important things were not right in my life. And there was my wife, ready to tell me what some of them were.

She told me that my biggest problem was that I was not a follower of Christ, and, with brutal detail, described how that caused pain and suffering in the family. I was honestly stunned and shocked. But since becoming a follower of Christ, I've had other such encounters with the Lord and my wife. I have discovered that even as a dedicated believer, a man can ignore important fundamentals and defend himself with rationalizations that are embarrassingly thin. It is one thing to give up overtly sinful behaviors. It is quite another to become faithful in the disciplines required to function as a husband and father. Proverbs 18:9 tells us that "One who is slack in his work is brother to one who destroys." That includes all of our work—the work we do to make a living, the work we do to lead our family, and especially the work we do to discipline ourselves in spiritual fundamentals.

Fortunately, "We do not have a high priest who is unable to sympathize with our weaknesses, but we have one who has been tempted in every way, just as we are—yet was without sin" (Hebrews 4:15). Every day with the Lord can be a new beginning. All a man has to do is say, "O Lord, correct me, but with justice; not in Your anger, lest You bring me to nothing" (Jeremiah 10:24 NKJ). The Lord is so faithful to this kind of prayer. He is always available to a man who will humble himself and ask for His help, whether as a new believer or a veteran who has fallen behind in his disciplines. His promise to each of us is, "Call to Me, and I will answer you, and show you great and mighty things, which you do not know" (Jeremiah 33:3 NKJ). All He requires is that we become diligent to His Word and "produce fruit in keeping with repentance" (Matthew 3:8).

Read and Study the Bible

I realized the importance of studying the Bible for myself, rather than depending on preachers to digest it for me, before I became a follower of Christ. I was attending a small congregation with my wife who had grown up in a close-knit group of Bible purists. The people were friendly and I felt comfortable attending their meetings, even though I was not very interested in reading the Bible or becoming more involved in the activities of the congregation. Their meetings were tightly ordered and there was always an emphasis on accuracy in discussing the Bible. Although I didn't understand all of their rules, their guiding concept of closely obeying the Bible seemed right to me. If you were going to teach people how to follow the mandates of God, it made sense to be careful how you did it.

Their teacher had begun a series on Paul's first epistle to the Corinthians. He had provided some good examples that helped me listen and his presentations appeared to be logical and believable. So, after attending for several weeks, I decided to read the Bible before I went to class. I began reading in 1 Corinthians 12, as that was the next chapter to be discussed, and I read several chapters ahead. The following Sunday I was actually eager to go to church. To my surprise, the teacher dramatically picked up the pace of the class. He described and discussed Chapters 12, 13 and 14, all in one meeting. I noticed that he was not nearly as fascinated by these chapters as I had become. I thought they contained so much practical information that I assumed he might take several weeks as he had on other chapters. But instead, he was summarizing the chapters and moving quickly through them. Then he quoted 1 Corinthians 13:10 (KJV), which says, "But when that which is perfect is come, then that which is in part shall be done away." He said that this verse explained why the things that were written in Chapters 12 and 14 were no longer valid. I was stunned by the teacher's assertion because I had become morally persuaded to "believe" as I read those chapters. But his torturous and illogical explanation left me feeling confused and disappointed.

When the meeting ended, my wife explained to me that there were all kinds of controversial things in the Bible about healing, prophecy, speaking in tongues, and other topics, which the leaders of their church had concluded were not for today. But I was not so much interested in defending or explaining any of the controversies, as I was in being able to understand the kind of logic required to come to those conclusions. Why would there be such a vague phrase in the middle of this "letter" that invalidated many of the verses directly preceding and following it. This was completely inconsistent with the kind of order and purpose that was so clearly outlined in the two chapters the teacher had so presumptuously dismissed. My concerns were simple. If the words of the Bible were really that tricky and subjective, it could not possibly be depended upon as instruction for living. And if it were true that, "All Scripture is inspired by God and profitable for teaching, for reproof, for correction, for training in righteousness; that the man of God may be adequate, equipped for every good work" (2 Timothy 3:16-17 NAS), then why would anyone take the risk of altering what it says?

Although it didn't help me much at the time, the lesson I had learned was a good one. What people have to say about the Bible can be helpful, but it can also put a limit on the grace of God in our lives. Ultimately, we must read and study the Bible to gain understanding for ourselves. 2 Timothy 2:15 (NAS) says every person should "be diligent to present yourself approved to God as a workman who does not need to be ashamed, handling accurately the word of truth."

No one answered the tough questions for me back then, so I left the church. Years later, after finally making a serious commitment to become a follower of Christ, I visited a local bookstore with my wife to buy a new Bible. I had decided to apply myself to learning what the Bible said, so I could properly respond to the Lord and lead my family. I didn't know there were so many different kinds of Bibles or that some of them had commentaries to help the reader understand various passages. My wife pointed out that a commentary was really just someone's opinion, which could be helpful or harmful depending on his point of view. That reminded me of my previous church experience, so I decided to buy one without commentaries and read it several times myself, before I asked anyone else for their opinion. I wanted to learn and be influenced by the literal words of the Bible. I could always turn to others when I needed help finding or understanding something.

I started reading the Bible every day for several hours. I carried one in my car and even listened to the Bible on cassette tapes. Between appointments I saturated my life with the Word and quickly learned some key strategic points. One of them was that God had arranged a new covenant with His people through His Son Jesus. In Hebrews 8:10-11 it says,

> This is the covenant I will make with the house of Israel after that time," declares the Lord. "I will put my laws in their minds and write them on their hearts. I will be their God, and they will be my people. No longer will a man teach his neighbor,

or a man his brother, saying, 'Know the Lord,'
because they will all know me, from the least of them
to the greatest.

It was wonderful to know that there was no special class of ministers who got to communicate with God. Every believer had access and everyone could read and understand the Bible. In fact, God had gone to the trouble of putting his laws in our minds and writing them on our hearts, probably so that we could have a conscience about what we see and hear. And not only that, in John 14:26 (NKJ) Jesus said, "the Helper, the Holy Spirit, whom the Father will send in My name, He will teach you all things, and bring to your remembrance all things that I said to you."

The story of Jesus' temptation by the devil in Matthew 4 shows us how important it is to know the Scriptures. Jesus had fasted for forty days and nights when the devil tempted him several times. Apparently trying to take advantage of His physical weakness and hunger, the devil said to Him, "If you are the Son of God, command that these stones become bread" (Matthew 4:3 NKJ). But Jesus answered and said, "It is written, 'Man shall not live by bread alone, but by every word that proceeds from the mouth of God'" (vs. 4). This is a strategically important statement, especially since men are notoriously guided by their appetites. Each time Jesus was tempted He responded with what had been "written" in the Old Testament (vs. 4, 7, 10). He knew the Scriptures. In fact, He was the "living Word of God" (John 1:1-14 NKJ) and when temptation came, He responded with the words and wisdom of the Bible. That's what studying the Bible should produce in us–a comfortable knowledge of how to follow Christ, resist temptation, and live and work successfully. Here are three important things to remember about Bible study:

1) Studying the Bible is not just about gathering information. It is a way of gaining revelation about ourselves and the world that will lead to actions of faith. "The word of God is living and active. Sharper than any double edged sword, it penetrates even to dividing soul and spirit, joints and marrow; it judges the thoughts and attitudes of the heart" (Hebrews 4:12). When we read the Scriptures

we enter into fellowship with God through His Holy Spirit. "And He, when He comes, will convict the world concerning sin, and righteousness, and judgment" (John 16:8 NAS). This work of the Holy Spirit is intended to help us conform to His will in our daily lives and be "transformed into his likeness with ever increasing glory" (2 Corinthians 3:17-18). When we read the Bible, He is able to open our hearts and minds to receive the truth we need, and to see the sinful behaviors that entangle us.

As we study the Scriptures, we can have the same experience as the men on the road to Emmaus (a village near Jerusalem) when Jesus joined them on their walk. As they walked along together and He explained what the Scriptures had to say about Himself, they did not recognize Him (Luke 24:13-32). Later, after they realized who He was, they said to each other, "Were not our hearts burning within us while He talked with us on the road and opened the Scriptures to us?" (vs. 32). This is the privilege of a follower of Christ. As He walks with us by the presence of His Spirit, His words come alive and burn within us as the transforming power of truth. Jesus said, "If you abide in My Word, then you are truly disciples of Mine; and you shall know the truth, and the truth shall make you free" (John 8:31-32 NAS).

2) There is no mystery to Bible study. When I was a pastor, a retired Naval Officer came to my office for a visit. He was a man who had commanded huge ships with thousands of sailors, and as a leader he was accustomed to diligently seeking the answers to critical questions. He had been struggling with a personal problem and told me that he was not satisfied with his study of the Bible on the topic. I opened my Bible to the passage he was reading and then pulled my concordance from the shelf beside us. I began to show him how to identify key words and how the concordance provides the literal meaning of the word (in the O.T. Hebrew or N.T. Greek) along with every Scripture verse in which it appears. We read some of the Scriptures together and he quickly realized how reading several Scriptures with the same key word gave us a better understanding of what it meant.

Suddenly, he looked up and said, "Is this how you guys prepare your sermons?" I said, "Yes, this is basically it." He responded,

"Well, why aren't you teaching us how to do this from the pulpit every week? All the rest of us need this information, too. This is important stuff!" I was dumbfounded by his honesty. As he hurried to the bookstore to buy his own concordance, I pondered again how fundamental the study of the Bible is to our lives and how accessible it is. Anyone who has a question and wants to know how the Lord feels about it needs only to study the Bible. And it's available in so many forms. There are single computer disks that contain several versions of the Bible, their corresponding concordances, and all kinds of indexes. These tools make serious Bible study practical for the man who knows that "the fear of the Lord is the beginning of wisdom, and the knowledge of the Holy One is understanding (Proverbs 9:10 NKJ).

3) I am often asked how much time we should spend studying the Bible. The answer is very simple–enough! It depends on many factors including: how much you already know, what responsibilities or problems you are dealing with, how much sin is in your life, how easily you learn, and how motivated you are. Jesus said in John 6:63 (NKJ), "It is the Spirit who gives life; the flesh profits nothing. The words that I speak to you are spirit, and they are life." Each person must make his own decision before God about how much time to dedicate to spiritual things. I believe a man should urgently study the Scriptures until he attains a practical, working knowledge. Then he can set a reasonable pace for the rest of his life. Proverbs 4:20-22 exhorts us, "My son, pay attention to what I say; listen closely to my words. Do not let them out of your sight, keep them within your heart; for they are life to those who find them and health to a man's whole body."

Continue to Repent and Forgive

Repentance and forgiveness are directly linked to each other. They affect not only our prayer life, but also our ability to mature in the Lord. Hebrews 12:1 exhorts us to "throw off everything that hinders and the sin that so easily entangles, and let us run with perseverance the race marked out for us." This is a simple mandate to rid ourselves of all sinful behaviors that prevent us from fully obeying the Lord. When we continue to repent of our own sins and forgive those who have sinned against us, we are progressively set free to become obedient in all areas of our lives. James 1:22-25 says,

> Do not merely listen to the word, and so deceive yourselves. Do what it says. Anyone who listens to the word but does not do what it says is like a man who looks at his face in a mirror and, after looking at himself, goes away and immediately forgets what he looks like. But the man who looks intently into the perfect law that gives freedom, and continues to do this, not forgetting what he has heard, but doing it–he will be blessed in what he does.

It is impossible to regularly read the Bible and not become aware of both the sins we have committed and the sins that have been committed against us. As we read and meditate, one thought can lead to another and we can be taken back in time to remember a sinful event and understand its affect on our life. A revelation of our own sin calls us to repentance. A revelation of sins against us calls us to forgive the ones who have harmed us. Revelation always comes for a reason, so we must be careful not to "show contempt for the riches of his kindness, tolerance, and patience," but realize "that God's kindness leads you toward repentance" (Romans 2:4). It causes us to turn away from what we did that was sinful and forgive the things that were done to us. These fundamental acts of faith can set us free from regrets about our past and help us live our lives without the hindrance of unwanted behaviors.

In Matthew 6 (NKJ) we find what is commonly known as the "Lord's Prayer." It is preceded by several comments that Jesus makes about prayer in general. He exhorts us not to pray "to be seen by men" (vs. 5) and not to pray using "vain repetitions as the heathen do" (or as the NIV says, "babbling like pagans") who "think they will be heard for their many words" (vs. 7). He goes on to say, "Your Father knows the things you have need of before you ask Him. In this manner, therefore, pray" (vs. 8-9). He then prays a simple, yet profoundly strategic prayer as an example for His disciples.

Our Father in heaven, hallowed be your name, your kingdom come, your will be done on earth as it is in heaven. Give us today our daily bread. Forgive us our debts, as we also have forgiven our debtors. And lead us not into temptation, but deliver us from the evil one.

Matthew 6:9-13

In effect, He is showing His disciples that their prayers can be short, to the point, and real, knowing that their prayers are to God, not man, a God who knows what they are going to say before they say it. With that in mind, it is interesting to see how much of His prayer is devoted to the topic of dealing with sin and evil.

In verse 12 He prays, "And forgive us our debts, as we forgive our debtors." And then in verse 13, "And do not lead us into temptation, but deliver us from the evil one." Then, immediately following His prayer, His focus returns to instructing the disciples. As if to remind them of the importance of what He has prayed, He says in verses 14 and 15, "For if you forgive men their trespasses, your heavenly Father will also forgive you. But if you do not forgive men their trespasses, neither will your Father forgive your trespasses." Jesus was saying that receiving forgiveness for the sins you have committed and granting forgiveness for the sins committed against you, are linked together. You cannot have God's forgiveness of sin if you are not willing to forgive those who have sinned against you. This means that a prayer of repentance about a sinful behavior in our life is virtually a "vain repetition" unless it is accompanied by specific forgiveness for anyone who may be associated with that behavior. To be free, we must forgive the people who have sinned against us, caused us to sin, or led us into temptation.

I can think of many times when another person's sin has caused me to sin. My sin was the anger, bitterness, and resentment I held against the people who hurt me. But I rebelliously justified my own sin by focusing attention on the injustice or unfairness of the harm the person caused me. This is a place where many men stumble. When we think of sinful behaviors in our lives, we might honestly have godly remorse and repent of them, but not fully obey

191

God's revelation about the sin. When we remember when, where, and how we began sinning, and who might have been involved, we should not be looking for an excuse or someone else to blame for our sins. Instead, we should be searching for how we can take ownership of our sins and who to forgive. Then we can receive cleansing from the "sin that so easily entangles" (Hebrews 12:1).

Mark 11:23-25 (NKJ) is an example of the relationship between the effectiveness of our prayers and our willingness to forgive. Jesus said,

> For assuredly, I say to you, whoever says to this mountain, "Be removed and be cast into the sea,"and does not doubt in his heart, but believes that those things he says will come to pass, he will have whatever he says. Therefore I say to you, whatever things you ask when you pray, believe that you receive them, and you will have them. And whenever you stand praying, if you have anything against anyone, forgive him, that your Father in heaven may also forgive you your trespasses.

Here again, as He instructs His disciples about faith, Jesus takes time to emphasize the importance of forgiving another person's sins. This is a tremendous example of an act of faith. I cannot imagine commanding a real mountain to be cast into the sea. I am sure, though, that if I did so in the Name of Jesus and did not doubt in my heart, it would happen. I believe it because I have actually commanded mountains of sinful behaviors to leave my life and know that they have left me. I had absolutely no doubt in my heart because I had thoroughly repented of my sins, forgiven those people associated with them, and rejected the sinful behavior from my will. I knew that the mountain of sin was gone after I prayed, because I no longer struggled with it as before.

I have also tried to unload sinful behaviors, by the authority of Christ, when I had failed to fully repent of the sins involved or to forgive others. The difference in the two experiences was remarkable. When the mountain of sin failed to move, I knew it. I didn't have to wait until the old temptation surfaced again to know that something was incomplete following my prayer. But as surely as I knew in my heart that it was not gone, the sinful behavior remained. Yes, there was doubt. Any person, who has not fully repented of his sin and forgiven others, will doubt his own faith to cast away a mountain of sin. That doubting feeling is a cue to more completely and accurately repent or forgive.

In Matthew 18:23-35 (NKJ) Jesus tells his disciples a parable to again emphasize the need to forgive the sins of others.

> Therefore the kingdom of heaven is like a certain king who wanted to settle accounts with his servants. And when he had begun to settle accounts, one was brought to him who owed him ten thousand talents. But as he was not able to pay, his master commanded that he be sold, with his wife and children and all that he had, and that payment be made. The servant therefore fell down before him, saying, "Master, have patience with me, and I will pay you all." Then the master of that servant was moved with compassion, released him, and forgave him the debt. But that servant went out and found one of his fellow servants who owed him a hundred denarii; and he laid hands on him and took him by the throat, saying, "Pay me what you owe!" So his fellow servant fell down at his feet and begged him, saying, "Have patience with me, and I will pay you all." And he would not, but went and threw him into prison till he should pay the debt. So when his fellow servants saw what had been done, they were very grieved, and came and told their master all that had been done. Then his master, after he had called him, said to him, "You wicked servant! I forgave you all that debt because you begged me. Should you not also have had compassion on your fellow servant, just as I had pity on you?" And his master was angry, and delivered him to the torturers until he should pay all that was

> due to him. So My heavenly Father also will do to
> you if each of you, from his heart, does not forgive
> his brother his trespasses.

This parable presents a clear picture of a person who has become a follower of Christ and has been forgiven a great debt only to be tortured in his daily life because of his unwillingness to forgive another brother. This is a very common theme among men who struggle with addictions, compulsions, obsessions, and other torturing behaviors. No matter how much they try to repent of their sins, they cannot find freedom from them until they forgive the people associated with their sins. They often say as Paul said in Romans 7:15-17, "I do not understand what I do. For what I want to do I do not do, but what I hate I do. And if I do what I do not want to do, I agree that the law is good. As it is, it is no longer I myself who do it, but it is sin living in me." The sin of unforgiveness can be a powerful and tormenting force living within us. To be free, we must be prepared to repent and forgive the people who have harmed us.

Repentance and forgiveness should be practiced as routine disciplines of prayer. By asking the Lord to show us the sins we are committing and whom we might forgive, we are aligning ourselves with the most fundamental acts of faith. As the prophet Hosea said in Hosea 10:12, "Sow for yourselves righteousness, reap the fruit of unfailing love, and break up your unplowed ground; for it is time to seek the Lord, until he comes and showers righteousness on you."

Yield to the Holy Spirit

One of the primary objectives for a follower of Christ is to progressively eliminate sinful behaviors from his life and to yield himself more and more to the Holy Spirit. Jesus said in John 14:15-17,

> If you love me, you will obey what I command. And
> I will ask the Father, and he will give you another
> Counselor to be with you forever – the Spirit of
> truth. The world cannot accept him, because it

neither sees him nor knows him. But you know
him, for he lives with you and will be in you.

Then, in John 16:13-14, He said, "When he, the Spirit of truth,
comes, he will guide you into all truth. He will not speak on his
own; he will speak only what he hears, and he will tell you what is
yet to come. He will bring glory to me by taking from what is mine
and making it known to you." This is an amazing relationship.
God's Spirit comes to live within us, to help us obey His Word and
to become more like Him.

In 1 Corinthians 6:17 (NAS) we are told that, "One who joins
himself to the Lord is one spirit with Him." There are also a number
of places in the Scriptures which refer to being "filled with the Spirit."
Acts 13:52 says, "The disciples were filled with joy and with the
Holy Spirit." And then in Ephesians 3:19, the Apostle Paul prays
that "you may be filled to the measure of all the fullness of God."
In Paul's letter to the Ephesians (5:18-20) he says, "Do not get drunk
on wine, which leads to debauchery. Instead, be filled with the
Spirit. Speak to one another with psalms, hymns and spiritual songs.
Sing and make music in your heart to the Lord, always giving thanks
to God the Father for everything, in the name of our Lord Jesus
Christ."

Then there are many references to the Holy Spirit coming "upon"
people or people being "baptized in" or "with" the Holy Spirit. In
Luke 1:35, the Holy Spirit came "upon" Mary the mother of Jesus.
In Luke 3:22 He came "upon" Jesus in "bodily form" as He was
being baptized. John the Baptist speaking of Jesus in Luke 3:16
said, "He will baptize you with the Holy Spirit and with fire." Using
a concordance you can find several Scriptures that fall into each of
these categories. It is clearly God's will that the Holy Spirit be
actively involved in the life of a follower of Christ. So we should
welcome the Holy Spirit to come upon us, to live in us, fill us, and
baptize us; in other words, to saturate us with His presence and to
have free access to our lives.

In Matthew 13:33 Jesus said, "The kingdom of heaven is like
yeast that a woman took and mixed into a large amount of flour
until it worked all through the dough." Just like yeast is worked

into every part of the dough, the Holy Spirit begins working His way into every part of our lives as soon as we become followers of Christ. Dough gets squeezed, folded, and pressed; and with each kneading the yeast is spread throughout the dough. The same thing happens in the life of a disciple. As the events of life squeeze and press us, we have opportunities to behave like we did before or to allow the Holy Spirit to change how we think and act. In each situation we must make a decision whether or not we are going to continue in our old ways or yield to the Holy Spirit so that He can make us more like Christ. In James 1:2-4 we are told to "Consider it pure joy, my brothers, whenever you face trials of many kinds, because you know that the testing of your faith develops perseverance. Perseverance must finish its work so that you may be mature and complete, not lacking anything."

Some aspects of our behaviors are easier to bring into obedience to the Scriptures, while others are not so yielding. I can remember praying for help in some difficult financial situations I was facing just after I became a follower of Christ. When I picked up my Bible and began reading, this is what I found:

> Therefore, since we have been justified through faith, we have peace with God through our Lord Jesus Christ, through whom we have gained access by faith into this grace in which we now stand. And we rejoice in the hope of the glory of God. Not only so, but we also rejoice in our sufferings, because we know that suffering produces perseverance; perseverance, character; and character, hope. And hope does not disappoint us, because God has poured out his love into our hearts by the Holy Spirit, whom he has given us.
>
> Romans 5:1-5

I liked the first part of this passage about having peace with God, but I really did not like the implications of the other verses. I felt like God was telling me that I was not going to be let out of my troubles quickly and that I should somehow rejoice in the process as I persevered. Since I was facing the possibility of losing our home, I could not understand how I should be rejoicing. I was so caught up in my own perspective of my problems, I completely overlooked the part that said, "And hope does not disappoint, because God has poured out his love into our hearts by the Holy Spirit."

God can reach us with just the right picture or metaphor to help us make sense of our circumstances. During one of my trials, He let me see myself as a sponge, an image that has really stayed with me. The word sponge is used only once in the Bible and it is in the account of Jesus' crucifixion. In Matthew 27:48 it says, "Immediately one of them ran and got a sponge. He filled it with wine vinegar, put it on a stick, and offered it to Jesus to drink." This picture of Jesus being comforted by a wine-soaked sponge is a beautiful picture of the Holy Spirit helping and comforting us in our tribulations. But the sponge the Lord had shown me was not a soft and pliable one that could be easily filled with wine and offered to anyone as help or comfort. It was hard and crusty like the one sitting on the bench in my garage.

The Lord showed me that when I came to know Him, it was as though someone filled a syringe full of wine, placed it deep in the middle of the sponge and emptied it. But the sponge was too brittle to absorb much of the wine. For the most part I was still crusty and dry, unable to act consistently with the Lord's will. But I had His Spirit deep inside of me waiting for me to yield every area of my life to Him. Each trial or decision gave me the opportunity to consider my ways versus His ways. As the pressures of life squeezed me, I felt convicted about things that were wrong and I repented of them. Each time this happened and I yielded my thoughts and actions to the Holy Spirit, He filled the hard crusty areas with Himself and the sponge grew less and less brittle. But I was not always so eager to give up my will and yield to the Lord. In some cases I was sincerely convinced of the righteousness of my own ways and was not open to consider how wrong I might be. In those cases the Lord picked up the entire sponge and gripped it firmly in His hand, crushing the outer layers of hardness and releasing His Spirit into those areas I had protected.

For a long time I did not understand the Lord's mercy in this process. I noticed that I kept having trials and challenges that were more and more difficult. And after each one passed I could also see some improvement in my life. Nonetheless, I didn't appreciate getting battered around by what I had always thought were other people's shortcomings. Finally, after many years of complaining, I began to see that God was directly involved. The normal processes of life always supplied plenty of problems, but it became clear to me that the Lord was deliberately leading me into situations that were designed to break down my pride and soften my hardened, unyielding will. The pressures they produced at home and at work caused me to feel helpless and desperate for the Lord's intervention. It was during those times when I humbled myself to seek His help that He was able to get me to reconsider sins I had previously defended, and repent.

But what was His purpose in all of this? Jesus said to His disciples in Acts 1:8, "You will receive power when the Holy Spirit comes on you; and you will be my witnesses in Jerusalem, and in all Judea and Samaria, and to the ends of the earth." If we are to be His witness, we must be able to minister both the fruit and gifts of His Spirit to those who need help and comfort. The fruit of the Holy Spirit grows in our lives as we yield our will and our ways to His. Jesus said, "I am the true vine, and my Father is the gardener. He cuts off every branch in me that bears no fruit, while every branch that does bear fruit he prunes so that it will be even more fruitful" (John 15:1-5). So where there are unproductive sinful parts of our lives, He will prune them. Where there are productive areas in which we are obedient, He will prune them, too. His pruning does not mean He is upset with us. In His faithfulness, "God disciplines us for our good, that we may share in his holiness" (Hebrews 12:10). He wants us to manifest the fruit of the Holy Spirit, which is: "love, joy, peace, patience, kindness, goodness, faithfulness, gentleness, self control" (Galatians 5:22-23 NAS). The more we are pruned, the more fruit we produce.

Yielding to the Holy Spirit requires a level of openness and intimacy that many men think will make them feel uncomfortable. But yielding control of your life to the Holy Spirit is not the same as becoming weak and mindless. To the contrary, it requires us to humble ourselves to someone who has superior power and authority, and holds the strategic advantage; something we routinely do to receive a paycheck and other things we want badly enough. However, with the Lord, we must not only humble ourselves on the outside; but in our hearts. "Therefore, just as the Holy Spirit says, 'Today if you hear His voice, do not harden your hearts'" (Hebrews 3:7-8 NAS); "Devote yourselves to prayer, keeping alert in it with an attitude of thanksgiving" (Colossians 4:2 NAS); For He "is able to do exceeding abundantly beyond all that we ask or think, according to the power that works within us" (Ephesians 3:20 NAS).

Pray for Your Family and Friends

The job description of a priest is outlined in 1 Chronicles 23:13. It says, "Aaron was set apart, he and his descendants forever, to consecrate the most holy things, to offer sacrifices before the Lord, to minister before him and to pronounce blessings in his name forever." And then, in Deuteronomy 21:5 it says, "The priests, the sons of Levi, shall step forward, for the Lord your God has chosen them to minister and to pronounce blessings in the name of the Lord and to decide all cases of dispute and assault." Realizing that as followers of Christ we are all priests, these Scriptures lay out a daunting agenda for us at home and at work. Obviously, this job description would require a man to be actively in relationship with God through prayer and the study of the Scriptures in order to know what to consecrate, how to judge complicated issues between people, and to whom and for what purposes to pronounce blessings.

As priests, our job includes standing between God and people interceding for them in prayer, and standing between people to help reconcile personal conflicts. These potentially intense responsibilities emphasize the need for knowing the will of God and what actions to take in many situations. Our best example is Jesus who said in John 5:19, 30 (NAS), "Truly, truly, I say to you, the Son can do nothing of Himself, unless it is something He sees the Father doing; for whatever the Father does, these things the Son also does in like manner. I can do nothing on My own initiative. As I hear, I judge;

and My judgment is just, because I do not seek My own will, but the will of Him who sent Me." To follow this example, a man must be able to accurately apply the Word of God, and be ever yielding to the Holy Spirit.

An important part of our intercession for people is to pronounce blessings. To bless means to pronounce a benediction upon someone. In the Hebrew, the word translated as blessing (#1293) implies a specific benefit or prosperity to the recipient. When we pronounce a blessing upon someone, we are speaking favorable and prosperous things about them as a person or invoking good things into their life or future. There are many examples in the Bible of blessings being pronounced such as:

> By Melchizedek upon Abraham. "And he blessed Abram, saying, 'Blessed be Abram by God Most High, Creator of heaven and earth.'"
> Genesis 14:19

> By Moses upon the tribes of Israel. In Deuteronomy Chapter 33, he speaks a blessing over each of the tribes of Israel.

> By David upon the people of Israel. "After he had finished sacrificing the burnt offerings and fellowship offerings, he blessed the people in the name of the Lord Almighty."
> 2 Samuel 6:18

> By Solomon upon the people of Israel. "May the Lord our God be with us as he was with our fathers; may he never leave us nor forsake us. May he turn our hearts to him, to walk in all his ways and to keep the commands, decrees and regulations he gave our fathers."
> 1 Kings 8:57-58

By Isaac upon Jacob. "May God give you of heaven's dew and of earth's richness–an abundance of grain and new wine. May nations serve you and peoples bow down to you. Be lord over your brothers, and may the sons of your mother bow down to you. May those who curse you be cursed and those who bless you be blessed."

Genesis 27:28-29

By Naomi upon Ruth and Orpah, her two daughters-in-law. "Go back, each of you, to your mother's home. May the Lord show kindness to you, as you have shown to your dead and to me. May the Lord grant that each of you will find rest in the home of another husband."

Ruth 1:8-9

A blessing is not just something we make up out of our own imagination. The will and Spirit of God guide it. These are things we can know only through the study of the Scriptures and personal fellowship with Him. When we bless someone, we intercede (or stand between) him and God, and bless him in His Name. We can also stand between God and someone who has sinned, blessing him with a favorable judgment as the Levite priests did for the nation of Israel, and as Abraham attempted to do with Sodom and Gomorrah in Genesis Chapter 18. Unfortunately, Abraham's deal with God required ten righteous people to be in residence for the cities to be spared. There were not enough and the outcome was fire from heaven. So obviously, intercession is not a method of imposing man's will on God, but of expressing God's will toward someone through our prayers and blessings.

In Numbers 30:1-16, there is a very interesting example of God delegating authority to man, which allows him to intercede, judge favorably, and invoke a blessing for his wife or daughter. In this case, a man is given delegated authority to release his wife or daughter from a vow, pledge, or rash promise they may have made, even if it was to the Lord. Throughout the record of God's dealings with his people there have been men, acting in the role of priests, who could intercede between the people and God; and help them disentangle themselves from sin. Hebrews 7:23-25 says,

> There have been many of those priests, since death prevented them from continuing in office; but because Jesus lives forever, he has a permanent priesthood. Therefore he is able to save completely those who come to God through him, because he always lives to intercede for them.

> No one takes this honor upon himself; he must be called by God, just as Aaron was. So Christ also did not take upon himself the glory of becoming a high priest. But God said to him, "You are my Son; today I have become your Father."
>
> Hebrews 5:4-5

Just as Jesus received this authority from His Father, we as priests unto Him also receive the authority to intercede for one another's sins. In Matthew 9:2-7,

> Some men brought to Him a paralytic, lying on a mat. When Jesus saw their faith, he said to the paralytic, "Take heart, son; your sins are forgiven." At this, some of the teachers of the law said to themselves, "This fellow is blaspheming!" Knowing their thoughts, Jesus said, "Why do you entertain evil thoughts in your hearts? Which is easier: to say, 'Your sins are forgiven,' or to say, 'Get up and walk'? But so that you may know that the Son of Man has authority on earth to forgive sins." Then he said to the paralytic, "Get up, take your mat and go home." And the man got up and went home.

Here Jesus was demonstrating that healing a man's body was a greater expression of authority than to forgive sins. This simple truth sometimes baffles people, especially the proud "teachers of the law" that Jesus confronted here and in Matthew 23.

In 1 John 5:14-16 we are exhorted by the Apostle John to come before God and intercede for the sins of our brothers.

> This is the confidence we have in approaching God: that if we ask anything according to his will, he hears us. And if we know that he hears us—whatever we ask—we know that we have what we asked of him. If anyone sees his brother commit a sin that does not lead to death, he should pray and God will give him life. I refer to those whose sin does not lead to death. There is a sin that leads to death. I am not saying that he should pray about that.

How did John know that such a thing was according to the will of God? He knew because he was a witness when Jesus delegated the authority to forgive sins. After Jesus' resurrection He appeared to His disciples several times.

> On the evening of that first day of the week, when the disciples were together, with the doors locked for fear of the Jews, Jesus came and stood among them and said, "Peace be with you!" After he said this, he showed them his hands and side. The disciples were overjoyed when they saw the Lord. Again Jesus said, "Peace be with you! As the Father has sent me, I am sending you." And with that he breathed on them and said, "Receive the Holy Spirit. If you forgive anyone his sins, they are forgiven; if you do not forgive them, they are not forgiven.
> John 20:19-23

The Amplified version of the Bible says, "Now having received the Holy Spirit and being led and directed by Him, if you forgive the sins of anyone they are forgiven." So John is exhorting us to use delegated authority that He personally received from Jesus. But why is this wonderful authority granted to us? In 2 Corinthians 2:10-11, the Apostle Paul says,

If you forgive anyone, I also forgive him. And what I have forgiven–if there was anything to forgive–I have forgiven in the sight of Christ for your sake, in order that Satan might not outwit us. For we are not unaware of his schemes.

The devil is actively trying to entangle people in sin. In John 10:10, we are told that Satan's ultimate goal is to destroy us with sin. Jesus said, "The thief comes only to steal and kill and destroy; I have come that they may have life, and have it to the full." So since we know that our "enemy the devil prowls around like a roaring lion looking for someone to devour" (1 Peter 5:8), it makes perfect sense that Jesus placed authority in our hands to help disentangle our brothers from sin and the grip of Satan. In the same way as the Levites served and assisted their high priest in the ministry of the temple, we serve and assist our High Priest, Jesus Christ by interceding to bless, forgive, and reconcile people to one another and to God.

My wife and I have benefited enormously from this kind of intercession. We tried for years to counsel one another; each of us trying to get the other to see his or her sin. But our discussions often ended up with her defending her fears and me expressing my anger. We weren't just arguing about personal offenses between a husband and wife. There were many times when our sins were not against one another. It could have been an attitude one of us had about a friend, a fear that kept us from being able to participate in life freely, or a misconception about faith and obedience that caused us to sin against God. It was frustrating for us to watch one another continue to entangle ourselves in the same sins and live under the confusion and guilt they brought. We were no different than most people who tend to be blind to their own sins and only see other people's sins clearly.

One morning, while we were arguing about a particular fear that was plaguing her life, she said something that surprised me, "Since you see it so clearly and I don't, when you see me expressing fear, why don't you just forgive me for it?" When I left the house for work, her words were still ringing in my ears. So as I was driving along I began to pray for her. I had forgiven her many times for things she had said or done to me personally, but this time I was forgiving her for fear and unbelief that I was able to observe in her behaviors. I asked God to let me see her situation as He did, and to guide my prayers for her. Immediately I began to pray for her and to forgive her this way: *Lord, I forgive Dorothy for not trusting You. I forgive her for the unbelief and doubt that she speaks. I forgive her and I bless her in Your Name. I bless her with wisdom and I ask You to give her a revelation of her sin. Help her to see why she is this way and reject the old way of thinking. I bless her with peace and I rebuke the bondage of this fear from her in Jesus' Name.*

My prayer for her that day was considerably different from my usual, "Lord, please do something about Dorothy's fears." I found myself strangely at peace when I finished. I realized that, maybe for the first time, I was praying in the will of God for my wife.

When I returned home that evening she was bright-faced and eager to share what had happened to her. The thing she had never before been able to understand or receive from me as counsel, she now understood. God had shown her the roots of her fear. She had repented, forgiven the people in her life associated with her fear, rejected the devil's grip on her life, and was set free from her bondage. God had truly set her free. When I asked her what happened, she said it was like a mountain of sin-guilt had suddenly been removed from her life; and she was able to understand how her fear was causing her to sin. She said it actually became easy for her to see the fear as sin and reject it. As we discussed the dramatic effect of interceding in prayer this way, I discovered that she had been interceding and forgiving me for some time. In fact, some revelations I had reported to her concerning my own sins were things about which she had been specifically interceding in prayer and forgiving me.

Since then, we have had dozens of examples of the power of this kind of intercessory prayer. As the Lord has led us, we have forgiven and blessed one another, our family, and friends, and have seen astounding results. Now our counsel to one another takes place after intercessory prayer, and to confirm the results of the revelation we have received about our sins. Our conversations often start with, "I am being convicted about such and such. Have you been praying for me about that?" It has become an important expression of our love for one another, and a bond between us and God that is unshakeable.

I tried for many years to lead my family by exhorting and counseling them "on to good works," but with limited success. When I was finally willing to consider a new way of thinking and praying, I discovered the amazing truth of what the Lord said in Jeremiah 15:19 (NAS), "Therefore, thus says the Lord, 'If you return, then I will restore you–Before Me you will stand; and if you extract the precious from the worthless, you will become My spokesman.'" Learning to pray this way brought satisfaction to my prayer life that I had longed to experience. When I came before the Lord to bless, forgive, and reconcile, I knew that I was "extracting the precious from the worthless."

Stand Firm in Your Faith

When a man becomes a follower of Christ, his life takes a turn into an entirely new dimension of the spiritual world that has always been there even though we may have been unaware. People who have been involved in the occult before coming to Christ usually have no problem at all accepting the spiritual nature of the things we are called to do. They know evil spiritual forces are real and working to seduce people into wrong thinking and behaviors. "And no wonder, for Satan himself masquerades as an angel of light" (2 Corinthians 11:14). Satan and the demonic forces that follow him have one purpose, that is to "steal and kill and destroy" (John 10:10). When we intercede, pronounce blessings, judge favorably, forgive, or in any way use the spiritual authority given to us; we are literally maneuvering against the forces of evil that want to destroy people's lives.

The Scriptures give us many different glimpses of the unseen spiritual world and how it is ruled by the exercise of our faith. In Hebrews 11:24-27 Moses' exercise of faith is described. It says,

> By faith Moses, when he had grown up, refused to
> be known as the son of Pharaoh's daughter. He chose
> to be mistreated along with the people of God rather
> than to enjoy the pleasures of sin for a short time.

He regarded disgrace for the sake of Christ as of greater value than the treasures of Egypt, because he was looking ahead to his reward. By faith he left Egypt, not fearing the king's anger; he persevered because he saw Him who is invisible.

Like Moses, anyone who believes in Christ follows the "King [who is] eternal, immortal, invisible, the only God" (1 Timothy 1:17), and we do it by faith. So if we believe in and are willing to obey this invisible God, we should also believe what He has said to us about our invisible adversary the devil. When you look up the words Satan, devil, evil spirit, and demon in your concordance, you will be amazed at how much the Lord has to say about them. In Mark 16:16-18 Jesus said,

Whoever believes and is baptized will be saved, but whoever does not believe will be condemned. And these signs will accompany those who believe: In my name they will drive out demons; they will speak in new tongues; they will pick up snakes (Acts 28:3-5) with their hands; and when they drink deadly poison, it will not hurt them at all; they will place their hands on sick people, and they will get well.

This is a powerful list of spiritual acts, which believers can accomplish by faith and in the Name of Christ. The Gospels and the book of Acts are replete with examples of Jesus and His disciples engaging in the tactics of this great spiritual strategy to overcome the schemes of the devil. Jesus also said, "I tell you the truth, anyone who has faith in me will do what I have been doing. He will do even greater things than these, because I am going to the Father" (John 14:12).

A great end-time battle is described In Revelation chapter 12. In verses 10 and 11 it says,

Then I heard a loud voice in heaven say: "Now have come the salvation and the power and the kingdom of our God, and the authority of his Christ. For the

accuser of our brothers, who accuses them before
our God day and night, has been hurled down. They
overcame him by the blood of the Lamb and by the
word of their testimony; they did not love their lives
so much as to shrink from death."

This Scripture defines the fundamental battle strategy required
to prevail against the schemes of the devil. Relying completely on
the blood of the Lamb (Jesus), which is the price of our salvation,
the word of our testimony of faith in His Name, and an unshrinking
commitment even to death, we move confidently forward in life as
Christ's hands extended. There is no other authority and no other
ordination required to overcome Satan. "There is salvation in no
one else; for there is no other name under heaven that has been
given among men, by which we must be saved" (Acts 4:12 NAS).
Here the definitions of the Greek words offer helpful insight into
the broad intent of the Scripture. The word for salvation (#4991)
means to "rescue or bring to safety either physically or morally."
The word for saved (#4982) means to "save, deliver, or protect."
These words are translated throughout the New Testament as "save,
heal, preserve, do well, and make whole." So the promise of salvation
is broader than deliverance from judgment and hell. It is a promise
of a "full life" now as Jesus said in John 10:10.

As husbands and fathers we have a mandate to exercise the
authority the Lord has given us in His Name and lead our family
into deliverance and healing. But we must remember that the nature
of this battle is uniquely spiritual. Usually, when men think of battle,
they imagine testosterone-driven behaviors with aggressive
expressions of their soul power or physical strength. Our fixation
on these things is confirmed by our recreational activities, which
often include watching movies and sports that mimic warfare. There
appears to be an inborn capacity in man to engage in battle. As
disciples, we must learn to channel that inclination to the purposes
and methods of the Kingdom of God.

For though we live in the world, we do not wage
war as the world does. The weapons we fight with
are not the weapons of the world. On the contrary,

they have divine power to demolish strongholds.
We demolish arguments and every pretension that
sets itself up against the knowledge of God, and we
take captive every thought to make it obedient to
Christ.

2 Corinthians 10:3-5

In Ephesians 6:10-18, the Apostle Paul describes more of the
overall strategy, including the armor and weapons available to us,
and the tactics for engagement:

Vs. 10—"Be strong in the Lord and in his mighty power." (Our
first strategy must be to become an obedient disciple, depending
wholly on the Lord. We must yield our own strength to Him,
trusting in the power of His Spirit in us.)

Vs. 11—"Put on the full armor of God so that you can take
your stand against the devil's schemes." (We must reconsider any
limitations we have set for His Spirit in us.)

Vs. 12—"For our struggle is not against flesh and blood, but
against the rulers, against the authorities, against the powers of this
dark world and against the spiritual forces of evil in the heavenly
realms." (Do not be drawn into the deception that people are your
enemy. Keep focused on setting people free.)

Vs. 13—"Therefore put on the full armor of God, so that when
the day of evil comes, you may be able to stand your ground, and
after you have done everything, to stand." (The battle starts within
us as we learn to bring what we say and do under the control of the
Holy Spirit. Stand firm, don't waste effort attacking everything you
see or hear. Remember Jesus' example in John 5:19, 30. Use
reasonable judgment as directed by the Holy Spirit.)

Vs. 14 —"Stand firm then, with the belt of truth buckled around
your waist." (Our truth must be that found in the Word of God.
We must always be guided by the values of intellectual integrity and
moral conscience.) "With the breastplate of righteousness in place."
(We pursue righteousness by cultivating repentance and forgiveness.
It is like a bullet-proof vest against the threats and accusations we
face in life.)

Vs. 15—"And with your feet fitted with the readiness that comes
from the gospel of peace." (Stand firm, but be ready to move

forcefully in the Spirit, as you remain at peace with every person. Our battle is not *against* people, but *for* them.)

Vs. 16—"In addition to all this, take up the shield of faith, with which you can extinguish all the flaming arrows of the evil one." (Hold the shield of faith in front of you and your family by trusting God's methods. Repent, forgive, intercede, bless, and reconcile as acts of faith.)

Vs. 17—"Take the helmet of salvation." (Our salvation includes deliverance, protection, healing, doing well, and making whole.) "And the sword of the Spirit, which is the word of God." (Study to handle accurately the Word of God and speak what it says about life when we are challenged or tempted, like Jesus was in Matthew 4:1-11.)

Vs. 18—"And pray in the Spirit on all occasions with all kinds of prayers and requests. With this in mind, be alert and always keep on praying for all the saints." (Be task faithful and always yielding to the Holy Spirit.)

Imagine that you had to play a chess match with the devil, and that you knew almost nothing about the games' underlying strategies. To make matters worse, the results of each move during the game will have the potential of bringing you and your family into bondage to the devil's evil schemes, redirecting your career toward success or failure, and influencing many other choices and opportunities. Ultimately the outcome of the match may determine where you, and possibly your family and others, will spend eternity. What you say about your strategies and tactics will either perfectly target your moves or expose your plans to the devil's counter-attack. Your physical strength, although helpful, will only be useful to keep you alert and active under the stress of the battle. Beyond that, you will be limited to your intellectual abilities.

Then you discover that the Lord will observe and judge the outcome of the match. And to your great relief, He has offered Himself to you as a coach and strategist. You will have the option of having His Spirit reside in you, so that you will never actually be alone. This close relationship will increase your ability to see and hear what He would do in each situation before you move. He will guide you with nudges, words of wisdom, words of knowledge, and other revelations and references to His Word, which will be transferred via a secret channel from His Spirit through your own spirit and into your mind. Both the Lord and the devil will be invisible players, and you will sit at the table observing the subtle movement of the devil's pieces and watching his strategies unfold.

Considering the tremendous consequences of this match, where and on what would you focus your time and energy in preparing for battle? What would you be doing between moves and between games? Would you be seeking instruction about chess? Or would you be spending time with the Lord, reading His Word, praying, being filled with His Spirit, receiving instruction from Him, and learning how to see and hear what the Lord would tell you to do? If your faith is in your own abilities, intellectual or otherwise, you will learn only about chess. But if you recognize the realities of your situation, and have put your faith in the Lord, you will spend the time necessary to learn to yield to His Spirit.

The devil plays dirty. He takes every possible opportunity to steal, kill, and destroy. He also has many associates, both in the spiritual and natural worlds, ready to attack, confuse, and entangle us in his destructive schemes. When we get serious about being a disciple of Christ and embrace the values and strategies of spiritual accountability, we gain a strategic advantage in this battle. Then, as we discipline ourselves to follow the example of Christ, the word of our testimony can become consistent with Isaiah 50:4-10:

> The Sovereign Lord has given me an instructed tongue, to know the word that sustains the weary. He wakens me morning by morning, wakens my ear to listen like one being taught. The Sovereign Lord has opened my ears, and I have not been rebellious; I have not drawn back. I offered my back to those who beat me, my cheeks to those who pulled out my beard; I did not hide my face from mocking and spitting. Because the Sovereign Lord helps me, I will not be disgraced. Therefore have I set my face like flint, and I know I will not be put to shame. He who vindicates me is near. Who then will bring

charges against me? Let us face each other! Who is my accuser? Let him confront me! It is the Sovereign Lord who helps me. Who is he that will condemn me? They will all wear out like a garment; the moths will eat them up. Who among you fears the Lord and obeys the word of his servant? Let him who walks in the dark, who has no light, trust in the name of the Lord and rely on his God.

7

PERCEPTUAL CLARITY:
A MEASURE OF OUR TRAINING TO
DISCERN GOOD AND EVIL

Dr. Boris Ustinov was the cherub-faced young chief physician of the first privately operated nonprofit hospital in Russia since the 1917 revolution. The hospital was located on the campus of a famous seminary and only had forty beds, but supplying it with equipment and medicines was as much of a challenge as taking care of the patients. Boris considered it a great honor to represent the Russian Orthodox Church in their partnership with the city government and our foundation, and he spent most of his time at the hospital overseeing what had become a widely known and respected ministry to the elderly. He was the epitome of a gentle, caring healer with the administrative skills we needed to keep our project on track. Moreover, his studious pursuit of how to combine western medical methods with the compassionate care of believing nurses and doctors was a testimony to the failed Russian health care system about what the right leadership could accomplish.

Our foundation had helped the Russian Orthodox Church remodel and equip what had been one of the last church-run hospitals to close following the Russian revolution. To say the least, it was a tiny project with a huge profile as Russians and westerners alike monitored its progress and made humanitarian contributions to support its needs. On my frequent visits to St. Petersburg, I audited the usage of the medicines we had contributed as well as the expenditures of grants we had made for various remodeling and budget items. Each time, I found the records to be in immaculate condition, always balanced, and with the staff and accountants ready to provide whatever documents I requested. Dr. Ustinov and his colleagues had repeatedly proven their reliability, even submitting to surprise inspections of the pharmacy without reluctance. After nearly two years of operation, we had great confidence in Dr. Ustinov's integrity. Our only concerns were for his personal health and well-being. Still single and an active member of the Diocese, he had immersed himself in the routines of providing care for his patients.

During one visit, I had gone to the seminary offices on business unrelated to the hospital. I asked one of the administrators (who was also a good friend of Dr. Ustinov and had recommended him for his position) how Boris was doing. I had not yet met with Dr. Ustinov on that particular trip and the distinct change in the seminary official's countenance alarmed me. It was so unusual that I asked, "What's wrong? Is something bothering you about Dr. Ustinov?" He said, "Oh, it's probably nothing, but he has been acting irritable lately and has been uncooperative and difficult to reach. He's been away from the hospital a lot." This sounded nothing like Dr. Ustinov, so on my way out, I decided to stop by unannounced, as I had before, to have a cup of tea with him, and see for myself how he was doing. As soon as I entered the hospital, I sensed something was wrong. The atmosphere was tense and the beaming smiles were missing from the staff's faces. I nodded to a couple of nurses passing by and proceeded directly to Dr. Ustinov's office; my uneasiness growing with each step I took.

I knocked and no one answered, so I assumed he was somewhere else in the hospital. I stood in the hallway outside the door to his small, cramped office thinking that he would probably emerge from one of the patient rooms. In a few minutes, he suddenly burst out of his office and nearly ran into me, as though he was leaving in a hurry. He looked haggard and disheveled and said he had just awakened from a short nap after being at the hospital all night. He said that he was on his way home but invited me into his office to chat for a few minutes. Boris was nervous and uneasy and he sounded defensive when I asked a couple of simple questions about him and the hospital. I decided that I had caught him at a bad time, so I made an appointment to come back the next day. However, as I left his office and walked across the campus, I had a disturbing thought flash through my mind about Dr. Ustinov. What I had seen in his face and eyes was more than fatigue. Something significant had happened to him since my last visit, and it was not a good thing.

As I pondered what I could do to help the young doctor, I realized that my meetings at the seminary and with Boris had produced two gentle nudges to indicate that I needed to more diligently investigate the facts. Experience had taught me to be concerned that there might be something hidden from our view, so I asked a trusted friend who had well established relationships with both the Seminary and hospital staff to help me investigate the cause of Dr. Ustinov's decline. If Boris had worked himself into bad health, we had to stand by him. Nevertheless, his evasive, darting eyes, and oppressed countenance might indicate something more harmful, and we had a responsibility to our patients, staff, contributors, and many others to be sure. Visitors often compared the new Russia to Chicago during the "cops and robbers thirties," and I knew that Dr. Ustinov's behaviors could have very serious roots. I had to leave for the U.S. in just a few days and had little time to thoroughly investigate the matter. However, I could take no chances because a multi-million dollar shipment of medicines was on its way to St. Petersburg. So I quietly put several preventative measures in place and left for the U.S., expecting to return shortly to oversee the arrival of the specially licensed cargo of valuable narcotics.

The morning of our return, we discovered that Dr. Ustinov had been abducted in plain view of several witnesses. The startling significance of the event was simple. The thing we had been most concerned about might be taking place–a hostage for medicines trade. But we had not yet received a ransom call and the seminary was abuzz with rumors regarding Dr. Ustinov's disappearance and his possible linkage to a gang of young criminals trying to form yet-another mafia group. Some students had been standing outside the seminary when he arrived for work and as he approached the hospital, they saw three men force him into a car and drive away. They recognized one of the men as being a thug who had been hanging around the campus. We had excellent contacts with the police and called to ask for their special attention to the situation. They responded very quickly and soon arrived at our office to report that Dr. Ustinov had been badly beaten, but had been let go by his captors and was now safe at home. But in the words of the police, he had been beaten "by his colleagues not his enemies."

The information we now had from multiple sources merged into a clear picture of what had happened to Dr. Ustinov. The young doctor had become entangled with these men by accepting pornographic magazines and other favors from a childhood friend. Because he was a high-profile representative of the church, and feared being exposed, he was being blackmailed into cooperating in a scheme to sell our just-arriving medicines on the black market. However, the procedural changes I had put in place before I left made it impossible for Dr. Ustinov to deliver on his promises. What his mafia handlers thought was going to be a profitable relationship was not going to pay off and they were angry with him. We wondered how much of a threat we still faced because once someone opens the door to such people they do not easily leave. One thing was certain. Boris had crossed a dangerous and clearly drawn line, so we had no choice but to appoint a new chief physician. We narrowly missed what could have been a disaster for everyone associated with our project.

Perceptual clarity is a measure of our training to discern good and evil. To make good decisions about our family, work, or spiritual life, we must acquire reliable facts by asking questions, evaluating relevant information, and making accurate judgments about people and their circumstances. When we make mistakes, we must be ready to identify with the people involved and express empathy in a wise and practical way. By placing truth, kindness, and faithfulness, above loyalty to a person or organization, we can gain a clearer understanding of the facts. Then we must carefully decide what actions are required and how to apply mercy where it is needed.

"The heart of the discerning acquires knowledge; the ears of the wise seek it out" (Proverbs 18:15).

The Hebrew word that is translated as "discerning" (# 995) in Proverbs 18:15, literally means to perceive, understand, or consider a matter by mentally separating (or judging) its parts and pieces. It is very similar to the Greek word that is translated in Hebrews 5:14 as "discern," which means to distinguish, judge, or make a judicial estimation. Here it is in its context:

> For though by this time you ought to be teachers, you have need again for someone to teach you the elementary principles of the oracles of God, and you have come to need milk and not solid food. For everyone who partakes only of milk is not accustomed to the word of righteousness, for he is a babe. But solid food is for the mature, who because of practice have their senses trained to *discern* (#1253) good and evil."
>
> Hebrews 5:12-14 NAS

Discerning, or good judgment, comes as the result of practicing with both the spiritual and natural human senses. Spiritual awareness might include a moment of clear vision, wisdom, knowledge, or insight into good or evil, given to you by the Spirit of God. Our natural senses become sharpened through the disciplined practice of searching out the facts. When we feel uneasy or reluctant, (as I did with Dr. Ustinov) it may be that the Lord is using our spiritual senses to warn us that some fact or perception is not accurate or that there is more that needs to be known. Then by searching for reliable information and testing the validity of our perceptions, we can become certain of what we think the Lord is trying to show us. Discerning is not a guessing game about what our spiritual impulses mean or from where they are coming. It is a disciplined search for the truth and for hidden or disguised problems. Over time, and through the sometimes-distasteful repetitions of many difficult situations, we can produce a reservoir of wisdom and insight with which to more effectively discover the facts and make good judgments.

Pursue the Truth with Heartfelt Empathy

The dictionary definitions of truth, knowledge, and wisdom follow an interesting sequence. Truth is defined as "the actual state of a matter as it conforms to fact or reality." Knowledge is based upon our "acquaintance with truth, facts, or principles, as the result of study or investigation." And wisdom is "knowledge of what is true or right, coupled with good judgment." These definitions establish truth as the essential element of wisdom and judgment. In other words, a good or just decision is entirely dependent upon reliable facts, or truth, that has been studied or investigated. Proverbs 9:10 says that "The fear of the Lord is the beginning of wisdom, and knowledge of the Holy One is understanding." So the fear of the Lord—recognizing and respecting God as our Creator and Father— is the first truth. When we obey Him we have made a wise decision, one that will allow us to acquire further wisdom and separate the precious from the worthless in all that we do.

There are literally dozens of Scriptures that refer to truth, knowledge, wisdom, or judgment. For example, King David said in Psalm 51:6, "Surely you desire truth in the inner parts; you teach me wisdom in the inmost place." His son, King Solomon said in Proverbs 23:23, "Buy the truth and do not sell it; get wisdom, discipline and understanding." In Zechariah 8:16 the Lord said, "These are the things you are to do: Speak the truth to each other, and render true and sound judgment in your courts." And in John 16:13, Jesus, speaking of the Holy Spirit. said, "But when he, the Spirit of truth, comes, he will guide you into all truth." These Scriptures show us that truth is central to our relationship with God and our ability to make reasonable judgments. It is also necessary to express empathy in a godly way.

To empathize means to "identify with the feelings, thoughts, or attitudes of another person." Mere human empathy is based largely on emotions. But for godly empathy to flow through us to another person, we must have knowledge of the truth and be able to correctly judge their circumstances. For instance, when a person tells us a heartrending story we might be emotionally moved. But empathy is based upon finding the truth and identifying with another person's predicament. When a person is not telling the truth, godly empathy does not naturally flow through us because God, who knows the truth, does not respond to lies. Instead of being driven by emotions, godly empathy is based upon reliable facts, which allow us to identify with a person's need and then reach out to him or her in a realistic way.

I remember a young man who came into our church offices one day to ask for financial help. Since I was the only man around, the ladies in the office asked me to help him. He had already told them a very sad story about being destitute and homeless and how he needed a bus ticket to get home. It was a heartrending story that had them all in tears. I immediately felt reluctance in my spirit as if the Lord was alerting me, but I agreed to talk with him. I asked him to repeat his story and as I listened I prayed for wisdom. I recognized some inconsistencies in both his story and his appearance. His hair and clothes were rumpled, but he was wearing expensive shoes that were not at all the attire of a destitute street person.

He was more likely a middle-class drug addict trying to pick up an easy $100 by scamming a church. If that were so, to him our meeting was like a sales call. Two or three quick interviews and he would have the money he needed for a couple days. As I asked him a few questions about his life in the streets he became noticeably uneasy and just at the moment I had concluded with certainty that he was lying, he said rather abruptly, "Are you going to help me or not?" I said, "No, not unless you tell me the truth." He jumped to his feet and stormed out of the office yelling nasty things at me over his shoulder. The ladies in the office looked out the window just in time to see him leap into a shiny new jeep and drive angrily away. Their benevolent feelings turned to anger when they realized how easily they had been deceived and led astray by their emotions. They had not even considered questioning his story because they misunderstood what it meant to express empathy.

But how did I know his story was phony? Actually, I didn't at first, but I had learned not to ignore that sinking feeling in the pit of my stomach and to keep asking questions until I knew for sure whether or not it was a false alarm. Chaplain Max Jones, a prison chaplain with over thirty years experience, had trained me. My first day as a volunteer he explained to me how difficult it is to discern whether or not a person is lying just by looking at them and listening. "The more they have lied to get their way, the easier it is for them to look and sound innocent. You have to keep talking and asking questions until you are sure." He knew what he was talking about because he had led some of the most famous criminals of his time to Christ. He understood God's love and was willing to spend whatever time was necessary to get to the truth. He believed that dealing with the truth was the only thing that would fully and completely set a man free.

After I had gained some experience, Chaplain Jones took me into a "lock-down" facility. It was a prison within a prison where they kept what the other inmates referred to as the "crazies." The men in these cells were so deeply troubled that they were a constant danger to themselves and others. There were yellow lines painted down the hallway in front of the cells to remind you not to get close enough to the cells that they might grab you. You could be seriously hurt in an instant because in their psychotic state, they often had almost superhuman strength. It was like visiting a cellblock full of demoniacs (Mark 5:1-17). My job was to quietly walk down the hall, stop briefly in front of each cell, greet the person, and see if he wanted to talk. The visits were simple acts of mercy intended to demonstrate that God still loved them.

I was easing my way down the hall when I saw an inmate whose condition literally stunned me. He was a young man who appeared to be no more than twenty years of age. He was short, about five feet, four inches tall and as completely muscular as any body builder you might ever see. He had huge shoulders and arms and a tiny waist. He was standing in the middle of his small cell with his shirt off, flexing his muscles and looking straight into my eyes with the terrifying look of a predator ready to attack. His head was shaved and he had a huge tattoo of an eagle that covered his entire back and head. The beak of the eagle came down over his forehead onto his own nose, and its wings spread out across his arms. When he flexed his muscles the eagle nearly came to life.

I stood there speechless just looking into his lifeless eyes. They were like deep dark holes with no discernable expression except the occasional surge of intense hatred. We stood only about six feet apart separated by what then felt like thin little steel bars. Finally, I was able to get out the words, "Good Morning," sounding as friendly and cheerful as I could. He only grunted, but I knew from my training that in this case it qualified as communication. At least he wasn't throwing feces at me or doing some other vulgar things to express his rage. "My name is Larry." Another grunt. As I spoke to the man, I was praying, asking God for wisdom to know what to say. The first thing that came to my mind was a vision of a toddler standing in a small, dilapidated crib with that innocent look that every parent knows. Then the Lord spoke to my heart, "This man was someone's baby boy."

Compassion flooded my soul. I was overwhelmed with feelings of deep sympathy and sorrow for whatever suffering or misfortune had brought him to this place. My training reminded me that his crimes were extremely violent for him to have ended up where he was today. But I was not ignoring his crimes or the penalty he was rightly paying for them, I loved him as the Holy Spirit loved him through me. Although I didn't say anything very spiritual, I knew that I was transmitting God's love. That was the purpose of my visit. I could not possibly identify with him or empathize with his pain. There was no place in my brain that could fully understand it. But my words were being carried to his heart by the overwhelming love of God. He said nothing until I turned to leave and then in a low tormented voice he said only, "Thank you." It was more than enough.

I have learned that everyone has a story that, if you knew and understood it, would cause you to have compassion for him or her. Sometimes all we can do is listen and express God's love. But before we can take any effective actions to help, we must first try to identify with them and make a reasonable judgment by gathering the information we need to make a just decision. Unfortunately, there are lots of people in our world who will say absolutely anything to get what they want or to get away with what they are doing. Each of us must learn to act wisely because some of the most dangerous people are not found in prisons.

Charles and Denise, a mature, middle-aged couple had come to me for counseling. They were experienced believers and I wondered what it might be that brought them to my office. I had begun receiving a steady stream of unexpected appointments, usually from people who had visited one or more of the other pastors on our staff before coming to me. I hoped that, unlike the others, it had nothing to do with Pastor Joseph, who had left the church under a hail of accusations about infidelity. He had denied most of the accusations and only admitted to "grave mistakes" before he resigned, so there were many issues surrounding his behaviors that were still unsettled.

As they sat down in my office, Charles and Denise began to speak very quietly, almost in a low whisper. Both their countenances were downcast and sullen. They were obviously depressed and suffering under some kind of oppression. They told me how confused they had become in their walk with Christ and how they no longer felt confident to make decisions or judgments about simple problems in their life. I asked them a quick series of questions about how long they had been confused, what might have happened at about the time it began etc., trying to discover if there might be a proximate cause for their tormenting disorientation. They looked at each other as though they were afraid to answer, then Charles said, "Actually it started about two years ago when we first confronted Pastor Joseph, but the other pastors we have spoken to about our problem have told us we were probably wrong in getting involved or that the incident probably had nothing to do with our confusion."

At my urging they told me about how they had been praying for Pastor Joseph one night and were shocked to hear the Lord saying to them that some of the inconsistencies they were seeing in Pastor Joseph's ministry were because he was involved in a sexual relationship with a woman named Sonia they knew about in the music ministry of the church. They kept this information to themselves and continued to pray, occasionally receiving what they thought were confirming impressions from their prayers, Bible reading, and personal observations. They felt the Lord urging them to speak directly to Pastor Joseph, so one morning as the service ended, they approached him and shared their story. They said he appeared really disturbed but spoke kindly to them, explaining that what they had heard was clearly not from the Lord because he had no such relationship with anyone. They knew that he had later admitted to "mistakes," but their impressions had been very specific and they had heard nothing about Pastor Joseph and Sonia. The other pastors had told them that they didn't need any specifics and that it was just better to forget the whole incident. It was after their discussions with Pastor Joseph and his colleagues that confusion overcame Charles and Denise and their spiritual struggles began.

The truth was that we didn't have enough specifics to know how to counsel people like Charles and Denise, which left a lot of unanswered questions for many confused people. But one thing was clear, it was wrong to tell them these things were not important. They had either heard from the Lord or they hadn't. And if they were right, then Pastor Joseph had probably lied about a lot of things to a lot of people. We scheduled another appointment and as they closed the door behind them I lowered my head in anguish, frustrated that I was unable to help them. As I called on the Lord for help he brought to my mind Isaiah 16:3-4 (NAS), "Give us advice, make a decision; cast your shadow like night at high noon; hide the outcasts, do not betray the fugitive. Let the outcasts of Moab stay with you; be a hiding place to them from the destroyer." I knew that the Lord was asking me to help them find the truth and set them free from this torment. At that moment I saw in my mind's eye an older woman who I knew to be a serious intercessor and who prayed for the church. The Lord said to me, "Go and see her."

I arrived unannounced and knocked at her door. Before I could finish explaining the purpose of my visit, she said, "I know why you're here, it's about Pastor Joseph and Sonia isn't it?" I was dumfounded. I told the lady about Charles and Denise and how Pastor Joseph had denied any relationship. She was very involved with Sonia, who was divorced. She told me how she often baby-sat her children and about the incident she observed one night when she had stopped by for a visit. The kids answered the door and took the lady directly to their bedroom to play as they often did, and she had assumed that Sonia was busy in another part of the house. A few minutes later she heard the sliding glass door to the patio open and expected it to be Sonia coming through the living room and down the hall. But through the crack in the door she could see that it was Pastor Joseph who walked down the hall and into Sonia's bedroom where she was waiting, never realizing he passed so closely to the well-respected, retired missionary. The dear old lady tearfully provided other irrefutable facts that Sonia had later admitted to her.

Armed with this evidence, I was able to confirm the word of the Lord to Charles and Denise. As I led them in a prayer of forgiveness for Pastor Joseph and others who had either wrongly rebuked or misled them, each of us experienced relief. They were no longer under a cloud of confusion and doubt about their discernment. And I was no longer trapped between my empathy for these dear people, my obligation not to judge without the facts, and my lack of information. The empathy and compassion they needed and that I wanted to express was connected to an accurate judgment of Pastor Joseph. Then we could apply mercy to everyone involved. Charles and Denise left my office beaming, free from the condemnation that had tormented them.

Inquire, Probe, and Investigate Thoroughly

The pursuit of the truth involves much more than an empathetic attitude. It requires reliable methods to discover the facts. Remember "truth" is defined as "the actual state of a matter as it conforms to fact or reality" and "knowledge" is based upon our "acquaintance with truth, facts, or principles, as the result of study or investigation." Sometimes the truth is not as obvious as it may appear and finding the "whole truth" can take some effort. The first question most people ask about pursuing truth is "how much information is enough?" The answer is found in Deuteronomy 13:12-15:

> If you hear it said about one of the towns the Lord your God is giving you to live in that wicked men have arisen among you and have led the people of their town astray, saying, 'Let us go and worship other gods,' then you must inquire (#1875, ask or question), probe (#2713, examine intimately, search, and explore) and investigate (#7592, earnestly request or demand) thoroughly (#3190 until you do well and are successful and right). And if it is true and it has been proved that this detestable thing

has been done among you, you must certainly put to the sword all who live in that town. Destroy it completely, both its people and its livestock.

Serious questions require serious amounts of information. But in every case there must be enough information to be certain you have the truth. I learned very early in life how important it was to be sure of the facts. Everyone in the aerospace industry wanted things to be certain. For instance, every supervisor wanted to know "enough" facts about the work their crew had just performed to be comfortable with putting his or her signature on a pre-launch checkout document. If there were to be a failure (which commonly meant a very large explosion in my dad's days of rocketry and/or the possible loss of life when I was working in the Apollo program), the first thing the investigative team did was search for the root cause and begin to "earnestly request or demand" answers from the person who approved the work on the failed subsystem. The investigative team's objective was not to find someone to blame. It was to find the person with the information that could possibly lead to the "truth" of the matter, what actually went wrong and why, so that it could be corrected. That's the real value of truth–being able to do things right.

But the more important question is "how do I know my information is reliable?" Simply put, reliable methods produce reliable results. The method I have learned to rely upon and which has repeatedly proven its dependability at home and at work is called the "scientific method." All of the activities of the scientific method are characterized by an attitude that stresses "rational impartiality" or the unbiased search for reliable facts and truth. Although this method of inquiry involves some detailed techniques for investigation and analysis, my intention is to emphasize only its basic tenets, which are very user-friendly. Following are the steps of the scientific method:

1) Observation. When we become aware of a specific problem, circumstance, event, question of fact or phenomenon that requires an explanation, the first step is to gather enough information by simple observation or inquiry to clearly state the problem and its significance.

2) Hypothesis. On the basis of the initial information that is acquired, a hypothesis (or general idea) is formed about what the information means or how it explains an unknown or unproven issue.

3) Investigation. The implications of the hypothesis (the facts that you think can be proven to be true) are then further considered and tested by additional observations, investigations, and, when possible, experiments.

4) Testing. If the investigation produces additional facts that are in disagreement with the original hypothesis or its implications, the hypothesis is modified or discarded in favor of a new hypothesis, which is then subjected to further investigation and tests. This process is repeated until the results of investigating and testing a hypothesis and its implications are all in agreement and can be easily repeated by another investigator.

5) Conclusion. When a hypothesis and its implications are consistently proven to be accurate by each aspect of investigation and testing, they are considered to be reliable.

As a follower of Christ, we are guided by the ultimate truth of the Scriptures as we work through each step of the scientific method. This enhances our ability to analyze information and determine how to use it. Not only that, we can receive wisdom from the Holy Spirit, as He nudges us through the process as our all-knowing Mentor. Researching the facts does three very important things. First, it proves whether or not we have the truth. Second, it is a discipline that builds patience and restraint in us. And third, it provides opportunities for the Lord to tutor us in the ways of life. Proverbs 25:2 says, "It is the glory of God to conceal a matter; to search out (#2713) a matter is the glory of kings." There is nothing quite as satisfying or assuring as doing your homework to make sure your natural and spiritual senses are in sync. When they agree with one another and the Scriptures, you can be much more confident that your facts are reliable and that you are walking in the truth.

But like any method or technique, these things are only effective when they are consistently applied. And even then, they are not a guarantee for avoiding mistakes, only limiting them. Ultimately, it is our dependence upon the Lord's mercy that keeps us on track. The years I spent working in Russia helped me learn some important lessons about the mix of our diligence and God's ultimate grace. Russia was a tough place to do business and we were surrounded by people who were willing to lie, cheat, steal, or extort their way to prosperity, creating a constant pressure to check and double-check facts. So when I received a call from a well-known Christian leader in America who wanted to fund a significant contribution of medicines and equipment to one of our projects, I should have been completely thrilled. I was so weary from battling with unscrupulous people that I hoped his call would provide some welcome relief. But I immediately felt a nudge of caution from the Lord, and my heart sank. I wondered for a moment if I had become paranoid or if there was a problem hidden in this blessing.

The gift would be made through the Christian Helpers Fund (CHF) a humanitarian organization that specialized in medical assistance. From my first moments on the telephone with Stan Tracey, their president, I felt uneasy. He was a fast-talker whose conversation oozed with religious phrases. His demeanor was very unsettling and I knew it probably meant trouble. I sent him my "A" list of the things we needed, figuring that would end our discussions. Two days later he called back saying he was ready to ship. I was so surprised that I questioned him about several of the items. We badly needed help, but sometimes the expense of shipping and handling was more than the gift was worth. He brashly reminded me that I was dealing with the CHF and reeled off a list of impressive credentials. I was still troubled, so I made a couple of calls to see what I could discover. Since everyone I spoke with had only wonderful things to say about the CHF, I decided to put my misgivings aside.

I waited anxiously for the report of the shipment's arrival in St. Petersburg and when the fax finally came my heart started pounding. "My Dear Brother in Christ," it started. "In anticipation of the arrival of the container, we arranged for a delegation of city and church officials and news media to attend the opening. We are sorry to report that the contents of the container are unusable. The equipment is faulty and the medicines are expired. It has caused a great uproar and embarrassment." I was so angry with myself I could barely think. I was in the middle of an international public relations disaster and my mind was racing with thoughts of what I should have said or done. By most people's standards, I had used reasonable judgment. But I hadn't completely lost that uneasy feeling, and I knew that I should have continued my due diligence until I either got rid of it or found out why it was there.

I flew to St. Petersburg to see the shipment for myself. It was abominable. There was not a single piece of equipment that was usable. It was literal junk and some of the medicines were so old they had crystals growing in them. I made a detailed report and took pictures of every item. Then I got on the phone to complete the work I should have done before I accepted the shipment. This time I asked the right questions and all the responses were negative. Several people told me of similar experiences with the CHF. What Stan Tracey did, and was well-known for by both recipients and competitors, was called "creaming." He sent really good things to high-profile destinations where he was sure they would receive great publicity. The leftovers were sent to what he hoped were obscure or politically unsophisticated recipients. One person even told me how the CHF shipped snow shovels to Jamaica.

His scheme was to appear to be the most efficient provider of humanitarian support measured by dollars per pound delivered. One good shipment and one shipment of junk divided his actual equipment and medicine expenses in half and doubled the reported value of what he actually shipped, leaving his Christian and secular competitors far behind. He had won several humanitarian awards based upon his fraudulent numbers, which he then used as propaganda to raise more funds from unsuspecting supporters. Those who had attempted to protest were successfully labeled as ungrateful recipients or envious competitors, and there had never been a serious investigation.

Stan Tracey seemed unmoved by what I reported to him, as though he knew that he would not be held accountable. He had always depended upon the political and self-preserving nature of the leaders of the institutional church to operate his scam. And, like his competitors, I found widespread reluctance to hold him accountable. The philanthropist who had underwritten the shipment didn't want to be associated with the demise of the CHF, nor smudge his own philanthropic exploits. Another person, who had encouraged me to accept the shipment, was a board member of a major denomination's charity that, on his recommendation, had long supported the CHF. He didn't want to pursue the matter either. Even my list of witnesses, who were privately very frank in describing the CHF's unscrupulous deeds, feared retribution from established members of the humanitarian and Christian communities if they went public. They knew that exposing the CHF could embarrass important people and affect their own efforts to raise funds.

I reported the situation to my Board of Directors and we held a telephone conference to pray together and decide what to do. As we asked the Lord for wisdom and discussed all the facts, our choice became clear. We had a responsibility to be faithful to our work. That meant doing what was right for our partners in Russia, and the poor and elderly we served. We decided to complete our investigation, make our findings known, and trust the Lord to redeem my mistake. It was quite a battle, but we eventually received a letter of apology from the chairperson of the CHF, who removed Stan Tracey from his post in order to avoid serious problems with the IRS and the State Department.

Our management of the incident actually increased our credibility with several international agencies as well as the people of St. Petersburg. Not only that, we caught the attention of the agent for a major pharmaceutical firm. It was someone whose humanitarian career had been mercilessly crushed many years before when he had questioned the value of the CHF's shipments and Stan Tracey's ethics. As a result of our reports, his company contributed millions of dollars in high-grade medicines to our projects each year for several years thereafter. What started out as a disaster had drawn me into a much greater vision and we eventually delivered humanitarian supplies to over one hundred hospitals and clinics.

But I knew in my heart that our success had only been possible because the Lord had squeezed a Romans 8:28 secondary benefit out of my mess, and caused "all things to work together for good." It might have been that He was looking for an opportunity to end Stan Tracey's scheme, and bless our ministry. I don't know. But I do know that not fully trusting and obeying the gentle urgings of His Spirit could just as easily have ended my ministry to Russia. And there were some situations that came later where ignoring His nudges could have cost me my life. It has been events like this that have caused me to more deeply appreciate being led by the Spirit.

Carefully Examine the Crucial Facts

When I hear someone repeat the phrase "If it walks like a duck . . ." to point out how obvious a fact or someone's behavior might have been, I am reminded of my first duck hunting experience. Standing in waist deep river water at the break of dawn, with a twelve-gauge shotgun resting across my shoulder, it suddenly occurred to me that I didn't know what a "flying" duck looked like. Anyone who has hunted knows that birds have very distinctive flight patterns. As I squinted to see through the early morning fog with shards of light occasionally bursting through in a blinding glare, I realized that I did not have enough specific information or experience to be sure of what I was seeing and I had only a split second to decide what was sailing toward me.

Just breaking out of the fog about fifty yards away was what looked like a duck. But I wanted to be sure because my partner was depending upon me to check my portion of the horizon and quietly whisper alerts of oncoming birds. I didn't want to embarrass myself or shoot a protected bird (a sad mistake that could also carry a very heavy fine) so I waited until the approaching bird flew so close I could see the color of the ring around his neck. Then I impulsively yelled, "DUCK!" It rattled my hunting partner so badly that he swung his shotgun around just as I did and we simultaneously shot a startled mallard that had pulled up suddenly at my shout and exposed himself to two broadside loads of bird-shot at about fifteen feet. There was nothing left but feathers.

This story may sound vaguely familiar to anyone who wishes he hadn't been too proud or fearful to ask questions and do his homework before he had to make an important decision. Sometimes knowing that something "looks, walks, and sounds like a duck" is enough. But there are clearly times when you will need to know more and have greater confidence in your opinion. For instance, I have never really enjoyed Christian T.V. all that much. When I first started viewing its programming I was a new believer and although I didn't identify with its super-religious and sometimes effeminate-sounding spokesmen, I assumed that they must be legitimate because they claimed such wide support by people of faith. Nonetheless, I often got the "creeps" watching them. For me, that was enough. Since there was no mandate to watch or support them, I didn't, and as various televangelist scandals unfolded, I realized that my sense about some of them having a "bad spirit" was correct.

A few years later I found myself chairing a continuing forum on "Religion and Public Life" at the Council on Foundations in Washington, D.C. It was an educational and informational forum for foundation executives and we had many requests from our colleagues for a symposium on Christian T.V. Our foundations were regularly besieged by grant requests from broadcasters to support Christian programming and with all of the scandals, there were many unanswered questions about the viability of the medium. Most people would agree that a "few bad apples don't spoil the whole barrel," and the industry had continued to expand as believers came to its defense and propped up its faltering following. However, the kind of investments the men and women of the forum were being asked to make required much more detailed information.

The things we learned from the Christian T.V. operators and programmers were quite astounding. Fundamentally, they have such a consistently small audience (two to three percent of the market share in most areas) and such poor demographics (viewers are overwhelmingly women aged fifty or older) that their potential for advertising income, the lifeblood of television, is limited. They usually receive enough purchased air-time, donations from their audience, and "mercy advertising" from Christian businessmen to operate their transmitters, but there is little left for on-air personnel or programming. One of the more successful programmers said it was "like building an automobile factory, but never having enough money to buy materials and actually build automobiles." The economics of Christian T.V. are amazingly parallel to those of the institutional church in that most of the money received is consumed on maintaining the infrastructure, not furthering the mission agenda.

When you listen to the voices of Christian T.V., especially their fundraisers, they often mention the great positive effects their programs have for the Kingdom. But when you get down to the specifics of their claims, the evidence too often is not there. One on-air minister told me that one hundred people were coming to Christ each day as a result of his broadcasts in just one South American city. Over four years that would be a minimum of one hundred thousand new converts. In most cities, that many new constituents to anything, even hockey, would have a measurable effect on its culture. Interestingly, his claim of one hundred thousand new converts was being used to raise two hundred thousand dollars for new equipment, so we challenged him to make an on-air appeal to raise a dollar from each of their new constituents, which could then be matched by major contributors. The broadcaster asserted that the people were too poor to send in a dollar, even though "prosperity" was one of his major themes!

Another significant measure of performance that is often touted by Christian T.V. fund raisers is the number of households their signal "reaches." The listener might assume that he or she is talking about how many families are actually watching. In fact, that term really refers to the number of households who have the option of turning on their programming via local broadcast or cable. I'm sure one hundred thousand households reached by a signal sounds much more impressive to potential contributors than three thousand viewing households, especially when the production costs per viewer are considered. But it is not an accurate measure of its audience. Although some Christian T.V. stations do not subscribe to the Nielsen ratings, they are the industry standard. In one case where I needed to evaluate a broadcaster, I contacted someone with access to the Nielsen ratings for all the stations in his area. To my surprise his programs were viewed by only seven-tenths of one percent (.007%) of the households his signal reached.

Whether we are evaluating the pro's and con's of a decision to be made, trying to reconcile the conflicting stories of an interpersonal conflict, or checking out the reliability of someone's testimony, the facts that might be pivotal or strategic must be placed into their proper context or explained fully enough that their correct meaning is conveyed. This standard is consistent with both the previously mentioned Hebrew word *chaqar* (#2713, to examine intimately, search, and explore) and the Greek word *anakrino* (#350) which similarly requires us "to inquire, investigate, interrogate, question, examine, or discern in the forensic sense of a judge examining an accused and witnesses." The pursuit of the truth might involve careful research and study, as in the example of the Bereans, who are described in Acts 17:11 to have "examined (#350) the Scriptures every day to see if what Paul said was true," or questioning a person to get at the facts as in Acts 24:8 where the Jews accused Paul of wrongdoing and suggested to Felix that, "By examining (#350) him yourself you will be able to learn the truth about all these charges we are bringing against him."

A wise older man once exhorted me to be careful not to "leave my brain at the door" when I had dealings with "church leaders." It was good advice because they are not always what they appear to be, or even think they are. Not that they intentionally lie or manipulate the facts—although it does happen. But sometimes they are so affected by the culture of the institutional church that they fall prey to spiritual dishonesty. In other words, they may begin to believe that "the end justifies the means" or become influenced by a bribe. Deuteronomy 16:19 says, "Do not accept a bribe, for a bribe blinds the eyes of the wise and twists the words of the righteous." A bribe is a "gift or reward." It can come in the form of a donation, a personal gift, affirmation, or acceptance. One of the most powerful bribes that a man can receive is being publicly commended for his loyalty. With absolutely no money changing hands some men can be compromised by a simple complement or even the affection of a woman.

An example of how entangled these things can become is the case of Pastor Boulter and the Golden Clock. Pastor Boulter was an honest man who had left a successful sales career to pursue the ministry. Although he was a dynamic speaker he was ill-equipped, as most men are, to fulfill the institutional church's role of Pastor-

Teacher-CEO. However, he was so driven to be successful in the ministry that he refused to recognize his inability to fulfill all of the roles required of him. Instead of rejecting the faulty design of both the institutional church and his job description, he kept pushing himself to become the person he mistakenly thought God had asked him to become. However, like most men who have tried to press themselves into the mold of the institutional church, he began to surrender to organizational pressures and personal insecurities. Before long, he became aware of some criticism of his leadership and began to overreact to any hint of disunity, often arguing strongly to convince his congregation of the God-inspired nature of his vision for their future. Eventually, his reputation for personal integrity began to disintegrate as he sacrificed the need for unvarnished truth to maintain unity for various church-growth programs he had begun.

Professor Steck, the bearer of the Golden Clock, was a world-renowned manager who had retired to enjoy the fruits of his many business exploits and teach aspiring young businessmen how to succeed. He had become a follower of Christ very late in life and used his wealth to engage in various philanthropic endeavors. Like his keen business insight, his generosity was a genuine expression of his gifting and personality and he enjoyed widespread acclaim for his good deeds. He had become a member of Pastor Boulter's congregation at about the time they were beginning a new building program, a fact which Pastor Boulter considered to be an expression of God's blessing on his plans. But Professor Steck had serious personal problems that had brought his decades-long marriage to the brink of divorce. His compulsive interest in young women's breasts and his reluctance to become a whole-hearted disciple of Christ had led to many conflicts with his wife. He eventually turned to a young female assistant for solace, complaining that his wife demanded too much time be spent in prayers and Bible reading. But he wanted to feel justified in his actions and finally sought counsel from the church.

So there they were, Pastor Boulter and Professor Steck, each needing the other's approval to complete their agenda, and both deceived by the various fleshly impulses at work in their lives. If either of them had used his skills and experience to question the

234

other's values, objectives, or rationales, there might not have been an ill-advised building program, or a whitewashed divorce. But instead they spoke superficially about the matters, each achieving tacit approval from the other, while avoiding any legitimate responsibilities they had toward one another in Christ. In appreciation for Pastor Boulter's supportive counsel, Professor Steck presented him with a solid gold desk clock inscribed with his name. Both of their agendas eventually led to chaotic ends, in no small way influenced by their reluctance to examine one another's testimony. Pastor Boulter's congregation became divided over his decisions, leading to his dismissal and great confusion in the community. Professor Steck married his assistant and moved on to a new church, their consciences silenced by Pastor Boulter's approval and the aura of their good deeds. It was just like the adulteress in Proverbs 30:20, "She eats and wipes her mouth and says, 'I've done nothing wrong.'"

To those who knew about it, the Golden Clock was a bribe. But it was just a commemorative of the real bribe, which was the tacit approval each man gave to the other's goals. It's essential to understand the influence of a bribe on every kind of communication or transaction and not to underestimate its potential for invading even the most sacred venues. In a world that considers "spin" an acceptable business skill, constant vigilance is required. That's why some followers of Christ yearn to leave the business world to pursue a life in the "ministry," thinking they can avoid the corruption of working among unredeemed men. Unfortunately, even in the church, the facts are often skewed to misrepresent the truth. So each person must remain diligent to ask questions and investigate even simple matters to make sure they are reliable. If you are a discerning person who is diligent to seek out the facts, the truth is usually there for you to see. If not, the truth is still there, it's just of no benefit to you.

Test the Validity of Every Doctrine

When I first became a follower of Christ, I heard someone refer to the Bible as the "planet earth operations manual." The guy who made the comment was a scientist who was expressing his appreciation for how easy it is to test ideas and philosophies when you have the Bible as a standard. It was simple for him because he was a person who constantly tested facts using the scientific method. He was not biased by what he wanted the truth to be. He was completely focused on getting it right so he could serve the Lord the way He wants to be served. He conscientiously pursued the truth and was quick to question any strange theories or doctrines that a speaker might espouse. Although his questions created some embarrassing situations for some of the super-religious people he came in contact with, they were a perfectly legitimate expression of accountability, and something that each of us ought to be doing. The Apostle Peter warned us about the perpetrators of false doctrines saying:

> There will be false teachers among you. They will secretly introduce destructive heresies, even denying the sovereign Lord who bought them–bringing swift destruction on themselves. Many will follow their shameful ways and will bring the way of truth into disrepute. In their greed these teachers will exploit you with stories they have made up. Their condemnation has long been hanging over them, and their destruction has not been sleeping.
> 2 Peter 2:1-3

It's clear from this warning that there are people whose bad motives drive them to say things that are completely inconsistent with the Scriptures. But the people who have heard and believed the doctrines of false teachers and spread them like a virus throughout the body of Christ can be just as troubling. Being sincerely deceived, they have usually not taken the time, nor put forth the effort, to prove or disprove what they have heard, but zealously press their viewpoint wherever they go. Finding the proper balance between not being intimidated by such people and not being drawn into a worthless debate by their aggressive manner is a difficult thing to learn and one which I had to confront early in my ministry.

I had just finished baptizing the last of several new followers of Christ and was enjoying a time of fellowship and celebration with their family and friends. I was standing in the corner of the host's living room talking to several older men when I noticed a woman walking briskly toward us with a rather determined look on her face. To my surprise she walked right up to me, interrupted our conversation, and with a shrill tone said, "Brother Kennedy, do you realize the mistake you made when you baptized these people today?" I was startled and thought at first that she might be making some sort of joke, but I could tell by the way the men suddenly backed away that she was very serious. So I answered simply, "No ma'am. What did I do wrong?" She pointed her finger in my face and said "You didn't baptize them in Jesus' name!" I thought for a moment trying to recall what I had done. Then I said, "Yes ma'am, I did. I baptized them in the name of the Father, Son and Holy Spirit. Jesus is the Son, you know, and I'm sure that counts."

What a mistake! By indulging myself in a little frivolity I had only provoked her to further bickering. "No!" she screamed, "I mean *only* in Jesus' name, like the Apostle Peter instructed us to do in Acts 2:38." Then she rambled on for two or three minutes about some vague revelations she had received about water baptism. She finished by saying, "So you see you disobeyed what Peter told us to do!" I was perturbed by her loud insistence, which had by then severely dampened our celebration, so I said, "Well you can obey Peter if you want, but I am going to obey Jesus' command from Matthew 28:19 and baptize in the name of the Father, the Son and the Holy Spirit." She looked like she might explode, but before she could get started again, I said firmly but respectfully, "O.K. lady, that's enough." She jumped back as though someone had punched her in the gut. When she recovered, she spun around and stormed out of the house.

That was one of my first head-on collisions with a religious zealot. The lady sincerely believed that her legalistic, hair-splitting revelations about water baptism had come supernaturally; and I think she was right. They probably had come supernaturally, but not from God. That kind of divisive nit-picking is specifically condemned in several passages such as Titus 3:9, which says, "Avoid foolish controversies and genealogies and arguments and quarrels about the law, because these are unprofitable and useless." Sadly, whole denominations have been built on such controversies, with various groups thinking baptism or communion or some other essential should be done this way or that to be valid. My objective here is not to argue about the details, but to demonstrate how problematic some of these "doctrines" can become and how they can take on a life of their own.

When someone incorrectly believes that he has a "revelation from God," it is very difficult to convince him of his error, even when the Scriptures are clear on the topic. The more supernatural and untested the revelation, the more vulnerable people are to being misled. You might be surprised to know that some of the world's well-known institutional religions started as a result of a "revelation" or a "visit from an angel." And each new religion modified the basic covenant and doctrines of Jesus Christ.

In 1827, Joseph Smith started the Church of Jesus Christ of Latter Day Saints, or Mormons, on the basis of a visit from "a heavenly messenger named Moroni," who said that in mortal life he had been both a prophet and the son of a prophet. His father was named "Mormon." They were supposedly Nephite's, a branch of the House of Israel that had inhabited the American continent prior to Columbus. They created the Book of Mormon and also some new rituals such as baptizing the dead members of a family into Christ (lds.org).

The Islamic religion was founded by Mohammed, who said he received a series of visits and revelations from the angel "Gabriel" during the period of 610 - 632 A.D. With over a billion adherents, Islamic believers say Jesus was only a prophet (worldbookonline.com).

And once again, we must mention Constantine. In 312 A.D., prior to a final attack on Rome (at Milvian Bridge on the Tiber river), he attempted to consult pagan gods for guidance. He typically used diviners who acted as his intermediary and relied upon their ability to inspect and interpret the entrails of sacrificed animals as the basis for their predictions. Although it had been Constantine's custom to call on these pagan gods for assistance, he was apparently unable to engage them in this particular endeavor. However, he had a vision, or a dream, or a visit from an angel (history is divided on exactly what) in which he saw a bright light and the "monogram of Jesus Christ." He supposedly spoke to "the Christ of God" who assured him of success in battle if he would inscribe the monogram on his soldier's shields. In return for victory, Constantine promised to institutionalize Christianity by making it a state religion. There is no record of this monogram prior to Constantine, or of his personal testimony acknowledging Jesus as the Lord of his life. In fact, he apparently continued his contacts with diviners and pagan gods while serving as both the head of the church and the head of state. (See Appendix)

In Galatians 1:8 the Apostle Paul warned us that, "even if we or an angel from heaven should preach a gospel other than the one we preached to you, let him be eternally condemned!" Notwithstanding this admonition, Constantine's design for the church has been revered for centuries. His "vision" provided the platform for the abuses that Luther confronted, and has remained as the acknowledged framework of the institutional church. The lessons to be learned are very simple: No matter how good it may sound (and Constantine's vision might have been very appealing to a persecuted church), deviations from the basic scriptural pattern have consequences. And the channels through which they come should never surprise us. "Satan himself masquerades as an angel of light. It is not surprising, then, if his servants masquerade as servants of righteousness" (2 Corinthians 11:14-15).

There are two fundamental and strategic characteristics of false doctrine: First, it separates us from God and one another, dividing the body of Christ and diminishing its power. Jesus said, "Every kingdom divided against itself will be ruined, and every city or household divided against itself will not stand" (Matthew 12:25). And second, it is the devil's tool to damage or destroy the life of every individual and God's plan for them. Jesus said, "The thief comes only to steal and kill and destroy; I have come that they may have life, and have it to the full" (John 10:10).

Nothing is more divisive than denominational doctrine. Denominations actually take pride in emphasizing the special scriptural distinctive that sets them apart from each other. But they are quite simply dividing the Body of Christ among themselves and in the process slicing up the Bible and rejecting parts of the personality of God. I have attended many inter-denominational ministerial meetings where they tried to find unity in Christ while preserving their individual distinctions. It's like calling together an embattled family to help them find a peaceful common ground without resolving their important differences. Actually, they were just being polite and putting forth the appearance of unity as they privately clung to the tenets of the institutional franchises that held each of them captive. Nothing changes at those meetings even though the ministers return to their pulpits with dynamic stories about the body of Christ unifying.

When a new denomination or local congregation is formed around a doctrinal viewpoint, it usually represents either a failure to reconcile scriptural differences with a previous group, or a new revelation that supports one viewpoint over another. The problem with this very polite way of describing divisions is that someone lacked the humility and honesty to submit to the scriptural truth and commit to real reconciliation. My wife was once a member of a sorority that had a very interesting motto they invoked when there were conflicts in their local chapters. It was called "branch and grow" which was a euphemism for "leave those folks behind and start a new chapter." When you have been conditioned to think of the Kingdom of God as the sum of its institutions, there are very few options available but to "branch and grow," dragging along some of the confused and divided members of the body of Christ with you.

In all of my studies I have never found a Scripture that could be accurately and reasonably interpreted several ways. When the Hebrew or Greek text and literal context are considered along with any parallel Scriptures on the topic, there is always one very clear and overwhelming meaning. The more essential the Scripture is to life and godliness, the more easily and consistently it can be interpreted. It's amazing how effortlessly correct doctrine passes the common-sense test. When there is a serious debate with significant differences over what a Scripture means, it usually indicates that someone is holding on to a doctrinal position that requires some stretching and straining to explain.

It's dangerous to make Scriptures say what you want them to mean even when doing so sounds harmless. I remember one teacher who liked to encourage older people who were losing their memory by quoting a portion of Proverbs 10:7 which says, "The memory of the righteous is blessed." I'm sure his listeners were encouraged until they read the whole Scripture, which says, "The memory of the righteous is blessed, but the name of the wicked will rot." The meaning of the Scripture had been changed from how our lives are remembered by others to a trite application of false faith in our ability to remember things.

We are called to be responsible members of the family of God, not the local franchise of a denomination or the followers of a charismatic personality perpetuating false doctrine. As the Apostle Paul said,

> My brothers, some from Chloe's household have informed me that there are quarrels among you. What I mean is this: One of you says, 'I follow Paul;' another, 'I follow Apollos;' another, 'I follow Cephas;' still another, 'I follow Christ.' Is Christ divided? Was Paul crucified for you? Were you baptized into the name of Paul?
> 1 Corinthians 1:11-13

Doctrinal mistakes can have very destructive implications which are easily discernable by anyone willing to look honestly at the facts. One afternoon my assistant called to describe a counseling situation that had been going on most of the morning. A volunteer counselor had been unsuccessful in convincing a young woman to renounce her commitment to "Krishna" and give up drugs, and they wanted me to spend a few minutes with her before she left. She had apparently been a follower of this religion for some time and had since turned to drugs supposedly to expand her mind and find peace. She was thin and emaciated. Her hair was dirty and snarled and she had the general appearance of a homeless person. I was surprised to learn that she was a University student who had a job and an apartment.

As her counselor described the conversations they had been having, the young woman constantly interrupted her saying things like "Krishna is Lord, Krishna is wonderful, I love Krishna." She was clearly defensive and although she was in a drug induced state, was in control of her faculties to the point that she could make specific assertions when she wanted to argue a point. I recognized that she was not close to considering a change in her life, so I asked the counselor if she had a mirror in her pocketbook. She dug one out and I handed it to the young woman and asked her to look into it for a moment. Then I said, "It's clear that you are devoted to Krishna. I just wanted you to see what a great job he is doing." She looked up at me with fire in her eyes. "No, really," I said, "If that's you're idea of a good life, fine, but when you've had enough, I suggest you give up this foolishness and become a follower of Christ." Late that night in the loneliness of her apartment, the truth sank deep into her heart. She decided enough was enough and gave her life to Christ in a transforming moment.

The influence of false doctrine is not limited to groups we traditionally consider to be cults. When any institution's doctrine limits the power of God in your life and draws your affection away from Christ to itself, it is as much the tool of the devil as any cult. Like this young woman, each of us should judge doctrine by examining its effect on our life. "His divine power has given us everything we need for life and godliness through our knowledge of him who called us by his own glory and goodness" (2 Peter 1:3).

Follow the Facts to Their Spiritual Source

Keeping ourselves free from false doctrine or just fulfilling our responsibilities at home and at work requires wisdom. Remember, the dictionary defines wisdom as "knowledge of what is true or right coupled with good judgment." Jesus knew we would need someone to provide us with an occasional "word of wisdom" or "word of knowledge" (1 Corinthians 12:8 NAS) to help us understand the facts we have before us, nudge us toward the facts we need, or decide on a course of action, so He promised the help of the Holy Spirit. In John 14:26, He said, "The Counselor, the Holy Spirit, whom the Father will send in my name, will teach you all (#3956, every manner, means, and way of) things and will remind you of everything I have said to you."

There have been many times that I have thought about the next step to take in investigating a matter or how to advise a client, when the Holy Spirit would bring to my mind just the stimulus I needed to ask a question, make a call, or pull up some records that would reveal important facts. He has been so personally involved in helping me find the truth and gently guiding me to what I needed to see or hear, that sometimes His thoughts have become my own without my realizing it until I asked what I thought was a casual question that went right to the heart of a matter. The Holy Spirit has also directed me through the steps of the scientific method, quietly impressing me with an alternative hypothesis to check out before I got myself into trouble. Then there are the times when I have reflexively known not to do something, or felt reluctant to become involved with someone only to later discover facts that proved the wisdom of my choice. In each case, He has trained me to use all of my intellect and senses, but to ultimately depend upon His guidance. His will is to do the Father's will, just as ours should be. That's why He becomes so involved in helping us when we are trying to obey the Lord.

> For who among men knows the thoughts of a man except the man's spirit within him? In the same way no one knows the thoughts of God except the Spirit of God. We have not received the spirit of the world but the Spirit who is from God, that we may understand what God has freely given us.
> 1 Corinthians 2:11-12

Behind every motive, thought, or behavior there is a spirit that is human, demonic, or holy. Holy motives, thoughts, and behaviors are consistent with God's Word and bring us into closer fellowship with Him. Demonic motives, thoughts, and behaviors draw us away from God and His ways, often disguising themselves with good deeds and false doctrine. When we see a drug addict who has committed crimes to support his habit, we can easily accept the fact that he has been captured by demonic motives, thoughts, and behaviors. But what about the pastor who eloquently preaches an "inspired" sermon that draws us toward the institutional church, and then afterward meets his girlfriend for a rendezvous? Is he any less captured by demonic motives, thoughts, and behaviors than the drug addict? Or what about the follower of Christ who has spent his life loyally supporting and defending the actions of the institutional church? Are all of his motives, thoughts, and behaviors holy or is there some mixture?

The devil wants to entangle believers in demonic motives and make us unable to fulfill the commands of God. He accomplishes this by tempting us at the point of our fleshly desires and manipulating our will. Demonic manipulation cost Samson his physical power (Judges 16:4-31), Solomon his kingdom (1 Kings 11:1-13), and caused King Herod to have John the Baptist beheaded (Mark 6:17-29). Using subtle temptations and thoughts, demonic powers try to seduce and entrap all good men and corrupt their ways. We are tempted at the place of our greatest desires for security, identity, and belonging; or drawn away from our devotion to Christ into proud things like crusading and battling, coveting power or reform, leading the great project, or simply the pursuit of sexual gratification. Demonic manipulation causes us to misuse our strength and talents following after the things of this world or religion, diverting the energy and resources of the Kingdom of God to perverted purposes.

Over twenty years ago a federal investigator I had led to the Lord told me about the insidious nature of white-collar crime and how often it is connected to what he called "church people." I had spent an entire evening on stake-out with him watching known criminals go into and out of the offices of a deacon in one of the local churches, and trying to convince him how wrong he was to believe this was anything but a rarity. He laughed at my naive lack of knowledge and eventually used me as an operative where I got to see first hand how much money and raw power was involved, and how commonly and without challenge, it reached into the church for legitimacy. Years later, I was thinking about those things as I raised my right hand and promised to tell the truth to a grand jury investigator. As I took my seat, the bizarre nature of the moment rushed over me. I was about to testify to what I had inadvertently learned about a fellow believer's business practices, and the research I had conducted to discover the facts.

I had been doing some consulting work for a government official when one of the people I interviewed handed me a file with detailed information about corrupt contracting practices in his agency. The man providing the information knew that I was a believer and when he handed me the file he said in a gruff voice, "When you get into this one you will get to see what Bill Walden has been doing." I was stunned because Bill Walden was someone whom I considered to be a friend. He was also a pastor, and the facts in that file connected him, either knowingly or unknowingly, to some key players in a white-collar crime syndicate.

Pastor Walden's possible involvement in fraud and corruption had caused me to spend some significant time in prayer asking the Lord for guidance. As the Lord brought to mind several incidents over the years, I was impressed to call one or more of our mutual friends and ask some probing questions. For instance, I had once gone to Pastor Walden when I had heard his marriage was in trouble. I had challenged him to be faithful to his marriage covenant and work out his differences with his wife. As I thought back over that visit, I remembered the eerie little smile that crept across his face several times during our talk. So I asked someone who would know if he had ever suspected Pastor Walden of adultery. He laughed and said, "Which time?" He went on to tell me several stories of which he had irrefutable knowledge of Pastor Walden's infidelity over a period of twenty years. The same thing happened each time I made a call and for each topic that was relevant. It happened that several men knew of his corrupt lifestyle.

The amazing thing to me was how much some of these men knew and how long they had known it. I asked each one why he had not shared any of this with anyone prior to my call. Almost without variance they each described a failed attempt to confront him and how he had defied accountability by a number of other men. Their confused doctrines had trapped them between Pastor Walden's lack of accountability and what they thought was their obligation to protect the Gospel from ridicule. Pastor Walden had always made a big issue out of loyalty. He surrounded himself with good men who had one major flaw. They would be loyal to him no matter what they saw or heard, leaving him plenty of room to avoid accountability. A loyal person keeps his mouth shut, does what he's told, and ignores the inconsistencies. It was clear that Pastor Walden and I approached relationships from two very different perspectives. His was a religious world that demanded blind loyalty, while mine required me to think about how to express faithfulness and personal accountability in each situation.

Before I had an opportunity to sit down with him personally and share my concerns about what I had discovered, I received a call from special agent Foster, "inviting" me to be questioned under oath. In this situation, being faithful to the Lord required me to dig deep to be sure of my information, which I had done. It also required me to tell the truth about what I knew, if asked. Additionally, it also required me to go to my brother and discuss what I had found and give him the opportunity to accept responsibility and repent, or deny the corrupt nature of his involvement. When I finished my testimony, the investigators said I could not disclose the nature or topics of their interview with me. I agreed with one caveat. I had already told them about my relationship with Pastor Walden and so I explained to them how I had a responsibility to go to him as a brother. I promised to use only that information which I had already discovered.

When I met with him, he systematically lied about important facts, trying to convince me that he was not capable of such guile. But I was very well prepared and had thoroughly checked out the essential elements of his story. Had I not done so, he could have very convincingly confused the issues and put me on a guilt trip. We kept talking and he finally trapped himself behind the conflicting logic of his lies. When I pointed out the frailty of his arguments, he abruptly changed his tone and angrily said, "I don't owe you or anyone else an explanation. It's my business." Finally, he had spoken the sad truth. His hardened resistance was clear evidence of the controlling spiritual source in his life. His friends and colleagues had given him many opportunities to repent. But he had chosen to take refuge in a deceived life of corruption and self-indulgence.

After I discovered that Pastor Walden's controlling spiritual source was demonic, it was much easier to understand the significance of things I had seen and heard over the years and dismissed as idiosyncrasies, even though they were sinful. Behind his occasional off-color joke and inappropriate language was a man who was deeply involved in sexual sin. Behind his defense of the institutional doctrine of loyalty to spiritual authority was a man who controlled people like slaves. Behind his infatuation with the symbols of wealth and power was a man who had established a demonic covenant with a syndicate of white-collar criminals. Had I not stumbled across irrefutable facts that were too difficult to rationalize, I might never have followed the trail of evidence in his life to its logical source. But looking back it was clear. Here was a man who had yielded his life to the manipulating power of demonic temptation.

Almost anyone who has been surprised by the public scandal of a trusted friend or church leader can think back to see how the Holy Spirit tried to show them the inconsistencies in the person's life or ministry long before it became public. It is often the subtle "distinguishing (#1253, *diakrisis*) between spirits" (1 Corinthians 12:10) that tells us that something is wrong with a person's spiritual source. The Greek word *diakrisis* literally means, "to make a judicial estimation, or to discern or judge." It is related to *diakrino* (#1252) which is "a process of separating the facts thoroughly, and deciding mentally or judicially." These scriptural standards and my personal experiences have proven to me that wisdom from the Lord about the spirit behind a person's behaviors always connects to a specific set of facts. They are facts that will unfold before us if we simply pursue the truth. I believe this is why the Apostle Paul asked the question in 1 Corinthians 6:5, "Is it possible that there is nobody among you wise enough to judge (#1252) a dispute between believers?" After all:

Where then does wisdom come from? Where does understanding dwell? It is hidden from the eyes of every living thing, concealed even from the birds of the air. Destruction and Death say, 'Only a rumor of it has reached our ears.' God understands the way to it and he alone knows where it dwells, for he views the ends of the earth and sees everything under the heavens. When he established the force of the wind and measured out the waters, when he made a decree for the rain and a path for the thunderstorm, then he looked at wisdom and appraised it; he confirmed it and tested it. And he said to man, 'The fear of the Lord—that is wisdom, and to shun evil is understanding.

Job 28:20-28

8

SOVEREIGN DEPENDENCY:
A MEASURE OF OUR TRUST IN
GOD'S PROVISION

In his best known experiment, Dr. Ivan Pavlov (1849 -1936), a famous Russian scientist, inadvertently discovered how to manipulate perceptions, and thus behaviors, by linking a specific stimulus to a desired response. The procedure began with a ringing bell, which was immediately followed by food being given to a hungry dog. The sight and smell of the food caused the dog to salivate in anticipation of eating. Done repeatedly, the dog eventually associates the ringing bell with mealtime and begins to salivate as soon as the bell is rung, thus linking the stimulus of the bell to the salivation response. Once the dog is conditioned to expect food to come after the bell, it will salivate for a surprising number of repetitions, even when it is not fed. Then, only an occasional feeding is required to keep the salivating behavior in place.

It was upon these simple stimulus-response principles that Soviet doctrine was implemented. Once people had been conditioned to believe in and become dependent upon the state to meet their needs, they rarely questioned the facts. It was a tormenting life for those who could see the truth, because they knew the consequences they would endure if they gave any indication that they were not true believers. So they avoided social and economic retribution by speaking only about the promises that were fulfilled by their government, not those that were broken. The similarities between the people who rationalized the inconsistencies of Soviet life and those who have become dependent upon the institutional church to meet their needs for security, identity or belonging cannot be ignored. The Soviets and the institutional church have proven a simple fact about human nature: people can be easily misled by a political or religious doctrine if it is presented as the path to fulfilling their desires or escaping pressures.

Because of the cynicism that the Soviet doctrine created, the goal of the typical Russian I encountered was to gain control of my life, and thus my assets, by manipulating my perceptions and causing me to become dependent upon him in some way. And they were not amateurs. Many were trained in Soviet leadership schools where they learned the deceptive skills they needed to mislead their own people. Almost everyone had rejected the concept of moral restraint and had turned to gaining what they wanted by whatever means possible. As a result, I often felt like the dog in someone's experiment as a series of businessmen, politicians, bureaucrats, doctors, priests, and even plumbers tried to link one of my needs or desires to their bell. I routinely turned down offers of food, drink, sex, and money, as they tried to make me salivate.

And there were a number of things that could be done to lower one's resistance, like deliberately creating mistakes in documents or delays in approvals that were needed. I am certain that the hot water and heating system to my apartment were once turned off in sub-zero weather so that the culprit could then assume the role of helper and friend by getting the problems "repaired." But the most subtle manipulation was the "instigator/mediator" conspiracy method. In this scenario, a personal or business conflict is ignited by one player in the conspiracy, while the second conspirator offers his or her assistance in mediating. In the process of reconciling the situation, the friendly mediator gains your trust, causing you to become vulnerable to a misstated fact, manipulated perception, or devious tactic that you might otherwise have recognized and rejected.

During one period of particularly difficult challenges, I had sixteen separate conflicts involving people with evil motives. I had even received threats from people who opposed the level of accountability we imposed on our projects. I began to wonder if something was inherently wrong with our vision or me. So I prayed and asked the Lord why we kept facing such trials. He reminded me where I was and for whom I was working. Then He made it clear that He was purposely challenging the values of an amoral culture through our projects. The pressures of working under those conditions provided both the intense practice I needed to avoid becoming spiritually lazy, and the motivation to look within myself for adjustments. In the process, He was forwarding His agenda on both sides of the spiritual balance sheet, theirs and mine. Each phase of my life has allowed me to practice and prepare for the next. And in each phase, the tests and opportunities became greater. I had prepared for Russia and other business endeavors by learning to discern good and evil in the institutional church. Russia was teaching me to keep a constant vigil.

We had served many elderly patients in the city, both at our hospital and at free clinics we had sponsored. We had also distributed many tons of medicines to hospitals around the city. As a result, we often found an appreciative relative working in customs or at some other important intersection of authority. One such man, Mr. Paskevich, had shown a sincere interest in our efforts during my occasional visits to his office and he often asked very pertinent questions. When I explained some of the problems I had endured, he became openly irritated that I should have to be concerned with such things "while trying to do good deeds for the elderly of St. Petersburg." I couldn't have agreed with him more and I knew that he understood my situation, especially since he was known to be an influential member of the mafia counsel, a small group of men who ran the city.

"Do you think you need to carry a weapon," he asked? "I don't know," I responded, "I don't think so, do you?" As he reached into his coat pocket he said, "No! You don't need a gun, you need one of these." He pulled out what looked like a credit card made of black onyx and gold and handed it to me. When he did, his assistant gasped. "I will give you one of these," he said. "If someone walks up to you with a gun and orders you to give him your money, you can reach into your pocket and pull this out. When he sees it, he will throw down his gun and run from you in terror." What he had offered was a card which indicated the highest levels of membership and "protection" among his circle of friends.

At just that moment, one of his aides came into the room and whispered something to him. He turned back to me and said, "I must step away for a moment to deal with an important matter. I will return shortly and we will continue our discussion." While he was gone, I prayed silently and asked the Lord for wisdom about how to say "no thanks." There was absolutely no question that if I chose to accept this kind of help, I would be putting my faith in an ungodly man's organizational power instead of trusting God's favor. When he returned I knew exactly what I wanted to say. "Mr. Paskevich," I said, "I want to thank you for all the help you have given me in making my work here in St. Petersburg run smoothly." "But I have not interfered in your work at all," he said. "Yes," I said, "I know that, and I want to sincerely thank you." At first he looked startled, then, with a twinkle in his eye, laughed a great belly laugh. "Excellent, excellent, no problem, I understand completely. You are quite welcome."

"As to your very kind offer to give me one of these cards, I have no words to properly express my appreciation for your concern, but with all due respect, I must decline. I am not a serious businessman like you. I am a missionary with a very specific objective, which you well know. I would not want to become a source of difficulty or embarrassment for you with your important colleagues or to do anything that changes the nature of my mission." He smiled at me in an almost fatherly manner. "You are a good man and, of course, correct. As I think more about it, this would not be a good idea. But you should give no more thought to these men who are bothering you." I thanked him for the time he had given us and ended the meeting. As we sat silently in the car on our way back to our office, I felt the peaceful Presence of the Lord confirm that He was with us.

Sovereign dependency is a measure of our trust in God's provision. It is an expression of our faith in Him, personally, and our confidence that He has a plan for us that includes the measure of His power, favor, and sustenance we need for each day. And that according to His will and timing He will reveal His purposes about those events that challenge our understanding and test our emotional strength. For "God is faithful; He will not let you be tempted beyond what you can bear. But when you are tempted, He will also provide a way out so that you can stand up under it" (1 Corinthians 10:13). When we depend upon the Lord for our sufficiency, we are secure in every circumstance.

There were far too many ways to be taken advantage of in Russia for a person to depend upon his or her own strength, intelligence, or even the ability to discern good and evil. We knew that without the Lord's sovereign help, every day could be a crisis. Only He knows how many problems we avoided because of His intervention on our behalf. There were literally dozens of times that we know about, where we stumbled across critical information or were nudged to change a policy or procedure at just the right time. But there were many times when we had no idea that we were being moved around trouble until it had passed. Our covenant with the Lord is so precious, it is essential that we don't put our faith or trust in any man-made systems or organizations, but to ultimately rely on His ways, means, and grace. Our success was completely related to our trust in the Lord and a simple prayer of faith:

> O Lord, let your ear be attentive to the prayer of this your servant and to the prayer of your servants who delight in revering your name. Give your servant success today by granting him favor in the presence of this man.
> Nehemiah 1:11

Expect the Lord to Be Your Shepherd

While just a toddler and long before my schoolteacher grandmother taught me the alphabet song, she had me reciting the first verse of the 23rd Psalm. "The Lord is my Shepherd, I shall not want." Of course, I didn't fully comprehend the implications of those words, nor that they would be so meaningful to me almost twenty-five years later when I became a follower of Christ. But Grandma succeeded in her purpose: to instill in me a sense of God's sovereignty and His individual care for us. I almost automatically expected Him to be my shepherd and to take a personal interest in me; even though there were times I didn't quite understand or appreciate His will and purposes. But in this simple declarative statement, King David, who was himself an experienced shepherd, described the love and care that God has for each of us. When the Lord is your shepherd, you shall not "want, lack, or be without what you need" (#2637).

Psychologists and sociologists continue to debate about which human needs are the most important and how they should be met. Although there is no general agreement on such things, A. H. Maslow's "needs hierarchy" (Keith Davis, *Human Behavior at Work*, 1977, pages 42-45) is widely accepted as reasonably portraying the sequence in which humans seek to fulfill their needs. Most psychologists and sociologists fail to recognize God's place in our life so there is no mention whatsoever about relating to Him as a Person, dealing with our sins, or depending upon Him to shepherd us. Maslow's hierarchy categorizes needs only by what humans set out to do by and for ourselves, not by what we are able to accomplish with God's help. However, his insights into human behavior can be helpful in understanding some of our most fundamental thoughts and emotions. The five categories he describes are:

1. Physiological—These are our basic survival needs for things like food, water, rest, etc.

2. Safety and Security—After our physiological needs, we are concerned for our physical safety and assurances that our physiological needs will continue to be met.

3. Belonging, Social Involvement, and Love—These are met at home, at work, and socially with individuals and groups.

4. Esteem and Status—These are often referred to as "self-esteem" or the belief that we have an identity that has value in society.

5. Self-Actualization and Fulfillment—These are about inner motivation and our will to become all that we are capable of becoming.

We all think about these things at one time or another depending upon the kinds of trials and pressures we are experiencing. And most of us can remember a time when we turned to God for help even though we were not serving him day to day. I have vivid memories of sitting on a dock looking out over the Indian River wondering how I was going to find work if I lost my job in the Apollo space program, as I knew thousands of us soon would. The personnel cuts had already begun and there were so many people competing for so few jobs that you could find men with advanced engineering degrees working in drug store camera shops just to survive. Engineers were accustomed to transferring to a new project in another city, but there were no new projects. The situation was grim and I was sure that I would have difficulty competing with only an associate's degree. I realized my opportunities might be very limited, and the pressures of providing for my wife and baby boy had caused me to think well beyond the objective of meeting our physiological needs. I had begun to re-consider where I belonged in society, what my identity would become, and what I could do to improve my options.

The more I thought about the facts, the more hopeless my situation seemed to become, at least in my mind. I had sent out dozens of resumes with no results. I felt desperate and about ready to break down and cry. Then, from deep within my soul I could almost hear these words, "The Lord is my Shepherd, I shall not want." I had already sustained two rather serious collisions with the institutional church and had no intention of ever visiting church again. But at that moment the Lord seemed very close as though He were willing to listen to what I had to say. My prayer went something like this: "I know I haven't gone to church . . . ." Before I could explain why I really didn't like what I had seen in church, I felt nudged to skip over all of that, as though the Lord were somehow sympathetic. So I continued, "You know that I will work hard at any job I get. I just pray that You will help me find another job and give me the strength to get through all of this. Please help me. I'll try to do better." As I finished that simple prayer I noticed a very specific release of the tension in my body.

Not knowing what else to do I got up from the dock and started up the path to our mobile home, which was one of about twenty tucked away in a single row behind the home of a retired engineer. Everyone in the heavily wooded park was an engineer or technician who worked in one of the programs at Cape Kennedy. Just as I got to our doorway my neighbor pulled into his driveway, waving not as he usually did to say hello, but for me to come over. He excitedly told me that he had just heard a few minutes before leaving work that they were going to hire five engineers in flight crew training. He told me who to call and I went directly to the phone and made an appointment. As I look back upon the calls and interviews I had over the next week, the sovereign hand of the Lord was clearly working on my behalf. I interviewed with the General Manager and he decided on the spot to give me a "physics quiz," which I passed with flying colors. He didn't know it, but he had probably asked me the only questions I would have felt competent to answer. With each contact, one detail after another fell to my advantage, shifting the odds to my favor. I got a job as a Lead Systems Engineer in Flight Crew Training (a promotion and a raise) when I thought things were surely going the other way. But God had plans for my life, "plans to give [me] hope and a future" (Jeremiah 29:11).

What's amazing about all of this is that I still didn't understand the Lord's mercy, and that His helpful response was supposed to draw me closer to Him and cause me to want to obey Him above anyone else. I had no concept or model for obeying the Lord and following His commands without involving myself in the processes of the institutional church. The thought of going to church was still very grievous to me. I was a trained observer, and the ethical, moral, and theological inconsistencies I had already seen were more than I was able to reconcile. Although I continued to falter in my devotion to the Lord, two years after God intervened on my behalf with a new job, He did it again. As the aerospace industry continued to contract, I decided to pursue a business career. I had secured employment with an insurance company and was planning to give my notice following an afternoon meeting to finalize our agreement. While I was away at that appointment, seventy-five engineers were terminated, including me.

God seemed to be with me despite my conflict with the institutional church, and as I now understand things, maybe even because of it. The attempts I had made to follow Him were being undermined not only by my own lack of dedication but by the incomplete theology and inconsistencies of the institutional settings to which I had been exposed. In some respects my faith had fallen prey to denominational religions that "shut the kingdom of heaven in men's faces." Jesus said, "You yourselves do not enter, nor will you let those enter who are trying to" (Matthew 23:13). Ultimately every man is responsible before God for his own behaviors. But highlighting the contributory negligence of religious leaders was a common theme of Jesus' ministry as well as His Apostles. I am certain that I was benefiting from the mercy of God for a number of reasons that are all His own. However, I think one of them was my sincere lack of ability to get in sync with unreliable institutions that kept telling me that they were "the" church.

As I continued in spiritual limbo, I began to deteriorate morally. I could make no sense of the world, and my personal life and marriage were nearing collapse. One morning, after arguing with my wife and ranting at everyone and everything for several days, I awoke to the feeling of the Lord's Presence. It was as though He were right up in my face saying these words: "Today you must make a choice." That evening, with the help of my understanding brother-in-law, I finally turned to Christ with all my sins, not just my job requests, etc. This time it was with the full power and Presence of the Holy Spirit in my life. I was so free from oppression when I returned home that my wife actually gasped in astonishment. I had made a permanent connection with the Good Shepherd. I thought the "Spirit-filled" life might have been what was missing in my previous experiences and I'm sure that was a factor. About one thing I am certain: Turning back to the world was no longer an option.

At this point I was even willing to attend church. But to my surprise, I soon discovered some very troubling inconsistencies that exceeded even what I had seen before. I often heard messages with very conflicting spiritual viewpoints from the same pastor. One message would be about the transforming power of faith and how nothing was impossible with God. The other would be a kind of half-hearted, hand-wringing disclaimer about all of the moral and ethical mistakes our leaders made. As I understood the Bible, Jesus wanted to be the Lord of every man, offering each person the same access to His grace. If the leaders really believed in the power of

God to heal and change, why didn't they practice it in their personal lives the way they were preaching it to us. It seemed to me that it would eliminate the need for all the excuses.

Often one message would be about God's desire to prosper us, while at the next turn the pastors would be pressuring the members to give to their programs so that God could prosper them. I always wondered why, if the leaders really believed in "giving to get" they didn't do more of it themselves. Too much of what I saw and heard just didn't make sense. Even a casual analysis of most people's church experience will reveal the inefficiencies, idealistic delusions, and sincere miscalculations of its leaders. It's not just that things don't always work the way they should, it's worse than that. What I was seeing was a flawed system of organization and theology that undermined real faith and brought people into spiritual bondage. People's hearts were being routinely turned toward the institution instead of to the Lord. Sometimes it was subtle, indirect, and unintended, but at other times it was dangerously self-serving.

My wife and I once attended an ordination service that was chock-full of mysticism and ritual intended to elevate the importance of the pastor and the institution. It was such a confused mixture of faith and idolatry that my wife called out to the Lord for understanding. His response was very helpful. In a sentence He summed up what I had observed for many years but could not describe. "It's not of Me, but I am in it." This startling statement reminds me of what the Lord said in Jeremiah 2:8: "The priests did not ask, 'Where is the Lord?' Those who deal with the law did not know me; the leaders rebelled against me. The prophets prophesied by Baal, following worthless idols." The consequences of these behaviors are described in verse thirteen which says, "My people have committed two sins: They have forsaken me, the spring of living water, and have dug their own cisterns, broken cisterns that cannot hold water." Too much of what the institutional church has taught us to do just won't hold "living water."

Because He is faithful to us, the Lord invades our rituals trying to draw us back to reality and undivided devotion to Him. The Lord can speak to an errant pastor whose interests have become dominated by his fleshly desires through the words of his own sermon, calling him back to sobriety. The Lord can use the reports in a business meeting to rebuke a pastor whose outside interests have dulled his concern for the people he serves. The Lord can also speak to us through the quiet questioning of an elderly person who doubts the wisdom of a program. His voice can be heard in the angry accusations of a congregation stricken by a senseless scandal, or even in the grace of an unexplainable miracle that defies our man-made doctrine. These things expose the frailty and unreliability of our religious routines and how futile it is for both pastor and congregant to remain entangled in them. At some point we must take responsibility for the errors of our ways and give them up.

> Have you not brought this on yourselves by
> forsaking the Lord your God when he led you in
> the way? Now why go to Egypt to drink water from
> the Shihor? And why go to Assyria to drink water
> from the River? Your wickedness will punish you;
> your backsliding will rebuke you. Consider then
> and realize how evil and bitter it is for you when
> you forsake the Lord your God and have no awe of
> me," declares the Lord, the Lord Almighty.
> Jeremiah 2:17-19

I became so frustrated with the institutional church that I had to make a deliberate decision not to allow my disappointment to turn me away from the Lord. I was determined to find out what was really going on and why. I would later discover that the dilemma in which I had found myself was part of God's plan. He was sustaining me and helping me sift through all of the man-made substitutes to find His Kingdom. At the end of the day, it is His love and care that keeps me going. I know this because the Lord is my Shepherd.

Put Your Desires in Perspective

The secular world we live in is preoccupied by the desire to have or control the material things in life. And if, as followers of Christ, we have the same attitude, our prayers will be peppered with requests for the things we think are most important for our comfort or enjoyment. When I started attending church services I noticed the strong emphasis placed upon the necessity for each person to pray specifically for their needs. I remember being surprised to hear that the Lord had to be told so much detail, but the teachers said it was a matter of expressing our faith. Their premise was that the Lord expected us to express our faith in prayer or He wouldn't be inclined to do what we needed. However, I kept coming across Scriptures like Matthew 6:7-8, which says, "And when you pray, do not keep on babbling like pagans, for they think they will be heard because of their many words. Do not be like them, for your Father knows what you need before you ask him." This clearly contradicted the ritual of keeping lists and praying about my needs all the time. And it didn't align well with the idea of a Shepherd who wanted to "make me lie down in green pastures" and "lead me beside quiet waters" (Psalm 23:2).

As I listened to the sermons of some teachers, I began to realize how ineffectively they had researched the systems of faith upon which they were relying. There were often gaping holes in their theology and I was amazed at their willingness to take risks with people's lives. The confidence they exuded about very questionable matters of faith was bewildering. It was a thin veneer compared to the confidence I had seen the astronauts exhibit as they prepared to be strapped into a small spacecraft and propelled into orbit. Most people thought of them as "jet-jockeys" who were fearless about flight. It's true that a lot of them had been test pilots before becoming astronauts, but they were also highly trained engineers and scientists. Their "faith" was based upon an intimate familiarity with the math, science, and testing that had proven the reliability of each technology. They were "morally persuaded of the truth" about their safety. They understood the risks and were always open to anyone who could reasonably question their facts.

It was the lack of openness to critical analysis that bothered me the most about the leaders of the institutional church. They were too often concerned about the wrong things. Instead of being sincerely troubled that someone had a problem of faith that their doctrine could not explain, they would become focused upon preventing any "breach of faith" that such a question might bring to their congregations. For instance, someone might ask why when he or she prayed for two people to be healed of the same disease only one had been healed, while the other died. That's a hard question to answer for someone who believes that it is primarily our faith, not God's mercy, which brings healing. Being taught to put our faith in "faith" instead of the loving and caring nature of the Lord, might cause a teacher to say something unwise like, "The second man may not have had enough faith," when they should have simply said they didn't know and re-examined their doctrine.

As I became aware of various doctrinal questions, I decided to test and prove my faith like a test pilot—strap it on, fly it until it crashes, bail out, think about what happened, make the adjustments, strap it on again, and keep making reasonable adjustments until it flies peacefully without crashing. I would apply the scientific method to my faith and ask the Lord to help me find the truth about each doctrine I tested. It wasn't long until I had a series of incidents that began to sift and separate the facts in what I believed about God's provision, even though I sometimes missed what the Lord was trying to tell me. When He would intervene miraculously to make me aware of His shepherding, I would often mistake His involvement as the result of my pressing for a particular outcome. It took several years for me to understand that the Lord was uncovering an error of faith I had learned in the institutional church: I was inadvertently trying to serve God and mammon.

It started out innocently enough as I found myself asking the Lord to help me in situations where no one else could. I had gone through a downturn in my business and for several months we had very little cash. I had maxed out my credit cards and was paying interest-only or a token principal payment until I could get in a position to start paying them off. There simply was no cash to spare and I was trying to work my way out from under what could have easily been a bankruptcy. One day, as I headed toward an afternoon appointment in my little economy car I noticed that the gas tank needle was as far toward empty as it could be. There had been no money and little gas for several days, so I had limited my driving while I waited for a check that was coming. But the check did not come and I had to keep producing. As I turned toward the Interstate, I reached out to God for help. I laid my hand on the dashboard and prayed, "Lord, please help extend my miles; I really need to make it to this appointment." I looked down just in time to see the needle rise up to over half full. I wondered if the float valve might have just been stuck, so when I could finally afford some gas, I rechecked my records and trip meter to make sure. This was not an explainable anomaly. It was a miracle!

Not long after the Lord measured out some free gas for me, we came home to find that our air conditioner wouldn't work. It was a blazing hot summer day and I started checking all of the breakers and switches involved. When I got outside, I could smell the rotten-egg odor of a burnt motor coil, which probably meant the compressor motor was dead. I hit the start switch several times and I could hear the relays close as the engine grunted slightly without starting. With each attempt, the odor of the burning coil increased. As I sat on the ground thinking about what to do, I remembered a sermon I had heard about taking authority over inanimate things in Jesus' name. So I knelt beside the compressor unit, laid my hands on it and said, "In the name of Jesus I command this motor and compressor to be healed. I command it to work in Jesus' name." I yelled for Dorothy to lower the thermostat. The motor cracked and popped a couple of times and then snapped to life, never again faltering from its duty to supply cool air for my family.

The spiritual environment of the church services and home fellowship group we were attending was one that encouraged practical expressions of faith. When I shared my testimony about these experiences with my pastor and friends, they considered them to be a normal part of my spiritual growth. They told me that it meant I was able to believe God to answer prayers that were previously beyond my faith. So I enthusiastically began a prayer list for my business and family needs. It included outcomes I desired for appointments or meetings that were coming up as well as specifics about the kind of car and house I wanted and the goals I had set for my income. I put a check by each prayer request as it was answered so that my faith would be reinforced every time I looked at my list. There were quite a few items being checked off, but to be honest, not as quickly as I had expected. And there were some objectives that hadn't advanced or which had gone quite differently than I had prayed, so my prayer exercises had become both encouraging and perplexing, as I tried to discover more about God's will.

One afternoon, I was visiting a friend from church who excitedly told me about the latest prayer newsletter he had received. It was from a ministry that encouraged people to pray for the body of Christ worldwide. They published a list of strategic needs so that everyone receiving the newsletter could pray. It also had a teaching each month to help us learn more about prayer. "Did you know that the Bible says that God wants us to command Him to meet our needs?" John excitedly asked. I thought he was kidding, but he could not have been more serious. He must have seen the look of unbelief on my face and quickly added "Here it is in Isaiah 45:11. It says, 'Concerning the work of my hands command ye me.' The newsletter says that God wants us to be His operatives on the earth directing His work." John had some pressing business problems so he had decided to "command God to get rid of them." He asked me to pray with him but I was suddenly so fearful that I couldn't. So I stood quietly in his kitchen as he read the Scripture aloud and commanded God to save his business, in Jesus' name.

To be fair, John was naively and ignorantly doing just as he had been instructed. Of course the moment lacked wisdom, because even a casual reading of Isaiah 45:11 in its context would have shown that it actually says just the opposite of what John and the newsletter purported. God was asking a presumptuous people, "Do you question me about my children, or give me orders about the work of my hands?" The truth is that all of us in that particular faith community had become presumptuous, including me. I had started out humbly asking God to extend my gas miles. And when my damaged air conditioner was restored, it should have brought a sense of awe and security. But the false sense of power it gave me, ignited my desires. Actually there was no principal difference between John's "commanding" and my all-encompassing prayer list. Both of us were trying to control our material world instead of trusting it to the Lord.

Looking back, it's easy to see that God was using each item on my prayer list to help adjust my perspective on Kingdom life. Some of my prayers "were not of Him, even though He was in them." The only ones that really "worked" were those in the Lord's plan for me at the moment. It took years for me to stop trying to solve every problem with a miracle and realize how specifically God's will was related to each circumstance. I also had to learn how useless it was for me to attempt to set the agenda for when and how my needs would be met. I'm sure I missed a lot of quality time with the Lord because I spent so much time speaking to Him about my priorities instead of listening to what His were. It took ridiculous situations like the one created by the prayer newsletter for me to see how far I had drifted from dependence upon the Lord as my Shepherd. I had come dangerously close to relating to Him primarily as the means for obtaining my desires, whether they were personal, spiritual, or for what we all had falsely believed was the fulcrum of His Kingdom, the institutional church.

In the middle of Jesus' Sermon on the Mount, He took time to assure His followers that all of their needs would be met if they humbly trusted and obeyed Him. Matthew chapter six is a wonderful dissertation about God's concern for all of our needs and how foolish it is to be anxious about the things of life when the Lord is your shepherd. He also warned us about the risks of splitting our focus by treasuring or being drawn aside by the desires for the things of this world. In verse twenty-four He said,

> No one can serve (#1398, or be the slave of) two masters; for either he will hate the one and love the other, or he will hold to one and despise the other. You cannot (#3756 and #1410, there is absolutely no power to enable you to) serve God and mammon (#3126, or cravings, and desires that are deified or personified in money, wealth, or treasure).

The Greek word here translated as "mammon" literally means "avarice" which is a modern English word derived from the Latin for "craving." Jesus was clearly telling us not to be anxious, not to crave, not to let the desire for things become our god, and to trust Him to meet all our needs. In Matthew 6:25-33 (NAS) He said,

> For this reason I say to you, do not be anxious for your life, as to what you shall eat, or what you shall drink; nor for your body, as to what you shall put on. Is not life more than food, and the body than clothing? Look at the birds of the air, that they do not sow, neither do they reap, nor gather into barns, and yet your heavenly Father feeds them. Are you not worth much more than they? And which of you by being anxious can add a single cubit to his life's span? And why are you anxious about clothing? Observe how the lilies of the field grow; they do not toil nor do they spin, yet I say to you that even Solomon in all his glory did not clothe himself like one of these. But if God so arrays the grass of the field, which is alive today and tomorrow is thrown into the furnace, will He not much more do so for you, O men of little faith? Do not be anxious then, saying, 'What shall we eat?' or 'What shall we drink?' or 'With what shall we clothe ourselves?' For all these things the Gentiles eagerly seek; for your heavenly Father knows that you need all these things. But seek first His kingdom and His righteousness; and all these things shall be added to you.

One of the most practical ways we can express our faith is to trust the Lord to control both our life's agenda and the economic status and provision He chooses for us. This is especially relevant to the proper stewardship of our gifts and talents. In 1 Thessalonians 4:11, the Apostle Paul said, ". . . make it your ambition to lead a quiet life, to mind your own business and to work with your hands, just as we told you. . . ." So why doesn't the institutional church teach this simple approach to life instead of trying to instruct us how to serve God and get what we want? It may be because of its constant emphasis on its own needs. Just like the world, the institutional church is driven by its desires.

Refuse to Rely on the World or Religion

The task before us as followers of Christ is to keep things out of our lives that make us dependent on the systems of the world or religion. In Colossians 2:8, the Apostle Paul said, "See to it that no one takes you captive through hollow and deceptive philosophy, which depends on human tradition and the basic principles (#4747, or orderly arrangement of the systems) of this world rather than on Christ." In 1 Corinthians 7:31 he said, that we should ". . . use (#5531, or furnish what is needed through) the things of the world, as if not engrossed in them (#2710, or using them improperly or excessively). For this world in its present form (#4976, and its systems) is passing away." The ways in which we have become reliant upon the world or religion can be defined by the answers to two questions: 1) Can we receive what is needed for living through a product, service, system, process, or relationship, without becoming dependent upon it as our source instead of Christ? And, 2) can we follow the conviction of the Holy Spirit regarding what the Scriptures require of us for personal holiness, without fear of condemnation from an institution?

Both the world and religion pull at us in very specific ways, but no more powerfully than when they promise to meet our needs. Most people don't like to make repeated decisions and choices regarding their needs, but instead prefer easy access to sources that they can rely upon. This "craving" for dependable sources is the part of human nature upon which both the business world and religion build their constituencies. They know that people are very happy to pay an institution to give them leadership and to do the things for them that they consider mundane or undesirable. When the Israelites said they wanted a king, the prophet Samuel tried to explain to them the severe costs it would bring to them as a nation (1 Samuel 8). But their desire to have a human ruler "to lead us and to go out before us and fight our battles" (vs. 20) was so strong that they were willing to pay almost any price (vs. 11-18). They would not listen to Samuel because their hearts had already been turned to "other gods" (vs. 8). When Samuel prayed, the Lord told him: "It is not you they have rejected, but they have rejected me as their King" (vs. 6-7).

In a similar way, the institutional church draws its organizational strength from our desires for security, identity, and belonging. It emphasizes the importance of being loyal to "the church" and further asserts that good people do not judge one another, establishing a deceptively secure environment, free from the kind of effective accountability that would penetrate a man's entangled motives. In short, the institutional church endorses the authority of man-made doctrines and rituals "having a form of godliness but denying its power" (2 Timothy 3:5). In Galatians 4:16-17 (NAS), the Apostle Paul said this: "Have I therefore become your enemy by telling you the truth? They eagerly seek you, not commendably, but they wish to shut you out (#1576, or make you feel excluded), in order that you may seek them." This same kind of reverse psychology is used by institutions to make people feel like they are missing out on something (and maybe even going to hell) by not being a part of what they are doing. Their doctrines and activities create an "excluded" feeling with which very few people can feel comfortable, causing them to want to do what's necessary to feel "included."

I have seen far too many people stray from the path of provision the Lord had for them by holding on to stagnant relationships that made them feel included. As the Lord once said to my wife when she was having difficulty letting go of an institutional relationship, "Hold on to relationships lightly because people have decisions to make." People who have turned their hearts too much toward either the world or the mandates of religion, sometimes try to squeeze two quarts of God's will for their life out of a one quart relationship. Whether it is a business, personal, or spiritual relationship, we must recognize that God's plan for every person includes a diversity of people and circumstances to make us whole. When we begin to hang onto any relationship as though it were our source, its viability and usefulness will diminish. God's timing and grace mean everything and the relationships that are born of Him never die, they are only transformed as each person moves on to his or her next step of development in the Lord.

Another thing that makes the institutional church appealing to people is the perceived strength of its vertical authority. It usually has an impressive group of men who have established what they believe is a Biblical hierarchy headed by a pastor-CEO and ultimately the Lord Himself. People like the idea of being associated with a powerful institution, especially when it gives the impression that its leaders are trustworthy and will bring justice to your life when it's needed. This can be particularly appealing to a man who feels he does not have the communication skills or personal strength to go one on one with lawbreakers, or who does not have direct access to people in authority. It was this kind of situation that allowed Absalom to "steal the hearts of the men of Israel."

> He would get up early and stand by the side of the road leading to the city gate. Whenever anyone came with a complaint to be placed before the king for a decision, Absalom would call out to him, "What town are you from?" He would answer, "Your servant is from one of the tribes of Israel." Then Absalom would say to him, "Look, your claims are valid and proper, but there is no representative of the king to hear you." And Absalom would add, "If only I were appointed judge in the land! Then everyone who has a complaint or case could come to me and I would see that he gets justice." Also, whenever anyone approached him to bow down before him, Absalom would reach out his hand, take hold of him and kiss him. Absalom behaved in this way toward all the Israelites who came to the king asking for justice, and so he stole the hearts of the men of Israel.
>
> 2 Samuel 15:2-6

When I read those words I can't help but think of some of the pastors I have known. Their words sound so right, and when you consider the enormous size of the congregations they represent, you might feel something is wrong with your thinking to have any questions about their reliability. But besides the fact that it's difficult to find a man with the integrity to keep this kind of promise, if he is part of the institutional church, the promise almost automatically becomes conditional. Sooner or later your loyalty to them and their agenda or their doctrines and religious politics will become an issue. And at some point you can expect organizational and cultural pressures to force you to choose between the power of men or God to control your life. The tendency of the institutional church to make good men unreliable was one of the most difficult things for me to understand because of the cloak of goodness that disguises its incredible inconsistencies.

I wanted to make a difference in the church, so I had decided to become a part of the "system." I gave up my ministry as an itinerant teacher and counselor because the Lord had made it clear to me that he wanted to give me time to improve and deepen my character. The leaders of the church had also expressed their desire for me to come under their authority and work my way through the ranks. As we drove to a fellowship group meeting one night, the Lord spoke to me and said, "Two years from now you will be appointed to the staff of the church." I didn't realize at the time the importance of that word of encouragement. But the time would soon come that I would have to know with absolute certainty that He had sent me into the institutional church, and the Lord had mercifully given us a clear word so that we could persevere.

I had already served in almost every volunteer job in the church. Now I was going to start all over again. I thought they wanted to humble me and test my ministry. But as time went on it was clear that they primarily wanted to see if I would be loyal to their system. I became a member of a fellowship group, then a leader, and was active in the weekly men's prayer breakfast. I soon became a deacon and fellowship group director with several groups and their members under my care. Exactly two years to the day following the Lord's word to me, I was appointed to the church staff. A few months later, I was hired as a full-time associate pastor, and then ordained as an elder. I had always had some theories about what was right or wrong with the church and had studied its processes as any apprentice who was eagerly trying to please those in authority. But it wasn't until I was "on-staff" that I really got to see the "inner workings." To my dismay, I discovered that the processes I had hoped to change and improve were hopelessly entrenched in tradition, politics, and economics that would not budge.

Barely a year after I became an elder, the pastor decided that a lack of unity in the staff might be holding back a revival he had declared was coming. So he fired one of the most faithful men on staff whom he suspected of being less than enthusiastic about his agenda. Then he called me into his office for a pep talk and it was clear that he was not "asking" me to conform. Instantly, the Lord reminded me of what He had said to me about coming onto the staff and nudged me to speak up. I related the story about how the Lord had brought me to the staff, and said that I would also trust Him to tell me when it was time to leave. I promised the pastor that I would be faithful to my ministry and excused myself from our meeting.

As time passed, the pastor's religious zeal made it more and more difficult for anyone to perform routine ministry. I was heartsick about how twisted and confused life could be in the institutional church and had to keep reminding myself that the Lord had sent me there. One day, as I was remembering His promise, the Lord spoke to me again. He said, "Prepare yourself to leave here; and never again be dependent on a religious system for your support, or for the right to fulfill your ministry." Then He gave me this Scripture: "You will not go out in haste, nor will you go as fugitives; for the Lord will go before you, and the God of Israel will be your rear guard" (Isaiah 52:12 NAS). I really liked the news that we were going to leave what, to me, had become more of a prison than a platform for ministry. It had been very important for me to intimately observe the processes of the institutional church, so that I would never feel insecure without its approval or long for its benefits. But just as surely as the Lord had planned my entrance into church leadership in order to further my education and insights, He had also planned my exit, and there were some things He still wanted to accomplish in and through me before I left.

While I waited, I focused my energy on pastoral care. By the time I left the church, the twelve fellowship groups I had been given to care for had grown to thirty-three. This happened during a period when my colleagues reported their groups were diminishing. It was particularly interesting because I made no effort at all to make my groups grow numerically. My counseling ministry became widely recognized and I had trained dozens of volunteers to work in specialized areas of personal ministry, prisons, benevolence, and intercessory prayer. I had initiated a church-wide program to reach the poor and organized adult education programs ranging from advanced Bible studies, to nutrition, and first-aid. My pulpit time, although rare, was very well received and by any reasonable measure my ministry was a success. I mention these things because as they took place, the pastor and board of directors increasingly shunned me for not being unified with them in their misguided plans for church growth. It was part of God's plan to teach me to lean entirely on His grace.

Looking back, I can see that my faithfulness to the ministry God had given me had for many years been mistaken as loyalty to the institution and its leaders. It wasn't until I became a staff member that anyone realized how often I had questioned the ways and means of the things we were doing. It soon became apparent that I was not just along for the ride and my honest questioning was often perceived as disloyal, untrusting, or judgmental. These men did not appreciate the discomfort of having someone question the rules that ordered their world. *Religious institutions are born when people form into groups around the creeds they have conceived to support their particular system of faith.* And they don't like it when people challenge them to revisit the theories and scriptural interpretations upon which their way of life is built.

Our pastor and elders weren't strong enough spiritually to appreciate faithful men. They expected loyalty to their leadership and an unquestioning unity for their plans, and became increasingly frustrated when they could not extract them from me. The fruit of my life and ministry meant little to them in comparison to the value of keeping unified around their "vision." These good men had gradually become so institutionalized that they had unwittingly come to believe in the sanctity of their institution over the will of their heavenly Father, thinking it was the same. They didn't realize it but they had "rejected the law of the Lord and [had] not kept His statutes; their lies also [had] led them astray, those after which their fathers walked" (Amos 2:4 NAS). Our ongoing disagreements reached the point where little was being accomplished in our discussions, and they realized that I was not able to come into the kind of unity they required. Finally, they asked me to leave, and we parted peacefully, just as the Lord had promised. Like most people, I had to become convinced of the truth about religion by my experiences inside the institutional church:

> Do not seek Bethel (#1008, the house of God), do not go to Gilgal (#1537, the dwelling place of the prophets), do not journey to Beersheba (#884, the well of an oath). For Gilgal (the dwelling place of the prophets) will surely go into exile, and Bethel (the house of God) will be reduced to nothing. Seek the Lord and live. . . .
>
> Amos 5:5-6

Don't Burn inside Because of Evil Doers

I was twelve years old and our neighbor's son, Hank, was home on a weekend pass from "reform school." It was the juvenile prison of our day where violent young men were sent to "mature." Our neighborhood football game, which was usually competitive but peaceful, had been disrupted several times by Hank's bullying, and I had taken the brunt of his attacks. He was sixteen, taller, and heavily built, while I was thin and lanky, so he had a significant size and strength advantage. The game had ended and I was walking toward my home just across the street, when he hurled a final parting obscenity at me. Suddenly, I remembered my Dad's words. I had heard him tell many stories about "country justice" when he was a kid. "If it were me, I'd just pick up a rock and skin his noggin with it." Just then I looked down to see a jagged piece of sewer tile where the repairmen had been working. As I picked it up I noticed that it fit perfectly between my forefinger and the cusp of my hand. I was an all-star center fielder on my little league team and I was known for my rocket arm and pinpoint accuracy. Hank was only about one hundred feet away with the football resting on his shoulder and against his head with his hand on the top. With one motion I pivoted, yelled to get his attention and fired a near perfect strike for his temple. He turned at the last split second causing the lethal projectile to arrive with a loud "whack," hitting the football and barely missing its intended target.

Unharmed, he chased after me and I ran into my house closing and locking the door behind me. It would be years before I realized how narrowly I missed killing Hank and probably ending up in prison myself. Adrenalin was still pulsing through my body and I was gasping for breath, trying to overcome the effects of both fear and anger, when my Dad stepped out of my room into the hallway. "What are you running from?" he asked. He had watched the whole episode from my window. "Nothing," I said. "Then who's that out in the front yard yelling for you to come out? Now get out there and whip his butt or I'll whip yours." As much as I feared Hank, he was no challenge compared to my Dad, so I burst out the front door like a wild animal. Before Hank knew what was happening, I was all over him. With a blood-curdling scream I attacked, swinging wildly and landing punches with both fists. I was very afraid and very angry, a combination that created a terrifying experience for Hank, who turned and ran for his life.

From that day forward fear and anger played a major role in my life, one that God never intended. I didn't become violent. I had a couple of fights like most kids, but I didn't become an aggressor. However, I did develop the tendency to explode with anger in a violently aggressive tirade that usually ended anyone's fooling around. The people who triggered my rage were always doing something I perceived as unfair or unjust which also touched on one of my fears. If I feared personal loss, rejection, or someone impeding my path to success, my fear quickly turned to anger.

I once had a boss, a retired navy captain, who received an unfair complaint against me from a co-worker whose intent was to deflect attention away from his own malfeasance. My boss spent a lot of unrecorded time away from the office on personal business and my co-worker covered for him. Their reciprocal relationship had been obvious but not particularly bothersome to me until they tried to blind-side me with a false accusation. I'm sure the captain only meant to scare me a little with the threat of the loss of my job, but he really touched the wrong button. I went ballistic and could be heard yelling at him through the entire building as I delivered a litany of facts and threats that he could not misunderstand. The captain didn't know it, but the only thing that saved him from a terrific thrashing that day was one of my other great fears, losing my secret security clearance, which would end my career possibilities. So although I came to the very edge of physical violence, I never crossed the line. However, if you were the recipient of that kind of rage, the distinction was insignificant.

There were at least three things that kept reinforcing my bad behavior. First, I kept winning battles against very formidable foes. Each victory caused me to be less afraid to engage the next opponent and I began to regard the explosive power in me as an asset. Second, the people I attacked had usually been so unjust that others who had been victimized by them often commended me for my courage. This made me feel as though I were a white-horsed crusader and stiffened the pride within me. And third, after I became a follower of Christ, I felt so good about myself when I restrained my rage that I failed to recognize the disgust and hatred that was growing in my heart. I felt mature and justified to slowly burn inside instead of erupting in a tirade against evil. But the pressures within me were also evil and indicated my lack of trust in God. I had mistakenly spent my life defending myself when God wanted to do it for me. Even as a follower of Christ, I had not yet fully believed the promises and admonitions of Psalm 37:1-8, which says:

> Do not fret (#2734, burn, kindle, glow warm, or become furious with anger, zeal, or jealousy) because of evildoers, be not envious (#7065, or zealously angry) toward wrongdoers. For they will wither quickly like the grass, and fade like the green herb. Trust in the Lord, and do good; dwell in the land and cultivate faithfulness (#7462, enjoy the safe pasture of your Shepherd). Delight yourself in the Lord; and He will give you the desires of your heart. Commit your way to the Lord, trust also in Him, and He will do it. And He will bring forth your righteousness as the light, and your judgment as the noonday. Rest in the Lord and wait patiently for

Him; do not fret (#2734) because of him who prospers in his way, because of the man who carries out wicked schemes. Cease from anger, and forsake wrath (#2534, the fever, venom, or poison, of indignation, hot displeasure, or heated rage); do not fret (#2734), it leads only to evildoing.

I had a lot to repent about and many people to forgive, but I kept getting distracted from God's agenda for my own repentance by the incredible inconsistencies I encountered in the institutional church. I regularly found myself digging for the whole truth about what I had seen or heard because what some people tried to portray as a single error too often represented a lifestyle of scheming and abuse. And it was amazing how reluctant people were to deal with the truth, allowing pastors to escape to another venue and prey on yet another congregation. I did not understand the incredible lack of ethics and accountability people were willing to overlook in their leaders until I began to analyze what was taking place from the viewpoint of religious politics and economics. It was all about preserving the institution.

People's fears that their religion might be discredited by their leader's bad behaviors, or that they would not be able to make the mortgage payment on their new building, often caused them to protect liars, thieves, perverts, and pedophiles with ridiculous cover stories about being called away to this or that ministry. Honestly, it was hard to deal with the anger and disgust I had brought with me into the institutional church because of all the crazy things I saw that re-ignited them. The Lord went to great lengths to keep turning my attention back to my own sins and His Shepherding of my life. But I would barely get refocused on His agenda for me when another bombshell would draw me back to wondering about everyone else. I kept puzzling to discover whether the leaders of the institutional church were practicing deliberate deception or whether good people could possibly be that misguided. It took years for the Lord to convince me how misguided they were in setting their priorities and how that led them into error.

I had a good friend whose ministry was dramatically and unfairly harmed by some of the same people who had previously covered over the multiple sins of their pastor. Because he had such high regard for the institutional church, he took his wound far too seriously. I tried to help him see that he had been booted into the promise land not out of it, and that the people who had harmed him scarcely knew "their right hand from their left" (Jonah 4:11). But the wounds of the institutional church go deep just like those of a parent, and he never fully recovered. Most men find it more difficult to forgive the institutional church and move on than if a worldly businessman had treated them the same way. They either wrongly believe that they are required to reconcile and get in step with the institutional church or they fret and burn inside naively expecting institutional justice. As King Solomon said in Ecclesiastes 7:9-10 (NAS),

> Do not be eager (#926 alarmed, agitated or hasty) in your heart to be angry (#3707, vexed, indignant, wrought, or grieved), for anger (#3707, and provocation) resides in the bosom of fools. Do not say, "Why is it that the former days were better than these?" For it is not from wisdom that you ask about this.

As I began to find logical explanations for all that troubled me about the institutional church, I also found more grace to repent of my own sins and forgive others. But I still had a lot of questions to resolve which unfortunately kept the slow burning of my frustration alive in my soul. I was having a difficult time accepting the fact that I was on solid ground in my fundamental disagreements with the institutional church without allowing their lack of interest in change to ignite the anger in my heart. I found myself having to repeatedly repent until I stopped expecting too much from the institutional church. With all that you might hear about "revival" or "reformation," the organizational reforms within religious institutions rarely accomplish much more than trying to put new wine back into old wineskins, or to rebuild a slightly modified old wineskin with a new commitment to pastoral integrity or some other process detail. They keep missing the point that:

> No one sews a patch of unshrunk cloth on an old garment, for the patch will pull away from the garment, making the tear worse. Neither do men pour new wine into old wineskins. If they do, the skins will burst, the wine will run out and the wineskins will be ruined. No, they pour new wine into new wineskins, and both are preserved.
>
> Matthew 9:16-17

It's essential to remember that the institutional church is organized as an economic entity and that its processes are inextricably tied to the idea of congregating a constituency that can pay the bills of the infrastructure and overhead of a system that never really worked. In other words, the things that need to be changed the most are resistant to reform because of people's reluctance to let go of a failed organizational model that undermines the faith they need to follow the Lord as their Shepherd. So to slam your soul against the immovable object of a religious institution attempting to bring reform or revive a dry old wineskin may only produce more fretting and despair. At some point every man should embrace the practical reality of what is called the Serenity Prayer. "God grant me the serenity to accept the things I cannot change, courage to change the things I can, and wisdom to know the difference."

One Saturday morning while I was on vacation, I walked through a quiet Georgia neighborhood praying and thinking about these things. It was a cool overcast day and there was absolutely no one outside as I made my way down a residential street with houses lining both sides. As I approached the end of the street my eyes were drawn to a stand of tall straight pine trees alongside a house. They were all fifty to sixty feet tall and as I approached them one suddenly telescoped to the ground right in front of me. It didn't fall at an angle but fractured into several pieces and fell straight down upon itself into a pile no more than fifteen feet in diameter. As I stood there for a moment in stunned silence, I noticed that the fallen tree had green needles and mottled bark just like the others. It showed no signs of having been hit by lightning and by all outward appearances had been healthy and sap-filled just like the trees next to it. But in a single moment it had become a pile of rubbish not easily usable even in a fireplace.

Then the Lord spoke to my heart. "The things about the institutional church that have provoked you to fret will eventually collapse just like this tree. Its many schemes are causing it to slowly rot and die from the inside in ways that it has concealed from those who love Me. But after each perpetrator is given many warnings it will suddenly fall under the weight of its own error, no longer able to disguise its sins. Do not fear the institutional church, do not let it grip at your life, and do not allow its sins to anger you and create consequences for you that are avoidable."

Patiently Grow into Mature Eldership

One of the most misunderstood and abused concepts in the Body of Christ is "spiritual authority." There are so many opposing denominational viewpoints about how to establish and exercise spiritual authority that it has virtually lost its legitimate function among God's people. While one denomination rules its congregations by a board of "deacons," a board of "elders" rules another's, even though the Bible clearly distinguishes deacons from elders. One denomination might recognize the autonomy of each local fellowship, while another has layers of managing bishops and archbishops to do the job of the "overseer." While one denomination emphasizes a democratic process as the cornerstone of its authority, another presses each believer to "submit" to the delegated spiritual authority of its theocratic hierarchy. And while one denomination blithely provides third, and fourth opportunities for pastors to rehabilitate their moral failures, and even helps hide them, another is known for "killing its wounded servants," a euphemism created by adulterous pastors who claimed that their embarrassing "mistakes" received unfair treatment that was too harsh.

In a misguided effort to correct these kinds of constantly surfacing inconsistencies, one local church's "board of deacons" was replaced by a "board of elders," with the primary difference being that the new board was comprised of wealthy and influential contributors who "understood business." This was later replaced by a "board of presiding ministry-elders" who "understood ministry" and were all full-time ministers in the church. This was subsequently replaced by a new variation of an elder board intended to reduce the risks of having to confront another "tyrannical pastor-CEO." Unfortunately, it produced an equally frustrating organizational failure. Each attempt to reform their institution was accompanied by a whole new set of scriptural "proof texts" to support the illogical and at times improbable changes. Until I became a member of an institutional church staff I couldn't have believed how subjectively spiritual authority was delegated. From the viewpoint of the pew, our pastor's dissertations about holding to the purity of the Scriptures as a guide for recognizing and delegating spiritual authority sounded really high-minded and noble. But as I began to see more and more disparity in the kinds of men who were being ordained into service, I searched the Scriptures to find some answers.

The source of most of the confusion lies in the widespread misuse of the terms "elder" and "overseer." An elder (#4245) is "a senior or elderly person advanced in life." An overseer (#1985, or bishop) is someone who has the responsibility to "inspect, investigate, or supervise." And although Strong's says these terms are used interchangeably, they are not synonymous. They are separate descriptors for the same person. Since the age of an older person can vary from century to century and culture to culture, and does not alone indicate emotional or spiritual maturity, the Bible carefully describes the attributes of an overseer in practical terms that require both time and experience. So when Paul wrote to Titus about appointing "elders" (Titus 1:5), he meant "a senior or elderly person, advanced in life," who could fulfill the other criteria he outlined in verses six through nine. The word "elder" never means anything else, anywhere, ever, at any time, in the New Testament.

In 1 Timothy 3:1-7, Paul outlines the requirements of an "overseer" (#1985), which he distinguishes from a deacon in verses eight through thirteen. It is possible to look at verses one through seven outside the context of "eldership" and make an argument for a young, gifted, man to be an "overseer." But as soon as you put these verses and others like Titus 1:6-9 in the context of "a senior or elderly person, advanced in life," the rationalizations of the institutional church fail. Notwithstanding, they have regularly chosen older men who don't meet the qualifications, or younger men whose character has not yet been proven over time.

My objective is not to challenge each aspect of the character and experience that Scripture demands of an elder-overseer, but to emphasize that the institutional church has been unrestrained by these requirements in building its organizational structure. In the process it has confused the meaning of the Scriptures and created an impatient, self-serving atmosphere similar to the world, which is unwilling to wait for people or processes to mature. And it has compounded its error by misrepresenting the Scriptures to say that each believer is required to submit to its leadership, often labeling dissenters as "rebels." This condemning theology has enabled the institutional church to hold many men captive to its illegitimate authority. But the requirement for each believer to submit to spiritual authority presumes that we are free to recognize mature elders, with proven ministry, within a Biblically-based relationship. It was not intended to fulfill the arbitrary needs of the institutional church, which itself has no basis in Scripture.

Not long after I was appointed to the staff of my local church, the senior pastor called me into his office to inform me that I was being "made" an elder. He noted that I was carrying significant responsibilities, some exceeding those of men already recognized as elders and that he wanted me to feel "equal" to them. I had been serving as a deacon and had just finished a comprehensive Bible study of eldership. I realized that I was being trusted with important ministries but had decided it was because of my gifting, not my age or experience. I knew that I would (and should) feel insecure being called an elder so I respectfully declined the offer and asked to remain a deacon. To my surprise the pastor was angered by my response and he questioned me at length about my reasoning, none of which he could refute. Actually the more we argued, the more evident it became that not many of my colleagues should have been called elders. Finally I said, "I have one question. How is it that you intend to "make" a young man an old man?" His eyes twinkled a little and then he said firmly, "You are going to be an elder."

The pastor surely didn't want our discussion to spill over into an elders meeting. It would have created chaos, upsetting the order of their religious culture. Although I submitted to the new "title," I knew that it was important for me not to take it to heart. My wife and I agreed to keep remembering that this was an organizational decision, not a scriptural reality, lest we "become conceited and fall under the same judgment as the devil" (1 Timothy 3:6). The scriptural principles for spiritual authority do not work well within the institutional church and even less so when youthful "elders" skew them off course. When young men's gifts and talents are captured by the seductive approval of the institutional church, it stifles their natural development, turning their energies to speaking and acting like an elder instead of patiently becoming one.

Spiritual authority begins to take root in the disciplined responses of a young man to the conviction of the Holy Spirit. It is ultimately expressed through the seasoned wisdom of "a senior or elderly person," who is "advanced in life," and whose battle-tested reliability and shepherd's heart assures his fellow believers that our Father's will is always his first priority. It should be the goal of every man to properly steward his responsibilities and become a dependable voice in the deliberation of spiritual matters. "If anyone sets his heart on being an overseer, he desires a noble task" (1 Timothy 3:1). What we have failed to realize is that God has set in place a life-long process that allows the full expression of the gifts and talents He has given us as we grow and mature into eldership. An important purpose of the office of deacon is to give men a place to express their spiritual gifts in practical service to the body of Christ. There is no limit to the ministries that a deacon might perform. But like everyone else, he must be willing to subject himself to the spiritual authority of legitimate elder-overseers. As the Apostle Peter said in 1 Peter 5:1-6 (NAS):

> Therefore, I exhort the elders among you, as your fellow elder and witness of the sufferings of Christ, and a partaker also of the glory that is to be revealed, shepherd the flock of God among you, exercising oversight not under compulsion, but voluntarily, according to the will of God; and not for sordid gain, but with eagerness; nor yet as lording it over

those allotted to your charge, but proving to be examples to the flock. And when the Chief Shepherd appears, you will receive the unfading crown of glory. You younger men, likewise, be subject to your elders; and all of you, clothe yourselves with humility toward one another, for God is opposed to the proud, but gives grace to the humble. Humble yourselves, therefore, under the mighty hand of God, that He may exalt you at the proper time.

What the institutional church, its spiritually unqualified older men, and its young unproven overseers lack most is the patience to allow the work of the Holy Spirit to take its course in each man's life until he becomes a mature elder. Patience (#3115) is one of the fruits of the Spirit (Galatians 5:22) and it is defined as "endurance, constancy, steadfastness, perseverance, forbearance, fortitude, longsuffering, and slowness in avenging wrongs." It is this quality that enables men to delay gratification and wait on the will and timing of God. Every time a man resists following his own will or that of the institutional church and instead obediently submits to God's will, his patience grows stronger. As every real elder-overseer knows, each new test in life provides further evidence of God's sovereign provision and increases their faith. To an elder, patience is the purest form of faith in God; and it is part of his resume, not just his hope for the future. He knows that whether a man is just beginning his walk with Christ or is frustrated by a life mistakenly dedicated to the institutional church, that the Lord is faithful:

> He gives strength to the weary, and to him who lacks might He increases power. Though youths grow weary and tired, and vigorous young men stumble badly, yet those who wait (#6960, hope, expect, and patiently tarry) for the Lord will gain new strength; they will mount up with wings like eagles, they will run and not get tired, they will walk and not become weary.
>
> Isaiah 40:29-31 NAS

Since deacons have virtually the same moral and ethical requirements as an overseer (1 Timothy 3:8-13), it's easy to see how the institutional church, whether deacons or elders rule it, has rationalized around the requirement for an overseer to be "a senior or elderly person advanced in life." But when men begin serving as elder-overseers before they've had time to grow and mature, they often experience a creeping spiritual paralysis that makes them appear indifferent to even the most outrageous errors. After years of unresolved conflict and turmoil they gradually give up their high standards for integrity and wearily go through the motions of oversight.

Men who are growing spiritually and making good decisions eventually fall out of step with the institutional church. It is usually not a conscious or deliberate decision against institutional authority as much as it is a realization that the private decisions they make to obey Christ often put them at odds ethically or morally with practical matters within their congregation. They might even find themselves being held personally accountable by the Lord to a more reasonable standard than the institutional church is willing to follow. By the time most men endure several attempts to reconcile their differences with the institutional church, they begin to recognize that they will have to submit to its leaders and sit quietly, or leave. The institutional church sends a simple message to any man who is listening: "If you want to get along with God, you have to go along with us." Lots of men have been duped by this kind of proud, authoritative use of institutional power. That's one reason why there are so few spiritually mature men in most congregations; men who can be trusted to fairly and justly exercise spiritual authority. But King David said, "How blessed is the man who has made the Lord his trust, and has not turned to the proud, nor to those who lapse into falsehood" (Psalms 40:4 NAS). Again in Psalms 62:1-2 (NAS) he says:

> My soul waits in silence (#1747, and with trust) for God only; from Him is my salvation (#3444, deliverance, health, welfare, prosperity, and victory). He only is my rock and my salvation, My stronghold (#4869, defense, refuge and fortress); I shall not be greatly shaken.

Participate in the Restoration of the Church

People often ask me, "What's the alternative to continuing in the institutional church just the way it is?" I believe the most practical alternative is to become a reliable man of faith and practice who can effectively engage in the work of restoring the church to its New Testament glory. God needs authentic, ethical, morally pure men who can help restore the relational church life we have lost to institutional religion.

When God calls us into His Kingdom, it is first to Himself; second, to one another; and then to take His grace to the world around us. So a vital walk with Christ begins and is sustained in private worship and study, grows and prospers through our ministry to one another; and then produces help for people who are hurting and lost. Our daily goal should be to experience His peace and joy in all that we do. Likewise, the restoration of the corporate church must begin with the development of men with proven spiritual disciplines. Organizationally, we should avoid wrangling about personal preferences or process details. There is little to be gained by tinkering with the order of service or what the worship leader chooses to sing. Instead, we should pursue the root cause issues that have brought the church to where it is today, such as: the Constantine-Luther Pastor-Teacher-CEO form of leadership, the absence of ministry to one another, and the control and use of "the tithe."

You can start the restoration process by having reasonable conversations with family, friends, and church leaders about your concerns. You'll be surprised to discover how many people are troubled by the things they've seen and heard in the institutional church. But their choice of action will generally fall into one of three categories:

First, some will not see any great need for change or will feel unable to remedy their particular situation, choosing to continue with the familiar routines to which they have grown accustomed.

Second, there will be those who see the problems within their local church as an opportunity for reform and will take action by working within their system to bring improvement.

Third, there will be those who have tried and failed to bring reform and have gone on to a full, productive, relational church life; meeting in homes or developing new models with "first-century" roots.

Most people do not easily reconsider the value of strongly held beliefs and relationships until what they think or whom they trust causes them to endure pain, disappointment, or failure. So when believers talk about the restoration of the church they may, by necessity, be trying to resolve intense personal issues while at the same time expressing their doubts about institutional matters, thus making the process more difficult. They will also find that some pastors and church leaders are reluctant to engage in an open discussion because they feel obligated to defend themselves or the history and actions of their institutions. Even so, when pastors speak privately to one another, they often describe how they are "burning out" trying to fulfill the impossible agenda the Constantine-Luther model has created for them. It doesn't work any better for them and their families than it does for us. Over and over again, as one scandal after another wracks the church, each denomination, congregation, or ministry must find a rationale for the sudden disintegration of supposedly great men and their programs. But too many of them are unwilling to consider the possibility that they are trying to do a good thing the wrong way.

One such pastor stands out in my memory. He was one of the most dedicated and sincere young men I have had the opportunity to speak with, and on several occasions I spent some quality time with him discussing the vision he said God had given him. He had set forth what he thought was a great vision for church growth and although there were several parts of his "vision" that were questionable, what most disturbed me was the "aggressive" nature of his "faith." His sermons and personal explanations of his vision were filled with such bravado that it often sounded like someone who was whistling past the graveyard, terrified by what might happen in the dark cold night, but putting up an impenetrable front of confidence. It took me awhile to realize He was acting. But he wasn't doing it just to impress others. He actually thought the Lord expected it of him.

Twice I saw him put down opposition to his plans and with powerful language give the impression he was speaking by the unction of the Holy Spirit. He convinced even the most worried questioners that he had "heard from God" and he repeatedly declared that he would not turn back from "God's work." He was doggedly committed to "doing great things for Christ." But I realized that with the exceptions of the topic and the Scriptures he used to support his position, he sounded just like I had when I verbally attacked the man who had caused me to fear losing my job. His words were sincere, yet misguided, and they were empowered by the wrong spirit. As I began to pray about the situation and ask the Lord for wisdom, He spoke to me through Isaiah 16:14 (NAS) which says, "Within three years, as a hired man would count them, the glory of Moab will be degraded along with all his great population, and his remnant will be very small and impotent." This pastor was already speaking to a congregation of thousands and had predicted that it would become tens of thousands. Within about three years he had a congregation of four hundred people. During that period of time he declared so many of his ideas to be "of God" that weren't and so often rejected wise counsel, that he had no real understanding of what went wrong.

The Lord has provided me with many convincing proofs of the spiritual frailty of the institutional church, some of which I have shared on the pages of this book. As I prayed about each new event, I realized the Lord was using men's failures to open the eyes of His people to two important facts: First, as with the young pastor I just described, it is becoming increasingly difficult to have reasonable conversations with institutional church leaders about the failures of their vision and doctrine. And second, there is a dramatic shortage of reliable men who will challenge the institutional church's facts. The result is clearly demonstrated by the deteriorating condition of the Christian family, the church, and the world around us.

Some people believe that the church will eventually be reshaped by world events that will cause us to return to our New Testament patterns. If they are right, why shouldn't we seek the original design now? Why wait for the pressures of the world to direct us to a place we could reach through obedience? In the meantime, there are thousands of people in each of our communities who have either rejected the call of Christ or have given up on their walk with Him because of the inconsistencies of the church and its leaders. Now we are hearing about further thousands of strong, dedicated believers who are leaving behind institutional religion to pursue a more reasonable life in Christ. How long can we ignore the obvious? Instead of continually entangling the faith of new or "revived" believers in the suffocating web of institutional life, we should work to restore the ministries of the church to the simple, effective methods described in the Bible. For that, we need reliable men of faith and practice.

APPENDIX: HISTORICAL SOURCES

The historical facts and dates that appear in various portions of this text are widely accepted for their accuracy by scholars and historians, and/or, can be easily sourced through commonly available libraries and search engines on the Internet. Some original sources are designated by their Internet address such as: lutheranworld.org. For those facts which do not have a specifically designated source (and even for those which do) there are usually several sourcing options from which to choose. For example, there may be multiple books and articles related to a particular question about Martin Luther which can be found using the search format: martin luther AND *the key word(s) from the text.*

At the website, newadvent.org, you can access the Roman Catholic Church encyclopedia and connect with numerous sites and archives, which thoroughly describe the facts related to Constantine's build-up of the institutional church. He is honored for what the Roman Catholic Church believes was a great contribution to their growth and development, including the first church buildings, which historians and archeologists agree did not exist before Constantine. They describe his vision before the battle of Milvian Bridge and many interesting facts about his "conversion" to Christianity and leadership of the church. However, they do not emphasize that he continued to consult pagan gods as his plans for the church developed, and that he waited until his deathbed to be baptized. Fortunately, you can rely on an Internet search engine (yahoo.com, google.com, aol.com, etc.) for these and other very important facts and commentary about Constantine's effect on church life throughout the centuries.

Rather than quote a list of potentially biased or self-serving authors and sources, or the Internet addresses of each and every page I have read; I have chosen to describe my research process and invite you to join it. As you read through sections of the text, pull out key words and place them in your browser's search window. Then you can become morally persuaded of the truth about these facts as a result of your own investigation.